The Absent Father

The Absent Father:
Virginia Woolf
and Walter Pater

PERRY MEISEL

New Haven and London   Yale University Press   1980

82-967

Designed by Sally Harris
and set in IBM Journal Roman type.
Printed in the United States of America by
Edwards Brothers, Inc., Ann Arbor, Michigan.

Published in Great Britain, Europe, Africa, and
Asia (except Japan) by Yale University Press,
Ltd., London. Distributed in Australia and
New Zealand by Book & Film Services, Artarmon,
N.S.W., Australia; and in Japan by Harper & Row,
Publishers, Tokyo Office.

Library of Congress Cataloging in Publication Data

Meisel, Perry.
The absent father. Virginia Woolf and Walter Pater.

Includes index.
1. Woolf, Virginia Stephen, 1882–1941–Criticism
and interpretation. 2. Pater, Walter Horatio,
1839–1894–Influence–Woolf. 3. Aestheticism
(Literature) I. Title.
PR6045.072Z816   823'.9'12   79-19289
ISBN 0-300-02401-0

To the memory of Richard S. Sylvester

. . . face a teacher with
the image of the taught and
the mirror breaks.

—*Jacob's Room*

Contents

Preface

Although Virginia Woolf's achievement as a novelist will
always be subject to some dispute, as an essayist she is very
likely without peer in this century. Recognized as she is
today in the main line of English fiction, she is also in the
main tradition of English prose, from Browne and Johnson
and Gibbon to Coleridge, DeQuincey, Newman, Ruskin,
Arnold, and Pater. Modernist and feminist critics alike
tend to overlook this fundamental fact about Virginia
Woolf, much as they overlook the fact, too, that she was,
like Dickens, Defoe, or George Eliot, a hard-boiled professional of letters throughout a life of regular and unstinting
literary labor almost Victorian in its energy. No happy
curiosity among writers, Woolf succeeds Pater among
principal English critics, and it is with Pater that her principal literary relationship is to be found.

Pater's influence on modern writing proper, of course, is
no mean feature of the twentieth-century landscape. Joyce,
Yeats, Eliot, Pound, Stevens, Hardy, Conrad, James, even
Lawrence, each is obligated to Pater in particular ways.
But much as the study of English prose has provided us
with no real account of Woolf's relation to Pater as a critic,
neither has the study of modernism provided us with any
real measure of Pater's effect on Woolf as a novelist. Here,
though, the customary wisdom that modern novelists are

without precedent anyway succeeds in making two generations of Paterians guilty, as Woolf seems to be, of having
no influences at all.

Reasons for the omission from the feminist point of
view are obvious enough. Although it was once customary
to see Woolf and her circle as aestheticist, at least in the
popular 'nineties sense, the increasingly political tone of
Woolf studies has lately turned us away from the question
of Woolf's literary filiations altogether, and so obscures
the fact that she was, to use Avrom Fleishman's word,
a "learned" writer whose texts murmur with echoes of the
English tradition at large.[1] Of course, as a confirmed
misogynist and university man, Pater would in any case
appear to lie directly in the line of Woolf's lifelong attack
on the English patriarchy, and so seem less a precursor
than an enemy. And as a Victorian, however much an
intellectual renegade to some among his contemporaries,
the reclusive Oxford don looms, on the face of it at least,
antipathetic to the revolutionary and loquacious matriarch
of Bloomsbury.

It was, however, Wyndham Lewis, still carping about
Bloomsbury in a vendetta that had begun with his attack
on Roger Fry and the Omega Workshops in 1913, who
made the connection vividly apparent in 1934 despite his
belief that such a link was damning to all the parties concerned. For Lewis, " 'aestheticism,' though in truth ram-
pant and ubiquitous, is on all hands violently disowned;
and although the manner of Pater is today constantly
imitated, on the sly, and his teaching absorbed along with
his style, he is scarcely *respectable* in the intellectual sense."[2]
This is apropos of James, but with Woolf herself, "there is,

---

1. Avrom Fleishman, *Virginia Woolf: A Critical Reading* (Baltimore: The
Johns Hopkins University Press, 1975), p. x.
2. Wyndham Lewis, *Men Without Art* (London: Cassell, 1934), p. 145.

of course, a very much closer connection than people suppose between the aesthetic movement presided over by Oscar Wilde, and that presided over in the first post-war decade by Mrs. Woolf."[3] As a second-generation Wilde, Woolf, too, becomes a witting disciple of Pater, although in her case the discipleship is a veiled and secret one.

Lewis turns out to be more accurate than he knew, and succeeds inadvertently in valorizing the connection to which he alludes by charging it with the qualities of repression and strategic disavowal on Woolf's part that mark it out as a question central but hidden in her work. It is the contention of the present study that Lewis's estimate is a surpassingly rich and suggestive one despite its reverse intention, and that in the relation to which it points lies a repressed but decisive drama of influence fundamental to Woolf's whole enterprise as critic and novelist alike.

It is my purpose, then, to attempt to break through Woolf's manifest silence on the subject of Pater—for there is no single essay about him nor any significant discussion of his work to be found anywhere in Woolf's writing—and to recover what lies behind it. Such repression and the reasons for the anxiety that both causes and accompanies it may be unraveled by a psychoanalysis not so much of Woolf herself as of the texts, including the biographical ones, by which we know her. I have therefore attempted in my first chapter to reconstruct those historical circumstances in which Woolf came to read Pater's work and to study with his sister Clara during the years 1898 to 1905, circumstances dominated largely by Woolf's difficult relations with her father, Leslie Stephen, and by Stephen's history of antagonism with Pater himself. In the last section of the first chapter and in chapters 2 and 3, I have then tried to situate Woolf's characteristic stance and

3. Ibid., pp. 170–71.

rhetoric as an essayist within the Paterian framework from which her writing derives, particularly Pater's celebration of personality and the privileged moment, and his chemical vocabulary for the artist's crystalline or incandescent expressiveness. Indeed, like the rewoven and pasted pages of Woolf's early diary notebooks, the fabric of Woolf's formal prose is, in a manner of speaking, rewoven or layered over, too, with threads or pieces of Pater's text to be found underneath it even in ostensibly feminist works like *A Room of One's Own*.

Hence my working assumption throughout is that Woolf betrays her indebtedness to Pater by the recurrent and habitual use of particular figures of speech borrowed from the decisive moments in Pater's own vision, and that such borrowed figures betoken her capture by Pater on the level of stance as well. Style in the narrow sense, in other words, is not the issue here. Much as Pater's stylistic precursor, as Harold Bloom suggests, is Swinburne rather than the more important Ruskin,[4] so Woolf's stylistic precursor, at least as a novelist, is Dorothy Richardson, even though Pater remains the far more significant authority from the point of view of critical vision and sensibility as a whole. Indeed, if we ask if there is an imitative Paterian accent to Woolf's early literary exercises in her 1897 diary, for example, the answer is no, and applies to all notions of a Paterian trace in terms of style in the usual sense. One might even argue persuasively that the intricate diction of Pater's most characteristic sentences was one of Bloomsbury's principal and symbolic musts to avoid, and that the largely comma-free cadences of Woolf, Strachey, and Forster all may be accounted for by the reaction against such Victorian stylistic mannerisms for which all three writers are famous.

    4. Harold Bloom, "Introduction: The Crystal Man," *Selected Writings of Walter Pater* (New York: New American Library, 1974), p. xi.

Style aside, however, Pater uses a certain vocabulary, a certain series of key tropes or figures that make his rhetoric eminently recognizable, and that allow him to speak of art and the artist in a strikingly personal way. I have attempted to isolate these master tropes in my second chapter, and to trace in the third their return in Woolf's own criticism. And although the question of Pater's own influences is beyond the territory of the present study, it should be pointed out, too, that what I call the chemistry of Pater's crystal is prefigured for Pater in Ruskin despite the more customary links usually drawn between Pater and Arnold or Newman.

And although to present such a story of influence means to reverse the current political trend in Woolf scholarship, it is by no means to neglect feminism as a factor in Woolf, but rather to situate it within a more purely literary equation. Indeed, with the figures of father and authority identified with a tyrannical patriarchy in *A Room of One's Own* and, ultimately, with fascist tyranny itself in the late *Three Guineas,* the claim for a decisive influence or authority is itself ironic, and the claim for Pater particularly so. Notions of servitude, however, emerge only when tyranny is in fact operative, and Woolf's indictment of patriarchal authority in general is precisely the background and pressure against which the weight and anxiety of Pater's influence is to be seen and felt in her work. It is, in fact, the exemplary pressure of Pater's burdensome precedent that leads Woolf to attempt to expunge his authority despite, and because of, its lawgiving powers, and it is on the questions of authors, authority, and influence itself that we shall find the real lines of battle to be drawn between them.

Woolf's attempt to overcome Pater's authority is the subject of my fourth and fifth chapters. Although I try to suggest some partial means by which Woolf seeks to disavow Pater in the first half of the book, it is not until the full extent of the influence has been established there that Woolf's strategy for neutralizing and absorbing Pater can be properly presented in its own turn. Woolf overcomes Pater by doubling what I have called in the fourth chapter Pater's secondary or deindividuating profile. And though she doubles him here, as I try to show in the fifth chapter, in stance alone rather than in stance and figure together, such a difference from the master already suggests her success in distinguishing herself from him, a success that is realized in the way she establishes her own authority as a writer in his place by appealing to a theory of culture that she learns from him and that she turns against him.

I have also taken the opportunity in chapters 4 and 5 to read both writers at some length apart from the drama of influence in which I have situated them. Here I have attempted to tease out that secondary vision of art, personality, and culture in Pater that Woolf finds so appealing, even though its concern with all that is alien to the individual puts into question the manifest ideals of aestheticism adumbrated earlier on. With its unsettling complications, such an antithetical reinterpretation of Pater, particularly Woolf's transformation of impressionism into a theory of textuality in *Jacob's Room,* should in fact be read as an implicit reinterpretation of the central tenets of English modernism itself so far as it may be said to have a father in Pater at all.

My organizing attempt throughout, however, remains the single-minded one of tracing influence. Although I have attempted to articulate the secondary and discordant visions to be found in both writers side by side with their ideals, I eventually try to locate even these antithetical designs within the larger mechanics of Woolf's anxious relation to Pater as a whole. My justification for the single-mindedness is that a close reading of Pater contributes immensely to a close reading of Woolf, and makes her otherwise unfocused texts, particularly her many essays, cohere in unusual and unexpected ways. With more than a few ironies, Pater helps to show us how miraculously powerful and unified a sensibility Virginia Woolf possesses no matter what form she chooses to work in, and how capable her imagination can be when it is roused to handle its discordances as a resource rather than as a threat.

I should note here, too, that my treatment of Woolf's fiction is confined almost entirely to two sections of the fifth chapter, although even there the novels tend to be subjugated to the design to be found in Woolf's criticism, memoirs, and *A Room of One's Own*. I have also largely confined my reading of Pater to the formally collected *Works* in order to account for the exact Pater that Woolf knew.[5] As for the inevitable questions of how conscious Woolf is of Pater's influence and how intentional her strategies for overcoming it, they will be addressed at the close of the study in our writers' own terms. I have also cited both writers at some length so as to let them speak as much as possible for themselves.

It should also be said that the double and discordant designs that I trace in each writer are in each case compact in the same texts. Such simultaneity should suggest that the rhythm of influence and overcoming that I find in Woolf is not so much a drama that unfolds over the course of her career as it is the dialectical condition in which her work proceeds early and late. As such, the developmental flavor of the drama that unfolds over the course of the argument is properly the argument's rather than Woolf's own, as I try to clarify the mechanisms of influence one step at a time. My handling of each writer's work is there-

5. See p. 16, n. 24.

fore largely synchronic despite an occasional foray into developmental reasoning, especially since I take the genuinely diachronic biographical drama described in the first chapter to have been largely concluded by the time Woolf reached her early twenties and became a regular reviewer in the first decade of the century.

As far as Woolf's and Pater's writing is concerned, then, I have tried to read like Mrs. Ramsay, who reads a book or poem "backwards" and "upwards" as well as forwards (p. 184),[6] rather than like Mr. Ramsay, whose critical reasoning rarely strays beyond the purely conventional diachrony of the alphabet or the story line of a novel. Indeed, of the styles of reading presented in *To the Lighthouse,* it is the poet Carmichael's "acrostics" (p. 69) that actually provide the closest parallel to my own approach, which is also one of rearranging the various pieces in a textual puzzle so as to arrive at a combination that spells out multiple meanings at once. Only in this way can we read the two interpretations of Pater that Woolf requires simultaneously in order to accept and deny him in a single compensatory rhythm.

Hence my notion of Woolf's career, like my notion of Pater's, is, to use a Paterian word, really one of refinement, since the same designs tend to be present in the fiction and criticism of both writers early and late, with early and late different in terms of stress or accent alone. To be sure, the careers of both writers follow a similar movement away from a radical youthful solipsism and toward an increasingly conservative focus, in later years, on those communal structures beyond the self and no longer contingent to it. Nonetheless, the assertion of self in youth is put into question even there by the very terms both writers use

6. Virginia Woolf, *To the Lighthouse* (London: The Hogarth Press, 1927).

to establish it, much as later visions of community are pressured, in turn, by the persistence even in age of the early ideals. My notions about temporality in Pater and Woolf alike are eventually reduced to a single contention in the fourth and fifth chapters, and provide the key to Woolf's undoing of the Paterian knot as I attempt to trace it in the late portions of the concluding discussion, particularly in the reading of *Three Guineas* with which the argument concludes.

Above all, of course, it should be said that such a drama of influence and the particular character it ascribes to Virginia Woolf and her work are, finally, only a myth or fable of identity. I shall leave it to Woolf and Pater themselves to explain why.

I wish to thank the National Endowment for the Humanities for a summer grant award that allowed me to begin this study in 1977, and the New York University Graduate School of Arts and Science Research Fund for providing aid for its completion in the summer of 1978.

To J. Hillis Miller, Harold Bloom, and Walter Kendrick, I am grateful for counsel during the composition of the manuscript, and to them and to James Naremore for reading the manuscript when it was completed. My thanks to Mitchell Leaska for bibliographical aid and advice. My thanks also to Professor Quentin Bell and to the Henry W. and Albert A. Berg Collection of the New York Public Library for permission to quote from Virginia Woolf's unpublished early diaries.

P. M.

New York
August 1978,
March 1979

Textual Note

Since there is no standard edition of the works of Virginia Woolf, I have used first editions for the purposes of reference and citation. All references and citations from works prepared for book publication during Woolf's lifetime are from the first English editions, as are references and citations from the posthumous *A Writer's Diary* and *Contemporary Writers*. References and citations from the remainder of Woolf's posthumously collected works, including those volumes of the letters and diaries available at the time this study was completed, are from the first American editions. References and citations from Woolf's unpublished diary notebooks and from the "Introduction" to *Mrs. Dalloway* will be given separately in the text.

The following works by Woolf are cited; each is preceded by date of publication and followed by the abbreviation used to identify quotations from it throughout the discussion:

1915	*The Voyage Out*. London: Duckworth.	*VO*
1919	*Night and Day*. London: Duckworth.	*ND*
1922	*Jacob's Room*. London: The Hogarth Press.	*JR*
1925	*Mrs. Dalloway*. London: The Hogarth Press.	*MD*
1927	*To the Lighthouse*. London: The Hogarth Press.	*TL*
1928	*Orlando*. London: The Hogarth Press.	*O*
1929	*A Room of One's Own*. London: The Hogarth Press.	*ROO*
1931	*The Waves*. London: The Hogarth Press.	*W*
1937	*The Years*. London: The Hogarth Press.	*Y*

1938 *Three Guineas.* London: The Hogarth Press.   *TG*
1940 *Roger Fry: A Biography.* London: The Hogarth
      Press.   *RF*
1941 *Between the Acts.* London: The Hogarth Press.   *BA*
1944 *A Haunted House and Other Short Stories.* New
      York: Harcourt, Brace.   *HH*
1953 *A Writer's Diary: Being Extracts from the Diary
      of Virginia Woolf.* Ed. Leonard Woolf. London:
      The Hogarth Press.   *AWD*
1965 *Contemporary Writers.* London: The Hogarth
      Press.   *CW*
1967 *Collected Essays.* 4 vols. New York: Harcourt,
      Brace & World.   *CE* I–IV
1975 *The Letters of Virginia Woolf, Volume One:
      1888–1912.* Ed. Nigel Nicolson and Joanne
      Trautmann. New York: Harcourt Brace
      Jovanovich.   *Letters* I
1976 *The Letters of Virginia Woolf, Volume Two:
      1912–1922.* Ed. Nigel Nicolson and Joanne
      Trautmann. New York: Harcourt Brace
      Jovanovich.   *Letters* II
1978 *The Letters of Virginia Woolf, Volume Three:
      1923–1928.* Ed. Nigel Nicolson and Joanne
      Trautmann. New York: Harcourt Brace
      Jovanovich.   *Letters* III
1979 *The Letters of Virginia Woolf, Volume Four:
      1929–1931.* Ed. Nigel Nicolson and Joanne
      Trautmann. New York: Harcourt Brace
      Jovanovich.   *Letters* IV
1976 *Moments of Being: Unpublished Autobio-
      graphical Writings.* Ed. Jeanne Schulkind. New
      York: Harcourt Brace Jovanovich.   *MB*
1977 *The Pargiters: The Novel-Essay Portion of 'The
      Years.'* Ed. Mitchell Leaska. New York: The
      New York Public Library.   *P*
1977 *The Diary of Virginia Woolf, Volume One:
      1915–1919.* Ed. Anne Olivier Bell. New York:
      Harcourt Brace Jovanovich.   *Diary* I
1978 *The Diary of Virginia Woolf, Volume Two:
      1920–1924.* Ed. Anne Olivier Bell. New York:
      Harcourt Brace Jovanovich.   *Diary* II

1978 *Books and Portraits.* Ed. Mary Lyon. New
      York: Harcourt Brace Jovanovich.   *BP*

All references and citations from the works of Pater are from the New Library Edition (London: Macmillan, 1910), except for references and citations from *Marius the Epicurean,* which are from the Modern Library edition (New York, n.d.). References and citations from the suppressed essay "Aesthetic Poetry" will be given separately in the text.

The following works by Pater are cited; each is preceded by the date of its first issue in book form and followed by the abbreviation used to identify quotations from it throughout the discussion:

1873	*The Renaissance*	*R*
1885	*Marius the Epicurean: His Sensations and Ideas*	*M*
1887	*Imaginary Portraits*	*IP*
1889	*Appreciations*	*A*
1893	*Plato and Platonism*	*PP*
1895	*Greek Studies*	*GS*
1895	*Miscellaneous Studies*	*MS*
1896	*Gaston De Latour*	*GL*
1896	*Essays from 'The Guardian'*	*EG*

1
Relations

In 1875, seven years before the birth of his youngest daughter, Virginia, Leslie Stephen had written a bitter denunciation of aestheticism and published it in his *Cornhill Magazine*.[1] Entitled "Art and Morality," Stephen's fiery article was doubtless inspired by the debate surrounding Pater's *Studies in the History of the Renaissance* (1873), a book whose infamous first edition was still in circulation, complete with the noxious "Conclusion" that would be suppressed in 1877. Although Pater's name is conspicuously absent from Stephen's entire discussion, Pater is clearly the aesthetic critic whom the piece is designed to vilify. Couched in the form of a legal indictment, the article casts Pater as "the accused," who "sums up his general position by saying that art and morality are two different things" (91). Stephen, of course, is inclined to make franker distinctions than Pater himself, and such an absolute separation helps to sharpen his moral argument. "There are passions which ought to be suppressed," says Stephen, and "there are sentiments which imply moral disease as distinctly as there are sensations which imply physical disease" (94). "If," he proposes, "legal punishment is impossible"—with the trial of Oscar Wilde in

1. "Art and Morality," *Cornhill* 32 (July 1875): 91–101. Subsequent references to this article appear in the text.

1895, it turned out to be very possible indeed—then "the critic should step in and administer the lash with the full strength of his arm. The harder he hits and the deeper he cuts the better for the world" (92).

Even the religious Matthew Arnold, argues Stephen, is too aesthetic in his calculation that "the sphere of morality includes seventy-five per cent of our actions" (97). Although Stephen had published portions of *Literature and Dogma* just after he became editor of the *Cornhill* in 1871, his allusion to Arnold's judgment there that only "three-fourths of life . . . is conduct"[2] is really a chastisement: "Every action is good or bad," says Stephen in "Art and Morality," and "it is a legitimate and a curious question how far a man should indulge himself in purely aesthetic enjoyments" (97). Seeking thresholds in an attempt to preserve a judicious, even scientific, appearance, Stephen wonders "at what point a delight in the beautiful begins to enervate the character, and up to what point it exerts a healthy and elevating influence" (97–98). In an allusion to Pater's most celebrated image in *The Renaissance,* Stephen argues that the critic "may use the poet's fire to kindle passions when they ought to be checked, or check them when they ought to be kindled" (98).

That "the indolent epicurean" (94) presumes the first alternative rather than the second is, of course, beyond dispute. "There are people who prefer the morbid products," he continues, calling attention to Pater's fascination with death and decay, and perhaps even anticipating the funereal preoccupations of the imaginary protraits, "and who think that a great writer must necessarily be morbid" (100). On the contrary, Stephen concludes, art "should stimulate the

2. Matthew Arnold, *Literature and Dogma* (1873; rpt. New York: Macmillan, 1883), p. 19. In 1867–68, the *Cornhill* had also published *Culture and Anarchy.*

healthy, not the morbid emotions; and, in that sense, all art and poetry should be moral and even didactic" (101). By moral health, of course, Stephen means what is vigorous and robust, and it is in Scott, one of his favorite novelists and the writer whom Mr. Ramsay reads with tears in his eyes in *To the Lighthouse,* that such health is to be found in abundance. "Nobody can love Scott," says Stephen in a phrase that sums up his evangelical notion of artistic reponsibility, "who does not assimilate his most manly morality" (95).

Stephen's own "manly morality" had already been ruffled by stories about Pater's conduct only months before "Art and Morality" appeared.[3] Reports had reached Stephen that Pater had been impressed by a student's knowledge of French novelists during a water-party at Eton, where Pater was visiting his friend Oscar Browning. On the following day Pater had supposedly made the " 'profane remark' " to a woman who had been among the company that " 'when a boy of his years showed any kind of literary taste it was generally for poetry of a common-place nature, such as Alfred Tennyson's!' "[4] The woman passed the story along to Stephen's sister-in-law, Anne Thackeray, and Stephen in turn passed it along to his brother Fitzjames, a member of the Cambridge Apostles together with Tennyson and Oscar Browning alike, and whose son was a student at Eton at the time of the reported incident. Soon enough the story grew into a report that Browning had lent a copy of Gautier's *Mademoiselle de Maupin* to the student in question, prompting Fitzjames

3. Lawrence Evans dates the incident in question in the spring or summer of 1875 (see *Letters of Walter Pater,* ed. Evans [Oxford: The Clarendon Press, 1970], p. 16). Stephen's article appeared in July of that year.

4. H. E. Wortham, *Victorian Eton and Cambridge* (London: Barker, 1956), p. 60.

to write to Browning to protest and to add that Pater was reported to have stood by and approved the proceeding.[5] Such immoral intellectual behavior on the part of two men already suspected of pederasty only confirmed the judgment Stephen was preparing in "Art and Morality," and perhaps even prompted him to write the piece, whose energy is otherwise hard to account for given its appearance more than two years after the publication of the first edition of *The Renaissance*. Browning was in fact dismissed from Eton in September of 1875 on the strength of sexual allegations,[6] eventually returning to Cambridge, where he became a Fellow at King's.

By the 1890s, Pater and his popularizing followers surely remained among the principal objects of Stephen's wrath despite his increasing withdrawal from the life of the times as he grew older. "He had," wrote Virginia Woolf, "no feeling for pictures; no ear for music; no sense of the sound of words" (*MB*, 68). As Noel Annan gently phrases it, "he thought the contemplative life incomparably inferior to the life of action, almost an immoral existence."[7] Doubtless his children felt the strength of that opinion. "My natural love for beauty," said Virginia, "was checked

5. Ibid., p. 59. Pater, however, was not amused by Fitzjames's letters, which Browning had sent him for a laugh (*Letters of Walter Pater*, p. 16).

6. *Letters of Walter Pater*, p. xxxiv, p. 17; see also Wortham, pp. 126–41. Browning himself tells another story, and cites what appears to be an additional letter from Fitzjames received in the summer of 1875 in which the incident is put to rest as a mild disagreement as to " 'the nature of public school education' " (Oscar Browning, *Memories of Sixty Years at Eton, Cambridge, and Elsewhere* [London: The Bodley Head, 1910], p. 208). See also V. H. H. Green, *Oxford Common Room* (London: Arnold, 1957), for a compromising description from the diary of Mark Pattison of Pater and Browning at tea with undergraduates in 1878 (p. 307). Michael Levey's recent *The Case of Walter Pater* (London: Thames and Hudson, 1978) accents Pater's homosexuality and attributes Browning's original fascination with Pater to his perception that Pater shared with him a taste for boys (p. 99).

7. Noel Annan, *Leslie Stephen: His Thought and Character in Relation to his Time* (Cambridge: Harvard University Press, 1952), p. 240.

by some ancestral dread" (*MB*, 68). For Stephen, morality resided in what Annan calls "a way of life learnt unconsciously in the family where all that is most valuable in this kind of education is taught."[8] "All his devotion for many years had concentrated itself upon his home," wrote his daughter (*MB*, 40), although it was a devotion that seems to have expressed itself in a singularly pedagogical way. "It is a school they live in," said Lytton Strachey to Leonard Woolf after visiting the Stephen household in the summer of 1901.[9]

Strachey's image is hardly a fanciful one. Without the benefits, both social and intellectual, of any formal schooling outside the confines of 22 Hyde Park Gate, Virginia's education, like her sister Vanessa's, was conducted by Stephen himself in the years following their mother's death in 1895. Until Virginia's late adolescence, Leslie monitored her reading very closely, making "careful choices," as John Lehmann puts it,[10] from the various books he judged fit for use in her instruction. Given Stephen's tastes and opinions in literature, it is unlikely that any work by Pater was among these choices. Indeed, given "Art and Morality," it was clearly authors precisely like Pater whom Leslie sought to guard his daughter against. Although Virginia's reading was largely confined to the English classics during childhood and early adolescence, among the texts her father selected for her instruc-

    8. Ibid., p. 248.
    9. Quoted in Michael Holroyd, *Lytton Strachey: A Critical Biography*, 2 vols. (New York: Holt, Rinehart and Winston, 1968), I, 120.
    10. John Lehmann, *Virginia Woolf and Her World* (New York: Harcourt Brace Jovanovich, 1975), p. 9. The usual impression, reasserted recently in Mary Lyon's preface to *Books and Portraits*, is that Stephen gave his daughters "access" to his library from "earliest childhood" (*BP*, viii). In *Three Guineas*, Woolf herself recalls that "the education of the private house" included among its rules that one could "read this book, but was not allowed to read that" (*TG*, 68, 70).

tion were also to be included certain works of modern criticism and fiction—Coleridge, Macaulay, Thomas Arnold, Carlyle, Henry James[11]—most of them destined, with the exception of James, who was a family friend, to display Stephen's own clearly articulated system of values. "Literature," says Annan of Stephen's pedagogy, "must be regarded partly as a textbook to be censored for use in the schoolroom of society";[12] in the schoolroom of the home, censorship could be carried out with particular effectiveness.

Before setting Virginia free to read what she liked, Leslie watched carefully as his daughter's literary sophistication slowly grew before his eyes. If his impression of her emerging gifts was high, Virginia's respect for his own judgment and authority seems to have been equally profound. Indeed, among her earliest literary exercises is to be found a precocious text of praise for her father's "immense literary powers,"[13] written at age ten in a style so elevated yet so unimpeded by ornament that her model is clearly Stephen himself. That a bond of deep sympathy developed between them as Virginia's literary talents grew is, of course, undeniable. Sharing as they did what Quentin Bell calls "a common shop"[14] (even if, as Virginia later remembered, her father had in fact read little of what she had written [*MB*, 118]), literature and writing provided a wel-

11. Quentin Bell, *Virginia Woolf: A Biography*, 2 vols. in one (New York: Harcourt Brace Jovanovich, 1972), I, 50–51; Diary/Holograph Notebook, 1897 (Berg Collection, New York Public Library). "Father and I walked in the [Kensington] gardens, and he gave me the life of Sterling [*sic*] to read—I gave back the Coleridge . . ." (entry for Wednesday, 24 March 1897; in the entry for Monday, 9 August 1897, she notes, "I may read Vanity Fair and Jane Eyre").

12. Annan, *Leslie Stephen*, pp. 228–29.

13. Quoted in George Spater and Ian Parsons, *A Marriage of True Minds: An Intimate Portrait of Leonard and Virginia Woolf* (New York: Harcourt Brace Jovanovich, 1977), p. 10.

14. Bell, *Virginia Woolf*, I, 64.

come focus for even greater closeness in the years following the death of Virginia's mother, especially since Virginia's promise was apparently one of Leslie's few sources of delight in the atmosphere of "Oriental gloom" (*MB*, 40) that enshrouded 22 Hyde Park Gate as the last years of the century unfolded.

Such an early bond of sympathy between father and daughter had the positive effect of making Stephen largely responsible for the moral essayist Virginia was to become as her writing took more and more of a political turn in later years.[15] To the extent that she was eventually to envisage her work as serving a moral purpose, we can in fact ascribe it to the positive side of her father's earliest influence, with his insistence on the writer's responsibility to society clearly fueling the missionary zeal of works like *A Room of One's Own, Three Guineas,* and many of her shorter essays. That his legacy would be feminism is unsettling despite its compensations. With its antipatriarchal imperatives, this moral dimension of Virginia's work was obviously to carry with it more than a simple endorsement of her father's literary credo, since the social criticism through which his stance will be maintained also represents the call for his demise. Directed as her polemic will be against those forms of masculine tyranny nowhere more evident than in the life and work of Leslie Stephen himself, from a feminist point of view her father's influence will eventually be expelled even as its powers are being absorbed.

For the present, however, such a need to countermand her father's authority even as she submitted to it reminds us that her relations with him were by no means entirely positive or secure during these early years. "Passionate

15. For Stephen's influence on his daughter and on Bloomsbury, see Annan, *Leslie Stephen,* p. 270.

affection for my father alternat[ed]," Virginia later recalled, "with passionate hatred of him" (MB, 161):

> At . . . sixty-five he was almost completely isolated,
> imprisoned. Whole tracts of his sensibility had atro-
> phied. He had so ignored, or refused to face, or
> disguised his own feelings, that not only had he no
> conception of what he himself did and said; he had
> no idea what other people felt. Hence the horror and
> the terror of these violent displays of rage. These
> were sinister, blind, animal, savage. He did not realise
> what he did. No one could enlighten him. He suf-
> fered. We suffered. There was no possiblity of com-
> munication. [MB, 126]

Although in principle Stephen believed in the emancipa-
tion of women, his emotional dealings with the women in
his family betrayed a rather traditional feeling that their
place was to be restricted to the home and to society.[16]
Having witnessed during this formative period the death of
her mother Julia at the hands of what may arguably be
called her father's overweening emotional demands (MB,
114), Virginia had hardly reestablished congenial relations
with him (her first bout of madness had followed directly
on Julia's death) before her half-sister Stella, who had
taken over Julia's role of ministering to Leslie, met a similar end in 1897. "If, instead of words, he had used a whip
the brutality would have been no greater" (MB, 125). With
such fearful prospects in view, neither Virginia nor Vanessa
was to tolerate for long their father's proven abuse of his
women (MB, 56).

    16. Herbert Marder, *Feminism and Art: A Study of Virginia Woolf* (Chi-
cago: University of Chicago Press, 1968), pp. 11–12. See also Stephen's essay,
"William Godwin's Novels," where he refers to men as "the superior sex" and
worries that "colleges devoted to female education are, I fear, rapidly destroy-
ing that agreeable distinction" (*Studies of a Biographer* [London: Duckworth,
1902], III, 131).

If Vanessa rebelled openly (*MB*, 125), Virginia's reaction was covert, balancing her enduring love and sympathy for her father with a silent suspicion—whether true or not it does not matter—as to how seriously he was willing to take her early commitment to a life of letters like his own. For all their mutual sympathy, Virginia's inauspicious diary entry commemorating her father's birthday as late as 1928 recalls these suspicions in no uncertain terms: "His life would have entirely ended mine," she reflects in the well-known passage that celebrates his death more than his life. "What would have happened? No writing, no books;—inconceivable" (*AWD*, 138).[17] All this belated alarm despite—or perhaps because of—their "common shop" and the rather burdensome feeling of those early years captured in these phrases from the same entry: "I hear his voice, I know this by heart" (*AWD*, 138).

With Vanessa bustling off to the Royal Academy of Art each morning after breakfast in the years following Stella's death, Virginia was left to her own devices as her father shut himself up in his study until lunchtime, growing ever gloomier and more implacable as grief and bitterness overwhelmed him, together with deafness and the slow onset of the cancer that was to take his life early in 1904. Virginia's dominant emotion at the time was loneliness, and she worked at her reading and writing with a sense of isolation aggravated by the remoteness of her father's presence.

It was during these years that Leslie at last decided to grant her free use of his books, to read what she liked—and to reject what she did not—in accordance with a growing literary sophistication that was by now proceeding with little outside help at all. Apparently Leslie's policy of

---

17. Thus it comes as no accident at all that Virginia's first published article appeared in *The Guardian* just nine months after her father's death in 1904.

supervision, and with it the inevitable inculcation of his own literary values, had given way to a policy of intellectual laissez faire. Although this decision to allow Virginia free reign was evidently one sign of what Annan calls the "intellectual freedom" Stephen was willing to grant both his daughters,[18] his celebrated liberalism at this moment in Virginia's adolescence appears to be also a symptom of his own self-absorption and retreat from the responsibilities of paternity. Despite his daughter's need of a sustaining principle or authority to give shape and meaning to her expanding cultivation, the old authoritarianism was now exchanged for what may well have been no guidance at all.

With this abdication of paternal authority came a fraternal complication as well. In sharp contrast to Virginia's own isolation and loneliness was her brother Thoby's exciting new life at Cambridge beginning in 1899, which aroused in Virginia the inevitable resentment and jealousy of a more talented sibling denied like membership in a community because of her sex.[19] Despite evidence of Leslie's ritual continuation of guiding Virginia's reading (*Letters* I, 42), she was daily growing hungrier for books and talk. By 1901 she was ready to confess to Thoby why she must cram her letter with a rush of thoughts about *Cymbeline,* although the expression of her sentiments here is only partial and couched as an apology, complete with the conciliatory and pacifying remark that her difficulty in finding the play's characters human enough may well be the result of her "feminine weakness in the upper region": "Just as I feel in the mood to talk about these things," she writes in a weak attempt at humor, "you go and plant yourself in Cambridge" (*Letters* I, 45–46). At the time, of course, Thoby had already been at Cambridge for two

---

18. Annan, *Leslie Stephen,* p. 105.
19. See Bell, *Virginia Woolf,* I, 70–71.

years, and Virginia's belated recognition of it well accords
with the fact that this appears to be only her third letter
to him there, and only the first in which her appetite
for books is indulged and her sense of intellectual depri-
vation made at all clear to him. It was not until Thoby's
last term, however, that she was finally willing to express
the extent of her hurt and her profound sense of isolation:

> I dont [*sic*] get anybody to argue with me now, and
> feel the want. I have to delve from books, painfully
> and all alone, what you get every evening sitting over
> your fire and smoking your pipe with Strachey etc.
> No wonder my knowledge is but scant. Theres
> [*sic*] nothing like talk as an educator I'm sure.
> [*Letters* I, 77]

Like his father, however, Thoby "felt," according to
Virginia's recollection, that she and Vanessa "should
accept our place" (*MB*, 123).[20] Wedged between father
and brother like Cam on the voyage to the lighthouse
(even the name suggests the family university), Virginia was
clearly living an embattled existence at 22 Hyde Park Gate.
Although her Duckworth half-brothers were determined
to take both her and Vanessa into society, the brothers'
company, like the company of the innumerable family
friends and relatives who regularly descended on the sisters
out of sympathy, was hardly what either of them desired.
Besides, neither of the girls, particularly Virginia, was
comfortable in a world where, as George Duckworth put
it, " 'they're not used to young women saying *any*thing' "
(*MB*, 152). "We aint [*sic*] popular" was Virginia's terse summary (*Letters* I, 43). The Duckworths' demands, however,

---

20. It is significant, too, that Virginia endeavored unsuccessfully to fit the
redeeming but syntactically inadmissible phrase "allied by old ties" into the
same sentence in the manuscript copy of the memoir (*MB*, 123n.).

obliged Virginia to divide her life increasingly in two, with the morning hours devoted to reading and writing and the afternoons and evenings to the interminable boredom of social engagements designed to instill in her a proper feeling and respect for the duties expected of a young woman of her position and beauty (*MB,* 129–30).

During the mornings, however, Virginia was still free to read the books she was by now selecting on her own from her father's library. At last she might explore what had long been forbidden. In search of new principles and new authorities to replace those paternal ones now declining in strength and assurance (from the start these new principles could not be identical with the Cambridge of the male members of the family), she came at last upon the writer who challenged all that her father represented. Knowing long and well his mortal aversion to Pater, here was a remedy far stronger than even Vanessa's courageous personal resistance to his infuriating combination of authoritarianism and absence.

Before 1898, there was only a single volume of Pater in Stephen's library, a first edition of the *Imaginary Portraits,* presented to him in 1887 by Pater himself, who had inscribed the book and left his calling-card—perhaps because Stephen, who frequently barred visitors from his presence, had refused to see him.[21] Although by 1898 or a little later on a copy of *Plato and Platonism* was also to find its way into Stephen's library,[22] it was almost certainly in the form of the *Imaginary Portraits* that Virginia first experienced Pater directly.

21. "Early items from the library of Leslie Stephen &c," "Victoria Square Catalogue," in *Catalogue of Books from the Library of Leonard and Virginia Woolf* (Brighton: Holleyman and Treacher, 1975), sec. 1, p. 33.

22. Since *Plato and Platonism* first appeared in 1893, Stephen's 1898 copy is a reprint, and may have been acquired at a later date ("Early items from the library of Leslie Stephen," sec. 1, p. 33).

The logic of this first encounter is dramatic, especially if we recall the extent to which Woolf's fiction, like Joyce's, has no clearer anticipation in English prose than Pater's own fictional portraits.[23] With his careful attention to the movement of his characters' thoughts—in the opening sketch they are given in the diary form that Virginia had already begun to show a liking for—Pater anticipates the lavish care Woolf's narrator will also take in tracing the mood and tone of her characters' ideas and sensations. Even more to the point at this early moment in Virginia's career, however, is the degree to which the common predicament of the central characters in the *Imaginary Portraits* must have spoken directly to her present situation. With an attraction toward Pater already prepared for in her incipient rebellion against her father's values, the dreamy lives of Pater's imaginary figures, youthful ones played out in the vicinity of houses fortified like Virginia's own, must have solicited her immediate sympathy and identification.

The first of the sketches—and probably the very first Pater Virginia was to read—is told by a female narrator whose situation bears a striking resemblance to the one in which Virginia herself was now embroiled. Sitting out her existence at home while the male members of the house-

23. See James Hafley, "Walter Pater's *Marius* and the Technique of Modern Fiction," *Modern Fiction Studies* 3 (Summer 1957): 99–109; U. C. Knoepflmacher, *Religious Humanism and the Victorian Novel: George Eliot, Walter Pater, and Samuel Butler* (Princeton: Princeton University Press, 1965), pp. 169–70; Gerald Cornelius Monsman, *Pater's Portraits: Mythic Pattern in the Fiction of Walter Pater* (Baltimore: The Johns Hopkins University Press, 1967), p. 32; Ruth Z. Temple, "The Ivory Tower as Lighthouse," in Richard Ellman, ed., *Edwardians and Late Victorians: English Institute Essays, 1959* (New York: Columbia University Press, 1960), p. 34. See also Robert M. Scotto, " 'Visions' and 'Epiphanies': Fictional Technique in Pater's *Marius* and Joyce's *Portrait*," *James Joyce Quarterly* 11 (Fall 1973): 41–50; and William E. Buckler's recent *"Marius the Epicurean:* Beyond Victorianism," *Victorian Poetry* 16 (Spring–Summer 1978): 165.

hold make their fame and fortune in the great world outside, Pater's narrator doubtless provided a sudden shock of
recognition. Although the female accent in Pater's work
is ordinarily negligible and sometimes even abusive, in
Virginia's case this unusual instance of reasonable feminine
portraiture happily provided the initial point of contact.
To be sure, the narrator of "A Prince of Court Painters" is
no more overt about her plight as a woman than Virginia
herself was at the time, although it is just this fear and
reticence that adds to the identity between them. Pater's
narrator here is even inclined to apologize for her intellect
by ascribing its shortcomings to the inherent weaknesses
of a woman's mind, much as Virginia does in her letter to
Thoby. "There, is my simple notion," says Pater's narrator
in exemplary self-effacement, "wholly womanly perhaps,
but which I may hold by" (*IP,* 33).

It is, moreover, the narrator's father—himself a sculptor
of repute—who has guided her life in the absence of her
mother, but whose attention here is largely taken up by
the arrival of his godson, Antony Watteau, who comes to
paint under his tutelage. The narrator watches Watteau's
career unfold from afar, a melancholy and self-effacing
observer, and the victim not only of unrequited love for
Watteau himself but also—at least from Virginia's point of
view—the victim of sexual politics. "There are good things,
attractive things, in life," she writes in her diary, "meant
for one and not for another—not meant perhaps for me"
(*IP,* 28). "With myself," she laments, "how to get through
time becomes sometimes the question,—unavoidably;
though it strikes me as a thing unspeakably sad in a life so
short as ours" (*IP,* 25). In an effort to countermand
Watteau's rejection of both herself and her brother, Jean-
Baptiste Pater (with whom Pater himself was wont to
claim kinship), the "central interest" in her life becomes

the latter's work—"I bury myself in that," she writes, with a considerable stress on the verb (*IP, 26*).

While Pater's female narrator gazes at death, however, the sensibility Virginia encountered in the *Imaginary Portraits* pointed instead to a new lease on life. Indeed, Pater's book delivered exactly what its opening sentence had promised: "They have been renovating my father's large workroom" (*IP, 5*). Hence her delight at Pater's concern with purely formal perceptions, particularly by means of the visual arts she now associated with Vanessa's own independence, and with the pleasing absence here of the overt moral considerations and combative accents she associated with patriarchs like her father and the other Victorian writers he had given her to read. Instead of art and morality, here Virginia found art coupled with a concern for perception, vision, fineness; with the *aesthesis* that provides the narrator of "A Prince of Court Painters" with her single pleasure as she gazes at her beloved Watteau's pictures:

> Yes! Besides that unreal, imaginary light upon these scenes, these persons, which is pure gift of his, there was a light, a poetry, in those persons and things themselves, close at hand *we* had not seen. He has enabled us to see it: we are so much the better-off thereby, and I, for one, the better. The world he sets before us so engagingly has its care for purity, its cleanly preferences, in what one is to *see*—in the outsides of things—and there is something, a sign, a memento, at the least, of what makes life really valuable, even in that. There, is my simple notion, wholly womanly perhaps, but which I may hold by, of the purpose of the arts. [*IP,* 32–33]

Moreover, she saw morality in her father's sense of the term thrown to the winds by the ghoulish forces unleashed in the dark revelry of "Denys L'Auxerrois." Even the sanctity of family traditions was opened to question— like the disinterments that are so frequent in Pater's por- traits—in the book's two concluding sketches. It was not, of course, an explicit style of rebellion that Virginia found in "Sebastian van Storck," but a familiar tension between "the ideal of home" (*IP*, 87) and the need of sons —and daughters—to fashion "visionary escapes" (*IP*, 89). Rejecting his father's injunction to " 'be stimulated to action!' " (*IP*, 95), Sebastian instead prefers the contem- plative life, and, like Virginia, desires only the company of thinkers in his pursuit of a new ideal of "intellectual disinterestedness" and "a domain of unimpassioned mind" (*IP*, 104).

Next and last, Virginia encountered Duke Carl's growing impatience with his own family traditions and the gloomy and massive house—evocative of 22 Hyde Park Gate—that embodies them. Like Virginia, Duke Carl wants to "pur- chase his freedom" (*IP*, 138). And like the hopes that in- spire the young Watteau's "new manner of painting" (*IP*, 16), Duke Carl's particular desire as a writer is, in a phrase whose stance looks ahead to "Modern Fiction" and "Mr. Bennett and Mrs. Brown," "for a literature set free, con- terminous with the interests of life itself" (*IP*, 130).

Stephen's copies of the *Imaginary Portraits* and, later on, of *Plato and Platonism*, were by no means the only books by Pater to find their way into Virginia's hands. Perhaps as early as 1902, when the atmosphere at 22 Hyde Park Gate had grown more oppressive than ever, Virginia appears to have gone and bought herself a set of Pater's collected works,[24] a considerable expense for a young woman still living at home with a library hitherto large and

24. In her personal library is the 1900–01 Edition de Luxe of Pater's *Works* (London: Macmillan), with the following signature: "Each volume has a small bookplate pasted inside front cover with the initials 'A. V. S.' [Adeline Virginia

various enough to suit her needs, and with a card for the London Library whenever new needs arose. To be sure, Virginia, like Vanessa, then had a yearly allowance of £50 (*MB*, 131), most of which was already being spent on books and writing materials in anticipation of the way she was to handle spare monies throughout her life. So far as we can tell, however, the allowance usually bought no more than single volumes of favorite authors at a time long before it was her habit to buy collected works as a matter of course. With Pater, however, only the collected works would do, and by 1902 there was, as it turns out, nothing at all fortuitous about such a purchase.

Four years earlier, in September of 1898, Virginia had begun Latin classes with Pater's sister Clara.[25] Together

---

Stephen] enclosed in black parallel lines and the dates 1902 to 1905. In each case the last two figures have been written in in ink in the hand of Virginia" ("Items Belonging to or Presented to Virginia Woolf," "Victoria Square Catalogue," in *Catalogue of Books from the Library of Leonard and Virginia Woolf,* sec. 2, p. 5). Although the catalogue lists the edition of Pater's *Works* as "1900–1904", "1904" is doubtless a miscopying of "1901," since the only two collected editions ever published are the 1900–01 Edition de Luxe in nine volumes and the ten-volume Library Edition of 1910. The 1900–01 *Works* cost four guineas, and could be purchased in "sets only" (*The English Catalogue of Books,* vol. 6, January 1898–December 1900 [London: Sampson Low, Marston, 1901], p. 487). Since the contents of the Edition de Luxe are the same as those of the Library Edition, I have confined my reading of Pater to the latter so as to deal as strictly as possible with the Pater that Woolf actually read (for an account of Pater's uncollected essays, portraits, and fragments, both published and unpublished, see Samuel Wright, *A Bibliography of the Writings of Walter H. Pater* [New York: Garland, 1975]).

I am indebted to Brenda Silver for pointing out to me a passage in Woolf's unpublished diary notebook from Christmas 1904–May 1905 in which she reports going to Hatchards to buy Stevenson and Pater (entry for Monday, 13 March 1905). This would place the purchase of Pater as late as 1905, the terminal date on the bookplate. Silver also reports *The Renaissance* among Woolf's list of books from 1905 in the same diary, even though Woolf's recollection almost twenty years later has her reading *Marius* with relish at least as early as 1903 (*MB*, 160).

25. It appears that Virginia began Latin with Clara in 1898 and Greek in 1899 or 1900. (Before that, she had studied Greek in Dr. Warr's classroom at King's College in London [see *Letters* I, 10, 13].) Virginia refers to "Miss

with her older sister Hester, Clara had maintained a home in Kensington in the years following her brother's death at Oxford in 1894, and apparently took private pupils in the classics whenever finances were grim enough to require it.[26] Always close, the Paters—Walter, Clara, and Hester—had lived together since 1869, when all three had taken a house in Oxford to remedy the homelessness caused by the death of their Aunt Bessey, who had served in the role of mother following Maria Pater's death in 1854. In 1885, however, the family moved to London, presumably because Pater had grown irritated and hurt by the university's continuing suspicion about his work and his morals, despite more than ten years of diligent discretion. In town, however, a generous and salutary welcome awaited him in most literary and artistic circles,[27] which succeeded in raising Pater to unusually "radiant spirits," as Lionel Johnson put it after visiting him at home in Kensington in 1889.[28] Nonetheless, Pater and his sisters eventually decided to return to Oxford in 1893, probably the result, as with Hardy, of a certain temperamental dislike of society that prevailed despite the attentions of his disciples,

---

Paters [sic] Intermediate Latin class, on Tuesdays at 2" in a letter dated 17 September 1898 (*Letters* I, 20), and to "Miss Pater's Greek" in a letter of April 1899 (*Letters* I, 23). In October 1900, however, she writes to Emma Vaughan that she is going to her "first class with Miss Pater" (*Letters* I, 39); the most reasonable explanation seems to be that not until 1900 did she begin private lessons. The start of Virginia's lessons with Clara in 1898 may also explain the appearance of *Plato and Platonism* in Stephen's library that year or soon afterward. Moreover, despite Stephen's aversion to Pater himself, Clara was probably his choice for a teacher rather than Virginia's, at least according to Annan, who sees the choice as another example of Stephen's liberal treatment of his daughters (p. 106).

26. "The ladies are in great need of money," wrote Edmund Gosse to the literary agent William Colles a week after Pater's death (*Letters of Walter Pater*, p. 156).

27. A. C. Benson, *Walter Pater* (New York: Macmillan, 1906), p. 117.

28. Quoted in *Letters of Walter Pater*, p. xxiv.

and perhaps also because there was too much traveling for both Clara and himself to contend with during term-time.

For like her brother, as it turns out, Virginia's tutor had also been obliged to be at Oxford during the week. No stranger to teaching, she had assisted in the founding of Oxford's Somerville College for Women in the late 1870s and early 1880s, and had served as both its vice-principal and its first classics tutor, even though she had not come to learn Greek and Latin until well after she was twenty-five, despite being her brother's junior by only two years.[29]

Although it is hard to determine what Virginia's lessons with Clara were like, there are still accounts to be had of Clara herself. For Mrs. Humphry Ward, who had been a neighbor during the years her husband was Pater's colleague at Brasenose, Clara's personal and intellectual presence had been central to the Pater household at Oxford, and after Pater's death, both Clara and Hester (or Tottie, as she was called) "became the vigilant and joint guardians of their brother's books and fame."[30] Although Mrs. Ward is perhaps a little too "vigilant" in her own way here, that "Miss Pater represented," as one historian puts it, "the quintessence of Oxford aestheticism" is probably undeniable.[31] Even Virginia refers to her as "cultivated," although only after crossing out the word "sympathetic" that stands beneath it in an unpublished notebook from 1903.[32]

Doubtless Clara was "cultivated" and "sympathetic" at once, and we can be sure that, at the age of sixteen,

29. See Vera Brittain, *The Women at Oxford: A Fragment of History* (New York: Macmillan, 1960), pp. 43, 82, 258.

30. Mrs. Humphry Ward, *A Writer's Recollections* (London: Collins, 1918), pp. 124–25.

31. Brittain, *The Women at Oxford*, p. 42. See also Levey on Clara's "temperamental affinities" with her brother (p. 44).

32. Diary/Holograph Notebook, 1903 (Berg), p. 49.

Virginia was much impressed with the woman whose portrait now hangs in Somerville with a "serious, oval face"
and "contemplative eyes."[33] With her legendary Pre-
Raphaelite garb and her airy charm, Clara brought color
back to Virginia's world of gloom ("all blue china, Persian
cats, and Morris wallpapers," she remembered as late as
1931 [*Letters* IV, 411]). Clara probably recalled shades of
Virginia's mother as well, who had not only supervised the
children's lessons until her death, but had also been herself
immersed in the world of the Pre-Raphaelites in childhood and youth, a maternal inheritance that Quentin Bell
describes in *Bloomsbury* as a profoundly "un-Stephen atti-
tude" that was "concerned," as the Paters were, "with the
pleasures of the senses and above all with the pleasures of
the visible world."[34]

It is doubtless to the latter part of this period that
Virginia refers in "Old Bloomsbury"—the period from late
1902 to early 1904—when she remembers lying in bed at
midnight reading "a page or two of *Marius the Epicurean*
for which I had then a passion." And yet her passion was
not to be enjoyed unadulterated. In the same passage she
recalls how her reading was suddenly interrupted by one of
George Duckworth's nightly assaults, "in order, as he told
Dr. Savage later, to comfort me for the fatal illness of
my father—who was dying three or four storeys lower
down of cancer" (*MB,* 160).

Although tangled among such painful associations, as
a respite from these circumstances she had not only Pater
to read but Clara's sensibility to absorb, remember, and
assess. Given the strictures of intercourse between pupil
and teacher at the turn of the century, Virginia probably
managed to extract, at least in atmosphere, a blend of

33. Brittain, p. 42.
34. Quentin Bell, *Bloomsbury* (New York: Basic Books, 1968), p. 40.

aestheticism and women's educational rights from her tutor, both of which provided effective antidotes to life with father and the Duckworths. Soon after Virginia's Latin lessons began in 1898, the Pater sisters appear to have become the Stephen sisters' companions frequently enough to suggest that some special relationship had grown up between them. Between 1898 and 1901 Virginia was not only receiving Clara at 22 Hyde Park Gate for her lessons (*Letters* I, 26), but also inviting her (with much apprehension) for a weekend in the country (*Letters* I, 36) and meeting her and Tottie at parties, where they comported, she wrote to Emma Vaughan, "like Botichelli [*sic*] angels" (*Letters* I, 33).[35]

By 1902, however, Clara had suddenly become an "old wretch" (*Letters* I, 64), and a new public rhetoric toward her had begun even though she was still welcome at Bloomsbury parties as late as 1905 (*Letters* I, 179-80). Despite the fact that Virginia's reading of Pater's collected works was beginning in earnest, it was Janet Case who was now Virginia's Greek tutor. Case was to become a lifelong friend and Virginia's introduction to feminism proper, and she replaced cultivation and sympathy with toughness, probably slighting Clara's rigor when she grew exasperated with Virginia's syntax, and doubtless impugning Clara's politics, which were of the old-fashioned sort that the Paters' friendship with Mrs. Ward—who opposed Women's Suffrage—should have made clear to Virginia all along.[36]

That a revaluation of Clara was already under way is clear enough from the changes that set in under Case's

---

35. Note the uncannily similar description of the Stephen sisters by David Garnett: "Vanessa was the Virgin, with Quentin an infant Jesus in her arms; Virginia a Saint or Angel, with none of the beauty of maternity" (*The Flowers of the Forest* [New York: Harcourt, Brace, 1956], p. 160).

36. See Ray Strachey, *"The Cause"*: *A Short History of the Women's Movement in Great Britain* (London: Bell, 1928), pp. 319, 335, 355.

moral and political corrective to Virginia's burgeoning aestheticism. As a new authority in her own right, Case was to achieve immediate heroic stature in Virginia's eyes by protesting George Duckworth's public fondlings,[37] and succeeded in supplanting both Clara's attractiveness and the ideals she represented. Indeed, Virginia's decision that Clara was "cultivated" rather than "sympathetic" comes in an early literary exercise entitled "Miss Case," whom, we are told there, is a more "professional" tutor than Clara even though Virginia confesses to not liking her at first in a series of emendations and cancellations expressive of the changes that were now going into effect:

> But I am sorry to say—really now a little repentant— that she did not at first attract me. She ~~stirred a~~ was too cheerful and muscular. ~~I was not allowed to f~~ She made me feel 'contradictious' as the nurses used to say.[38]

Case's cautionary influence seems in fact to have been so strong that it caused Woolf even in 1939 to leave Clara's name dangling in the margin of her draft of "A Sketch of the Past," where she discusses her study of Greek in the text proper only in terms of her lessons with Case (MB, 127n.).

By now Virginia's overt dealings with the Paters were concluded. Her reading of Pater from 1902 to 1905 would be completed in silence, and the precursor and his family driven even deeper underground in the future. The story of the repression and some of its causes are to be found in the two portraits that commemorate Clara in Woolf's later fiction. Both present the Paters in considerable disguise, and both include some suggestions as to why the

---

37. See Bell, *Virginia Woolf*, I, 43n.
38. Diary/Holograph Notebook, 1903 (Berg), pp. 49–50.

enduring pressure to rewrite the Paterian interlude was as acute as it was.

The first portrait takes up an entire sketch, "Slater's Pins Have No Points," with the telltale prefix, "Moments of Vision," suppressed when the story was published during Woolf's lifetime in 1928.[39] The sketch is acknowledged by Bell to be drawn directly from the Paters,[40] with Clara the principal character (Miss Craye) and her recently deceased academic brother, named Julius in the story, a cipher for Pater himself. The names "Slater" and "Craye," of course, are a virtual anagram for the name "Clara Pater"—according to Woolf's diary, Clara's original remark was " 'Barker's pins have no points' " (AWD, 99), with the change to "Slater" obviously designed to suggest the name "Pater" instead—while the Crayes' family roots in Canterbury (HH, 104) recall the Paters' removal to that same neighborhood in 1853, when the young Walter became a student at the King's School. Even the domestic details of the Crayes' life before the death of Julius are drawn directly from what we know of the Paters' household habits—the proverbial floral displays; the keeping of cats; above all, the fact that "none" of the Crayes "married" (HH, 104). There was, says Woolf, "something queer" or "odd" about Julius (HH, 105), and "odd perhaps" about "Julia too" (HH, 105). The atmosphere of homosexuality surrounding Pater himself now seems to carry over to the Clara figure, Julia,[41] and it is met with ambivalence in Virginia's fictive persona here, Fanny Wilmot, the story's

39. See B. J. Kirkpatrick, A Bibliography of Virginia Woolf, rev. ed. (London: Rupert Hart-Davis, 1967), p. 127.

40. Bell, Virginia Woolf, I, 68n.

41. In a 1927 letter to Vita Sackville-West, Woolf refers to the just-completed sketch as "a nice little story about Sapphism" (Letters III, 397).

narrator and, like Woolf herself, the older woman's private pupil.

Julia's spinsterhood—the fact that she goes through
life "alone" (HH, 109) and somewhat frustrated—both
disturbs and intrigues Fanny, leading her to recall how
Julia used to attract "her brother's friends from Oxford or
Cambridge" in her youth (HH, 107) only to disappoint
them all. Here, of course, Fanny is granted extrapersonal
knowledge of Julia's past (it is a form of extended consciousness we encounter often enough among Woolf's
characters), and it is helped along, doubtless, by the way in
which Clara's history partially came to represent Virginia's
own in the years following Leslie's death, when she began
enjoying the company of Thoby's friends from Cambridge.
The difference, however, is that it was largely Thoby's
friends who were guilty of diasppointing Virginia—"there
was no physical attraction between us," she remarks in
"Old Bloomsbury," recalling how most of the men were
only attracted to each other (MB, 172). Here Bloomsbury
homosexuality also becomes a figure for the sudden absence of family life in the "manly" Stephen mold in the
period following his death, with Virginia's guilty ambivalence toward her dead father getting doubled in the
ambivalence she felt toward her new homosexual friends.
In the story, of course, both forms of ambivalence are concentrated in Fanny's tangled feelings toward Miss Craye,
whose "oddness" is not only disturbing, but, like her
brother's, also "seductive" (HH, 105).

Fanny's ambivalence toward Miss Craye is eventually
thematized or abstracted into a conflict between two
visions of life itself. What disturbs Fanny most about her
tutor is the "perpetual frustration" (HH, 106) caused by
her inability to "reach" out to the world (HH, 105), "to
break the pane of glass which separated them"—Julius as
well as Julia herself—"from other people" (HH, 104).

Structuring the sketch, then, is a tension between the practical side of life, signified by heterosexual love and "the pettiness of daily life" (*HH*, 110), and the Crayes' "cool glassy world of Bach fugues" (*HH*, 103), signifying in its turn the solipsistic and contemplative universe of Paterian *aesthesis.*

It is, of course, this same conflict between the worldly and the aesthetic—between social responsibility and procreation on the one hand and contemplation and homosexuality on the other—that structures the antagonism between Stephen and Pater themselves, and that may be seen here as the larger ancestral struggle in which Fanny's ambivalence toward Julia—and Woolf's toward her new Bloomsbury life—is to be situated as well. From this point of view, the very "tug-of-war" (*HH*, 109) between self and world that Fanny perceives in her tutor appears to be her own ambivalence projected outward, investing Julia with a conflict that really comes from within. With "An Unwritten Novel" and "Mr. Bennett and Mrs. Brown" reminding us that Woolf's sketches are often generated by the projections or misreadings of their narrators, it is hardly surprising that Julia's "frustration" here is really a version of Fanny's—or Woolf's—own ambivalence, so that the thematic structure of the story as a whole emerges as a displaced account of the conflict between father and Pater in Woolf's own imagination.

Most telltale of all, however, is the symptomatic confusion at the close of the story in which Julia remembers tending, not her brother's "sickness" but "her father's" (*HH*, 111). Without so much as a single mention of either the Crayes' father or an illness associated with him earlier in the story, it is surely brother Julius's fatal sickness that is alluded to here, although the silent substitution of the word "father" where "brother" alone is logical constitutes a parapraxis—the momentary intrusion of another, repressed train of thought into the otherwise uninterrupted flow of the manifest narrative. Of course, because Julia's (faulty) remembrance is given directly through Fanny's consciousness (*HH,* 110, 111), the slip seems to be Fanny's own, and suggests that Woolf reinvents her own paternity through Fanny by exchanging Pater the brother for Pater the father. Pater thereby covers the legal father, too, whom he replaces in the symptomatic posture of sickness.

Hence Fanny's ambivalence toward Miss Craye derives from an exchangeability or struggle to signify between Pater and Stephen themselves, a struggle which initiates all the isomorphic conflicts at work in the story. With Stephen representative of Hyde Park Gate, family life, and social responsibility, and Pater representative of Bloomsbury, homosexuality, and private contemplation, the conflict is both psychological and literary, with each paternal figure both originating and standing for the larger antiphonal contexts of politics and aesthetics in which Woolf's work is itself to be situated. Here, too, we may suggest sources for our customary understanding of Woolf's project as an active conflict between, for example, what Alice van Buren Kelley calls "fact" and "vision," although to say that the conflict is also one between what Nancy Topping Bazin calls the "masculine" and "feminine" in Woolf's search for the synthesis of androgyny would be to neglect the degree to which Woolf's feminism—which is not to be identified with the "feminine" any more than the "masculine"—is itself driven or powered by her father's insistence on the writer's responsibility to society.[42]

42. See Alice van Buren Kelley, *The Novels of Virginia Woolf: Fact and Vision* (Chicago: University of Chicago Press, 1973); Nancy Topping Bazin, *Virginia Woolf and the Androgynous Vision* (New Brunswick, N.J.: Rutgers University Press, 1973). Roger Poole's recent *The Unknown Virginia Woolf* (Cambridge: Cambridge University Press, 1978) insists on the irreconcilable nature of such differences in Woolf's work as a whole (p. 262).

In Woolf's second portrait of Clara, written and re-written over the course of the 1930s, the ambivalence of 1927 finally resolves itself into praise, affection, and the active repression of sexual feeling. One effect of such a resolution is to reinvest the tutor and the scene of instruction with redeeming social value, with the repression of homosexuality producing a tacit gain in social or procreative energy. Thus, if Clara's active participation in the founding of Somerville College contributed little in the way of worldly merit to the sketch of Julia Craye in "Slater's Pins," it becomes a considerable factor in this later portrait of Clara as Lucy Craddock, Kitty's history tutor in *The Years*. Although by no means a feminist, Miss Craddock is nonetheless an example to Kitty of almost solitary success as a woman at Oxford whose life is devoted to intellectual labor in a world dominated by men. It is, however, in a suppressed draft sequence of *The Years*, published recently as *The Pargiters: The Novel-Essay Portion of 'The Years,'* that we get Woolf's full portrait of Miss Craddock, which seems to have been considerably shortened and condensed by the time *The Years* itself was completed in 1936.

Like Leslie Stephen, it is Kitty's father, Master of Edward Pargiter's college at Oxford, who prefers a woman tutor to the alternative of Kitty's actually enrolling in classes, with the telltale and ironic possibility of Somerville itself being rejected (along with Cheltenham) as the first possibility for her continuing education (*P*, 100). The choice of Miss Craddock, however, is a happy one, since Kitty "loved Miss Craddock—perhaps she loved her better than anybody in the whole world" (*P*, 100). At the time of their lessons, Miss Craddock, like Clara, is already "over fifty, and very plain" (*P*, 111), although Kitty has nonetheless fallen "in love with something which seemed to her," as indeed it did to Virginia, "wonderful, new, exciting—the disinterested passion" (doubling and combining Sebastian's "disinterestedness" and "unimpassioned mind") "for things in themselves" (*P,* 112). Indeed, Woolf calls upon the authority of Mrs. Ward's autobiography to validate what she calls "this idealisation of the woman teacher" (*P,* 112) as a sign of the times, thereby confirming the portrait's source in that Oxford environment of the 1870s and 1880s, and drawing in its train once again the flowers (*Y,* 68; *P,* 112), the poverty (*Y,* 67; *P,* 100), and the taking of private pupils as her tutor's sole means of income.

If Kitty has fallen in love with Miss Craddock, Miss Craddock's love for Kitty is itself considerable, although unlike Miss Craye she is discreet about it and "considered it her duty to repress it" (*P,* 113). With such assurances, Woolf is free to say that Miss Craddock's liking for Kitty is "undoubtedly influenced by some long suppressed, almost extinct, sexual instinct" (*P,* 113), although it is precisely the achievement of what is already a kind of implicit sublimation that transforms Miss Craye's homosexual withdrawal from life into Miss Craddock's status as an exemplary and socially useful figure in the fight for women's rights.

If Miss Craddock has repressed her feelings toward Kitty, however, the men at Oxford have done little to repress their feelings toward Miss Craddock. Indeed, it is Miss Craddock's martyrdom that makes her the socially useful creature that she is in *The Years* and *The Pargiters* alike. With almost Dickensian pathos, Woolf tells us that "Poor Lucy's little book . . . was treated as the scribbling of an industrious child" (*P,* 124). Kitty's father has himself "dismissed Miss Craddocks [*sic*] little book . . . with a kindly smile"; it is, according to the Master, "quite unreadable" (*P,* 103). Indeed, when Kitty dreams of becoming "a learned woman" on the model of her tutor, she recalls that "Lucy Craddock was not learned at all in her father's sense of the word" (P, 103). " 'Why didn't they give her a professorship or something—a fellowship anyhow?' " she asks. But, "of course, that was impossible because Miss Craddock was a woman" (P, 119).

Woolf even sets Kitty's romance with her tutor within the explicit context of female activism at Oxford during the exact period of the Paters' residence there, alluding to Clara's considerable role in the movement by means of the real history deployed in the text side by side with its imaginary characters:

> Women were making efforts to establish some kind of College for themselves in Oxford in 1880; Somerville and Lady Margaret's were actually founded in 1879. But the contempt which these efforts roused in the ordinary don and undergraduate, the opposition [with] which all requests for money to build, or for the right to attend lectures or share in the educational advantages of men were received . . . could scarcely fail to impress the mind of an intelligent girl of twenty-one. [P, 125]

And yet immediately following the passage cited above, Woolf calls upon Pater himself by name to dramatize such contempt in a specific way. Citing an incident reported in Thomas Wright's 1907 *Life of Walter Pater*,[43] Woolf uses Wright's account of Pater's wilfully ungallant conduct at a reception at one of Oxford's new women's colleges for plainly political purposes:

> the lady Head of the house dropped her white kid glove in front of Pater; and Pater, at least, thought

43. For an account of Wright's notorious unreliability, see *Letters of Walter Pater*, p. xvi.

that she did it on purpose. Therefore, he "instead
of gallantly picking it up, walked on and trod on it."
[*P*, 126][44]

Woolf goes on to cite more of the incident related by
Wright, including Pater's reported remark that " 'it was an
insinuation of the devil that caused this woman to drop
her glove' " (*P*, 126),[45] although she stops short of relating
the conclusion of the account, in which Pater is said to
have condemned marriage by claiming that " 'women
won't pull our way' " because " 'they are so perverse!' "[46]
Coming as it does in the midst of Kitty's bitter reflections
in *The Pargiters* about the role and status of women at
Oxford (in *The Years* itself Kitty's thoughts on the matter
are considerably softened), the incident stands as a major
example of Woolf's condemnation of male university life
and the overriding symbolic role assigned to Pater within it.

Such a view, however, is surely a misreading, albeit
a necessary one for Woolf, of Pater's career at Oxford,
which could hardly be identified with mainstream life
there, especially during Jowett's reign. While Pater may in
retrospect be seen to derive in an Oxford line from Newman and Arnold,[47] or, as Harold Bloom suggests, from
Ruskin himself,[48] such continuities were by no means
clear at the time. Although Pater was, in the well-known
phrase, "vaguely celebrated"[49] during the late 'sixties and
early 'seventies, the appearance of *The Renaissance* in
1873 almost immediately alienated him from the univer-

44. Thomas Wright, *The Life of Walter Pater*, 2 vols. (1907; rpt. New York:
Haskell House, 1969), II, 130.

45. Ibid., p. 131.

46. Ibid.

47. See David J. DeLaura, *Hebrew and Hellene in Victorian England:
Newman, Arnold, and Pater* (Austin: University of Texas Press, 1969).

48. Harold Bloom, "Introduction: The Crystal Man," *Selected Writings of
Walter Pater* (New York: New American Library, 1974), pp. vii–xxxi.

49. Benson, *Walter Pater*, p. 22; see also *Letters of Walter Pater*, pp. xx–xxi.

sity community at large. Already known for "a certain want of balance" and "a certain recklessness of statement" in his conversation,[50] the publication of his "gospel," as Mrs. Ward called it, not only "stirred" Oxford but also "scandalised" it.[51] Indeed, within a month of the book's publication, John Wordsworth, a former pupil of Pater's and himself a fellow at Brasenose since 1867, felt obliged to write him that "no one can be more grieved than I am at the conclusions at which you represent yourself as having arrived."[52] Wordsworth, however, was speaking not only for himself, referring as he does to "the pain" Pater's ideas "have caused me and I know also many others."[53] Jowett's enduring anxiety about his own role as a contributor to the *Essays and Reviews* may have made him particularly sensitive about men like Pater, who threatened to become the kind of immoralist it was feared might emerge from the climate of intellectual latitude which his own actions had in some degree abetted. Here, in fact, Jowett could even join Leslie Stephen, otherwise an antagonist, in bemoaning the excesses both men ruefully awaited as one consequence of the loss of faith they had helped to produce.

Less than a year after the book appeared, in fact, Pater was refused the nomination for a university proctorship that he had expected to receive because of his seniority, the nomination going instead to the junior Wordsworth. By the 1880s, Pater had done what he could to reingratiate himself with the Oxford community, although even as late as 1885—only a few years after the time of the incident inserted in *The Pargiters*—he was passed over once

50. Ibid., p. 187. Mrs. Ward recalls the "great tumult" that arose at a dinner party when Pater slighted Christianity by saying that " 'no reasonable person could govern their lives [*sic*] by the opinions or actions of a man who died eighteen centuries ago.' " (p. 121).

51. Ward, *A Writer's Recollections*, p. 120.

52. *Letters of Walter Pater*, p. 13.

53. Ibid.

again, this time as the successor to Ruskin's chair as Slade Professor of Fine Art. Indeed, Pater's acute sense of "isolation"[54] at Oxford seems at last to have driven him to London with his sisters in the summer of 1885.

For Woolf, however, such internal Oxonian disputes could hardly have mattered with the college beadle in *A Room of One's Own* standing guard against women with strict indifference whether the gate was that of Balliol or of Brasenose. Despite Pater's embattled "modern" position at Oxford, by the 'thirties Woolf's early sympathies, particularly with the liberationist Pater of the *Imaginary Portraits,* seem to have been refined out of existence by the overweening demands of her growing political preoccupations, at least on the evidence of *The Pargiters, Three Guineas,* and those diary entries burdened with the real threat of fascism. Like the parapraxis in "Slater's Pins" and the graphic cancellation in the 1902 notebook, Woolf's splitting off of brother and sister in *The Pargiters* is another illustration of her need to repress the Pater connection even as it is being maintained, although here it expresses itself in a far more ingenious and evasive way than in either of the previous examples. For Woolf sets up as direct opposites siblings bound together by blood and vision alike, rewriting not only the story of Pater's Oxford career in the process but also the Paters' domestic life. The gain to be had from such a combination of disguise and displacement lies, of course, in rendering the old connection immune from the point of view of feminism, and, by valorizing Clara's activism, in making (at least one of) the Paters also consistent with it. Indeed, the "new form" of the "Essay-Novel" is part of the gain, too, since it allows Woolf to use real names or not as the occasion and the

54. Benson, p. 138.

necessity—may require. Having neutralized her father by arming herself with Pater, she is now able to neutralize Pater as well, by arming herself with a politics whose own source leads back to Stephen to put the compensatory apparatus in motion once again.

If we return to 1904 we can tease out another strand in the story of Pater's repression, although it is more elusive and harder to disentangle with ease or exactitude than the political repression required by Virginia's friendship with Janet Case. It appears in the form of the new male friends Virginia was making through her brother Thoby, with whom she, Vanessa, and their younger brother Adrian had taken a house at 46 Gordon Square, Bloomsbury—doubling with only a slight difference the domestic arrangements of the Paters themselves—in the autumn following their father's death in early 1904. Amid these new friends, chief among them Lytton Strachey and Clive Bell, Virginia seems to have discovered that to discuss Pater, especially by name, was neither fashionable nor sympathetic. With all that Cambridge love for talk and company, the solitude of Paterian meditation was largely an alien quantity despite the overlapping concern with the question of beauty and the status of the Good in relation to art. In fetching a copy of *Diana of the Crossways* to show Ralph Hawtrey what she meant by "atmosphere" in fiction in prewar Bloomsbury (*MB,* 168), Virginia had apparently learned already that one did not fetch a copy of *Marius the Epicurean* for such a purpose. To be sure, in 1922 Bell was publicly to proclaim himself an aesthete in his attack on Shaw in *The New Republic,*[55] while even as late as 1949

55. "The Creed of an Aesthete," reprinted in S. P. Rosenbaum, ed., *The Bloomsbury Group: A Collection of Memoirs, Commentary, and Criticism* (Toronto: University of Toronto Press, 1975), pp. 371-74.

E. M. Forster plainly confessed in a lecture to having been a lover of art for art's sake in his youth.[56] But in neither case are names named or intellectual pedigrees given (in Bell's case, just the lateral alliance with Proust)—all this despite so many obvious similarities with Pater, particularly those between "significant form" and the Paterian formalism adduced by Wimsatt and others.[57] Nor are the names of Pater or Wilde easier to come by in the work, diaries, letters, or memoirs of these Bloomsbury friends, with Wilde's name appearing even less often than Pater's own. Indeed, when Pater is discussed at all, he is usually handled in Strachey's fashion: "As for Pater," he wrote to a friend in 1901, "though I have not read much of him he appears to me so deathly—no motion, no vigour—a waxen style. . . . And after all does he say so very much that is worth hearing? In short I do not like the man."[58]

There appears to have been more than a question of literary manners or of temperament at issue here; there was also the question of social respectability. "The trial of Oscar Wilde," writes Cyril Connolly in connection with Strachey, "was responsible for a flight from aestheticism which had lasted twenty years." While Strachey may have been history's choice, as Connolly puts it, "to lay the ghost of Reading Gaol,"[59] like his friends he remained forever silent on whatever debts he may have owed to High

56. "Art for Art's Sake," in *Two Cheers for Democracy* (New York: Harcourt, Brace, 1951), pp. 88–95.

57. See William K. Wimsatt and Cleanth Brooks, *Literary Criticism: A Short History* (New York: Alfred A. Knopf, 1957), p. 490; Mark Goldman, *The Reader's Art: Virginia Woolf as Literary Critic* (The Hague: Mouton, 1976), p. 112.

58. Quoted in Holroyd, *Lytton Strachey*, I, 118.

59. Cyril Connolly, *Enemies of Promise*, rev. ed. (New York: Macmillan, 1948), p. 47. Strachey did, however, arrange help for the sculptor Jacob Epstein's work on Wilde's tomb (see Holroyd, II, 53).

Aestheticism beyond the obvious ones of dandyism and a languid demeanor. Moreover, the Wilde scandal, as Holroyd says of Strachey's undergraduate years, "was still very much present in many people's minds,"[60] and with Lytton tearing about the country in jealous pursuit of Duncan Grant and Maynard Keynes soon after their graduation, it was probably wisest not to discuss Pater or his school at all, much less to praise him or avow him as an influence. Besides, the temperamental differences were already sufficient to blunt and obscure whatever identities may have been latent between them. And self-proclaimed aesthetes as they were, these friends were also only cautiously bohemian, true children of the well-to-do whose insistence on the amenities as merely understood (particularly with Clive Bell in the company) was part of the freedom they required to do the work that would accord them their rightful places in the traditions in which they had been raised.

Moreover, with Leonard Woolf's return from Ceylon in 1911, the aesthetic tone of the circle that awaited him was, particularly for Virginia, soon to be exchanged for a more political one. From this point of view, Leonard represents the return of Leslie Stephen and a reinforcement for the work Virginia was now doing for the women's movement through Janet Case and her friend Margaret Llewelyn Davies. An often intolerant rationalist concerned almost exclusively with political, social, and moral questions despite his lifelong appreciation of aesthetic avant-gardism, Woolf was patriarchal in the Victorian mold. He even bested what Virginia called Stephen's prophetic or "Hebrew" qualities (*MB*, 40): "Woolf," says Keynes in

60. Holroyd, I, 137.

"My Early Beliefs," was "a rabbi."[61] For Virginia he became, or recreated, the cautionary and corrective figure who stood for social responsibility and moral authority, although with the saving difference that he provided sympathy instead of demanding it.

Besides, for the male members of Bloomsbury, it was not Pater but G. E. Moore who was decisive in their youth. Here, however, a latent connection tends to reassert itself. Even though this new Cambridge ethos was different in style from Pater's Oxonian romanticism, it nonetheless matched it with its equally insistent emphasis on the authority of one's personal judgment and the rejection of the authority of mere tradition and inherited taste. Although Moore himself rejected pleasure as a sign of what is good, he nonetheless found value to reside in one's "state of mind,"[62] in what Keynes was later to remember as "timeless, passionate states of contemplation and communion, largely unattached to 'before' and 'after.' "[63]

Different as they were, as influences, then, Pater and Moore were surprisingly similar in a stance common to them both in a heritage of Protestant revelation through personal witness.[64] Hence Virginia was, as it turns out,

61. John Maynard Keynes, "My Early Beliefs," in *Two Memoirs* (London: Rupert Hart-Davis, 1949), p. 81. Poole also emphasizes the rationalist in Leonard, and takes him as representative of male Bloomsbury as a whole (*The Unknown Virginia Woolf,* pp. 62 ff.); he suggests, too, the similarities between Leonard and Leslie Stephen in Woolf's mind (pp. 65–66). See also Phyllis Rose's recent *Woman of Letters: A Life of Virginia Woolf* (New York: Oxford University Press, 1978), p. 90.

62. G. E. Moore, *Principia Ethica* (1903; rpt. Cambridge: Cambridge University Press, 1966), p. 205.

63. Keynes, p. 83. Morris Beja links Moore's "states of mind" laterally with the Joycean epiphany (*Epiphany in the Modern Novel* [Seattle: University of Washington Press, 1971], p. 124).

64. Keynes himself accents another Protestant quality in the Moorish credo: "Our religion closely followed the English puritan tradition of being chiefly concerned with the salvation of our own souls" (p. 84). The almost parodic—and wholly unconscious—Paterian accents of Keynes's peroration in "My Early Beliefs" is unsettling (pp. 102–03).

well enough prepared for the Moorish predispositions of her new companions, although her own relish for a rejection of Victorianism through "visionary escape"—for individual judgment and the pursuit of passionately intense and immediate "states of mind"—was Paterian or aesthetic rather than patently analytic.

Moreover, whether any of the Bloomsberries realized it or not, the very chest in which the secret papers of their beloved Apostles were kept had been donated to the Society by a member with impeccable Paterian credentials —Oscar Browning.[65] Indeed, in the Society's early days in the mid-nineteenth century, it had even envisioned its mission in a way that had already allied it, unwittingly to be sure, with Pater's own position at Oxford—to countermand the power of Balliol's Jowett, Pater's chief political antagonist and a dictator of national taste whom the Cambridge Apostles sought to replace with their own intellectual authority.[66] With male Bloomsbury "a graduate Apostolic establishment in London,"[67] the drama had come full circle—the Apostles were indeed to be in imminent control of national taste (Desmond MacCarthy, for example, became literary editor of *The New Statesman* in 1920, and succeeded Gosse as senior literary critic at the *Sunday Times* in 1928), although with some irony as well, since they were to be indicted for their power and position in the name of Jowett's own domestic rival, Pater.

It was not until 1937, however, that Bloomsbury (so far as it continued to exist at all at so late a date) publicly avowed its position in the debate over Pater and his influence that had been taken up again in the 'thirties to Pater's profound disadvantage, and sometimes to Blooms-

65. Holroyd, *Lytton Strachey*, I, 162.
66. Ibid., p. 161.
67. Spater and Parsons, *Marriage of True Minds*, p. 36.

bury's as well, by Eliot and, more to the point for Woolf
and her circle, by Wyndham Lewis and the Leavises. The
platform was Desmond MacCarthy's controversial lecture
on Leslie Stephen himself, and the occasion, fittingly
enough, was the annual Leslie Stephen Lecture at Cambridge (the Woolfs, it should be noted, were out of the
country the night Desmond spoke). In a rare avowal of the
chain of influence in which Bloomsbury was itself situated
historically, MacCarthy sets up by name the critical
authority of Pater and Wilde against that of Stephen himself—"the least aesthetic of noteworthy critics"[68]—and
tactfully, almost inaudibly, endorses the creed of the
aesthetes against that of Stephen's muscular and "manly"
style of moral criticism.[69]

To Bloomsbury's perpetual antagonist Mrs. Leavis, of
course, MacCarthy did not seem tactful at all. "Those of us
who do not choose to linger in the aesthetic vacuum of the
'nineties," she wrote in *Scrutiny,* "can afford the courage
of asserting that we agree with Leslie Stephen and not Mr.
MacCarthy."[70] MacCarthy, however, was the likeliest
choice among the friends to make the confession (for
Woolf herself, it was obviously unthinkable), since Pater

68. Desmond MacCarthy, *Leslie Stephen* (Cambridge: Cambridge University Press, 1937), p. 11.
69. In MacCarthy's *Memories* (New York: Oxford University Press, 1953),
the essay on Stephen repeats the judgment that "Stephen is the least aesthetic
of noteworthy critics" (p. 84), although the general tone has been changed to
one of praise and the names of Pater and Wilde excised. Strachey had rendered
a similar judgment of Arnold in a 1914 review, and briefly handles Stephen
there much as MacCarthy handles him at greater length in the 1937 lecture
("Stephen," says Strachey, "frankly despised the whole business" of literary
criticism), although as usual the names of Pater and Wilde are nowhere to be
found in the piece despite its "aesthetic" refrain. See *Literary Essays* (New
York: Harcourt, Brace and World, n.d.), p. 210. See also Goldman, p. 123,
n. 13.
70. Q. D. Leavis, "Leslie Stephen: Cambridge Critic," *Scrutiny* 7, no. 4
(March 1939): 406–07.

had long been among his favorite writers.[71] Moreover, as a Cambridge undergraduate, he had even been introduced to what he called "Intellectual Bohemia" by no less an aesthete than Oscar Browning.[72]

The central struggle with Pater, however, lies, of course, with Woolf herself, who by the 'thirties found the energies that demanded Pater's repression to have grown to legionary proportions—the enduring ghost of her father, the increasing pressures of feminist politics, and, now, the accusing finger of serious literary antagonists,[73] all this superadded to the customary anxiety still surrounding Pater's name in conventional—and bohemian—literary society. It is perhaps the consummate measure of these pressures that nowhere in the length and breadth of Woolf's prodigious output of nonfiction is a single essay on Pater to be found. How unusual—or how fitting—it is that a writer who concerned herself with virtually every significant figure in English literary history should have fallen silent on the question of a precursor with whom her own circle was so often identified by its literary enemies. Even the number of passing references to Pater are surprisingly—or fittingly—few. In Woolf's collected formal writings he is mentioned only a handful of times;[74] although when he surfaces at all, Woolf's remarks are usually disparaging ones like those to be found in Strachey.[75] But considering her deep involve-

71. See Raymond Mortimer's foreword to MacCarthy's *Memories* (New York: Oxford University Press, 1953), p. 8.

72. See MacCarthy's sketch, "Oscar Browning," in *Portraits* (London: Putnam, 1931), p. 36. Roger Fry had had the same experience (*RF*, 44, 48–49).

73. The political and anti-aestheticist stance of the younger literary generation should also be added to the list (see Rose, pp. 195 ff.).

74. Excluded here are the diaries and *Letters,* although even there one finds the same pattern of silence interrupted only occasionally by a momentary reference (*Diary* I, 264, 300).

75. In a 1916 review of a study of Butler, Woolf mentions Pater only to recall Butler's judgment that Pater's "style" is to be "likened to the face of an

ment with the Paters in her youth, Woolf's silence can hardly be taken at its word. "All books," she writes in her diary in 1939, "now seem to me surrounded by a circle of invisible censors" (*AWD*, 315). To search out what Woolf has hidden leads us now to begin our comparison of her work with Pater's. Let us start with their notions about the critic.

If we look for the organizing principle at work in Woolf's criticism, it is, like Pater's, based upon a criterion of expressiveness in art, and generates a search for the temperament or personality of the artist behind what he has made. Thus, with Pater's criticism as her model, Woolf's essays almost always seek the unity of a career rather than the design of a particular text, becoming in fact historical portraits much in the same way that Pater's critical essays are really portraits, too. From this point of view it is Pater's concern with "the special history of the special soul" (*R*, 67) that fashions Woolf's search for "the peculiar quality" of "temperament" (*CE* I, 118) in the life and work of the famous as well as in the lives of the obscure. If Pater finds the value, say, of Michelangelo's

---

enamelled old woman" (*CW*, 29). Similarly, in "The Narrow Bridge of Art" (1927), "modern literature," says Woolf, "had grown a little sultry and scented with Oscar Wilde and Walter Pater," although it "revived instantly from her nineteenth-century languor when Samuel Butler and Bernard Shaw began to burn their feathers and apply their salts to her nose" (*CE* II, 223). In the biography of Roger Fry, of course, Pater's name is also to be found: once when Woolf cites Fry's opinion that Pater's service was to the "last" generation (*RF*, 106); once when she cites Fry's recollection of John Addington Symonds's disparaging remarks about Pater and Botticelli (*RF*, 74); and once when she compares Fry briefly, and a trifle unfavorably as a stylist, with Ruskin and Pater (*RF*, 227). With two notable exceptions that will be taken up in chapter 3, the few remaining direct references to Pater in the collected formal work consist of his mention in a catalogue of writers (*CW*, 145); in the preface to *Orlando;* and in the momentarily illuminating contrast drawn in 1922 between "the extravagant beauty of Walter Pater" and "the intemperate candour of Leslie Stephen" (*CE* II, 48).

poetry to derive from the fact that his verse is the "direct expression of his thoughts" (*R*, 94–95), so Woolf will praise Hazlitt because "his essays are emphatically himself" (*CE* I, 155). And if, in "Style," Pater's notion of artistic strength rests on the artist's ability to be "true from first to last to that vision within" (*A*, 23), so Woolf will find the contemporary novel in trouble in "Modern Fiction" because it "more and more ceases to resemble the vision in our minds" (*CE* II, 105). Like Pater, too, Woolf seeks the relation between the author and his work, not to tender an ethical judgment of the writer as Stephen does, but simply to "define the quality of the author's mind" (*CW*, 56).

Indeed, as an initial indication of the degree to which the critical projects and rhetorical procedures of both writers are similar, we have only to compare the following passages, the first from Pater's essay on Michelangelo, the second from one of Woolf's essays on Gibbon:

> The titles assigned traditionally to the four symbolical figures, *Night* and *Day*, *The Twilight* and *The Dawn*, are far too definite for them; for these figures come much nearer to the mind and spirit of their author, and are a more direct expression of his thoughts, than any merely symbolical conceptions could possibly have been. They concentrate and express, less by way of definite conceptions than by the touches, the promptings of a piece of music, all those vague fancies, misgivings, presentiments, which shift and mix and are defined and fade again, whenever the thoughts try to fix themselves with sincerity on the conditions and surroundings of the disembodied spirit. [*R*, 94–95]

> . . . Gibbon was rooted in the eighteenth century and indelibly stamped with its character and his own.

Gradually, stealthily, with a phrase here, a gibe there, the whole solid mass is leavened with the peculiar quality of his temperament. Shades of meaning reveal themselves; the pompous language becomes delicate and exact. Sometimes a phrase is turned edgewise, so that as it slips with the usual suavity into its place it leaves a scratch. [CE I, 118–19]

Despite the obvious and extreme difference between Michelangelo and Gibbon—the "vague fancies" of the former, for example, as compared to what is "exact" in the latter—here we find both our critics unmooring their respective subjects from the particularities of time, place, and even symbolism in order to trace instead, in microscopic detail and in rather similar figures, the movement of temperament as though its rhythms on the page were little different from its flight in the minds of fictional characters like Florian Deleal, Marius, or Clarissa Dalloway. For Pater and Woolf alike this means, as Christopher Ricks has inadvertently demonstrated in Pater's case,[76] subduing the critic's subject to himself, much as Shelley or Emerson yoke nature to their own purposes as writers, with the Paterian critic finding temperament in his author by realizing it first in himself.

Indeed, much as individual expressiveness is the standard by which both writers determine the success or failure of a given artist, so Pater's celebrated injunction in the "Preface" to The Renaissance—"to know one's impression as it really is, to discriminate it, to realise it distinctly" (R, viii)—becomes Woolf's own injunction so far as the writing of criticism and fiction alike are concerned. "The following pages," says Woolf at the start of her long essay

76. See Christopher Ricks, "Pater, Arnold and misquotation," Times Literary Supplement, 25 November 1977, pp. 1383–85.

on the novel, "Phases of Fiction," "attempt to record the impressions made upon the mind by reading a certain number of novels in succession" (*CE* II, 56), a prescription doubled in the well-known passage from "Modern Fiction" so often identified with her aims as a novelist: "Let us record the atoms as they fall upon the mind," she writes there, "let us trace the pattern, however disconnected and incoherent in appearance, which each sight or incident scores upon the consciousness" (*CE* II, 107).

As critics, it is the portrait of the artist that is their common point of departure and their shared formal ground, although, like Pater, Woolf is wont to extend it into the freer mode of the imaginary portrait proper—the legacy perhaps of that first encounter—in which the temperament of the artist becomes a model, as it does in Joyce, for the workings of temperament as a whole, whether in "the special soul" or, in Woolf's (like Joyce's) quotidianizing version of it, in "an ordinary mind on an ordinary day" (*CE* II, 106). Hence whatever formal boundaries may appear to exist in both writers between criticism and fiction, or, indeed, between history and imagination, tend to grow dim in the face of such a unified aesthetic project, making the moment at which history or criticism leaves off and the imagination takes over a difficult one to fix in the work of either writer.[77] Much of the reason for the admixture of forms is that both writers are metalinguis-

77. Knoepflmacher observes that "many of Pater's 'imaginary portraits' are almost indistinguishable from his presumably authentic portraits" (p. 156), and that his "stories fall into a twilight zone between parable and essay, romance and theory, autobiography and criticism" (p. 170); similarly, James Naremore notes that Woolf's fiction conveys "the impression of a sketch, a swift but accurate summary, a series of impressions strung out in apposition," and that "this style is indicative of a habit of mind that can be felt in almost every aspect of Virginia Woolf's art" (*The World Without A Self: Virginia Woolf and the Novel* [New Haven: Yale University Press, 1973], p. 101).

tic in their basic inclinations, concerned as novelists with the languages of sense and perception much as they are concerned as critics with the languages of art and literature.

Thus Pater's characteristic hybrid of autobiography and fiction in "The Child in the House," or of history and the imagination in *Gaston De Latour* or "Prosper Mérimée." In *Marius the Epicurean,* of course, the admixture of forms is exemplary and complex, although once again the accent on portraiture subdues the differences among the narrative's numerous formal components—history, biography, autobiography, criticism, and fiction—and transforms them into a unified effort to search out Marius's temperament as it is constituted by the various events, personalities, and arts that play upon him.

In Woolf, of course, such transgeneric expansiveness is also a measure of the gain to be had from portraiture as a ruling compositional procedure. A characteristic historical sketch like "The Strange Elizabethans," for example, follows the real but elusive figure of Gabriel Harvey to Cambridge, where Woolf's desire to "pick up something humble and colloquial that will make these strange Elizabethans more familiar to us" (*CE* III, 37) suddenly transforms what is supposedly an account based on fact into an imaginary portrait with rules of its own. Such generic transformations are in fact an enduring feature of many of Woolf's historical essays—"Rambling Round Evelyn," "Eliza and Sterne," "Four Figures," "Dr. Burney's Evening Party," "Outlines," "The Lives of the Obscure," and so on—and are obviously at work in longer works like *Orlando* or *The Pargiters,* the latter a text that reminds us how much Woolf wished to leaven the historical with the imaginary under the explicit and rather Paterian rubric of the "Essay-Novel." Even what Woolf calls "the new biography"—chiefly Strachey's work, but also Harold Nicolson's as well as her own—may be viewed as a derivation of the Paterian portrait, too, with its use of "the devices of fiction in dealing with real life" (fiction itself, presumably, deals with something else) in order to discover, as always, "those truths which transmit personality" (*CE* IV, 233, 229). Indeed, the only substantial difference between imaginary portraiture and "the new biography" is that in the latter the historical figures are foregrounded instead of the imaginary ones, much as they tend to usurp the focus of the Paterian and Woolfian critical essay, too.

Indeed, from our present point of view, *Orlando* is the consummate Paterian portrait, asserting as it does the ideality of a strong and unified temperament capable of subduing time and sexuality alike to the law of personality alone. Moreover, like Gaston, Marius, or Emerald Uthwart, the fictional Orlando moves in the air of real history and in the society of real personages, very often the poetic, philosophical, and political heroes of the day, with Orlando's Elizabeth, Shakespeare, and Pope doubling Marius's Marcus Aurelius and Apuleius or Gaston's Bruno in a kind of multiplied and concentrated use of the device in a single text, with *Marius* the structural prototype despite the immense difference in tone.[78] Above all, like Pater's portraits, too, Orlando's story is organized by means of its setting in a series of significant transitional moments in history like those that give *Marius, Gaston,* and *The Renaissance* a resonant metaphoricity and a problematic that focuses each book on questions of development and repetition.

Moreover, the usual criticism of Pater's portraits for being "static" compared to their modernist counterparts

78. Note, too, that Pater is not only listed in the preface to *Orlando*, but listed there conspicuously (*O*, 7) in one of only three such examples of praise in Woolf's work, and the single one in which Pater is at all acknowledged as a personal influence.

in Woolf or Joyce[79] actually confirms their status as
protraits as such, at least in the way the "portrait" was
understood as a literary form in the 1860s, as that kind of
narrative opposed to the sensation or action novel, whose
balancing designation was the figure of the chain.[80] As
a form, in other words, portraiture already means a bias
against action and an emphasis instead on the contemplation of character. Hence, too, portraits by Woolf and
Pater alike almost always bear the names of their heroes,
unlike, say, Hardy's novels, whose titles more often tend
to designate role or circumstance rather than the abiding
particularity of a given personality like Marius or Orlando.

If we wish to survey what allies our writers from a more
strictly thematic point of view, common concerns are in
abundant evidence, too, particularly in the fiction: an appetite for sensation and a careful attention to the patterns it
weaves in the mind; a Keatsian fascination with death,
decay, and dissolution, although a compensatory figuration of history as stratified (valorizing Woolf's characterization of Pater as archaeologist in "Slater's Pins"), by
which the past leaves "fossilised" vestiges for future
generations to collect and rearrange in the reliquary of
culture (*GS*, 12; *ROO*, 108); a modernist emphasis on the
loneliness and isolation of the individual and a concomi-
tant desire for companionship and the knowledge of
others; a prevailing atmosphere of loss and an elegiac mood
suffusing the narrator's imagination; pathos as the highest
affect possible in a world where heroism and nobility are
likeliest perceived in ruins; above all, the vision of a universe in constant flux, with an attendant, and once again

79. See, for example, Knoepflmacher (*Religious Humanism*, pp. 169–70)
and Monsman (*Pater's Portraits*, p. 32).

80. See Walter Kendrick, "The Sensationalism of *The Woman in White*,"
Nineteenth-Century Fiction 32 (June 1977): 18–22. Pater himself alludes to
the customary distinction when he refers to Mrs. Ward's *Robert Elsmere* as a
" 'novel of character' " (*EG*, 57). From this point of view, the subtitle of

compensatory, strategy for seizing and arresting the particularly intense and revelatory node of experience known as the privileged moment.

It is, of course, the moment that provides us with Woolf's most immediate and recognizable link to Pater, although in the kind of swerve we have by now learned to recognize as a token for denial of the precursor, she assigns the origin of the trope to Hardy and Conrad instead, at least so far as she is willing to concede a history to it at all. "His own word," she writes of Hardy after his death in 1928, " 'moments of vision,' exactly describes those passages of astonishing beauty and force which are to be found in every book that he wrote" (*CE* I, 258). Two years earlier we find her preparing the swerve by noting in her diary how "the year is marked by moments of great intensity. Hardy's 'moments of vision' " (*AWD*, 98). Similarly, it is Conrad whose "books are full of moments of vision" in an essay of 1923 (*CE* I, 312), with the phrase documented in another essay on Conrad a year later in which Woolf gives the figure's apparent—and wholly secondary— source by quoting the French officer in *Lord Jim* (*CE* I, 305).

Latecomers to the trope themselves, Hardy and Conrad doubtless derive their own "moments of vision" from Pater himself, although to fix the figure's actual birth even here, of course, is to mistake a strong thematic accent that must be deferred in the light of Pater's own relation, say, to those " 'spots' of time" in Wordsworth (*A*, 46)—those "select moments," as Pater interprets them, "of vivid sensation" (*A*, 51; *EG*, 102)—or, indeed, to Hegel's *Moment*. This is to name only two of the trope's strongest High Romantic examples without even suggesting its

---

Marius the Epicurean: His Sensations and Ideas suggests an attempted rapprochement between the two modes of novel-writing.

history before that in Protestant revelation and the epic temper of quest-romance both Christian and classical.

It is nonetheless Pater who provides the moderns with the categorical epiphany in a direct and already formalized way, and none, not even Joyce, accords it so central and unmediated a place as Virginia Woolf. Thus Clarissa Dalloway's exemplary plunge "into the very heart of the moment" (*MD*, 57) repeats the "privileged hour" (*M*, 255) at which Marius has arrived by willfully "arresting the desirable moment as it passed" (*M*, 136), with Clarissa composing her world "into one centre" (*MD*, 57) much as Marius has gathered his own life "into one central act of vision" (*M*, 259).[81]

For Pater, of course, the moment is an organizing ideal in his work early and late. Hence the "single sharp impression" (*R*, 236) that will "set the spirit free for a moment" (*R*, 237) in the "Conclusion" to *The Renaissance* is already prefigured in the 1864 "Diaphaneitè"—" 'to gleam for a moment,' " writes Pater, selecting a moment from Carlyle, " 'and in a moment be extinguished' " (*MS*, 253). It is central as late as *Plato and Platonism*, too, in which Greek genius continues to reside in the originating power of "immediate vision" (*PP*, 190) that informs Pater's idealization of the Greeks as early as the 1867 "Winckelmann" and throughout the *Greek Studies* of the 1870s. In "The Beginnings of Greek Sculpture," Pater celebrates the Greeks because they are above all "emphatically *autochthonous*" (*GS*, 216) or self-begotten, "creating themselves out of themselves," as he puts it in "Winckelmann" (*R*, 219).

Visionary autogenesis, then, rests on what Marius calls the " 'Ideal Now' " (*M*, 216), in which experience is per-

<hr>

81. Monsman's recent *Walter Pater* (Boston: Twayne, 1977) points to similar passages as tokens of Pater's influence on Woolf in a new and useful brief on Pater and the major modernists generally in the book's concluding chapter (pp. 180–83).

petually "new-born at home, by right of a new, informing
. . . spirit" (*GS*, 216). The "right" of the "new," of course,
is also at the heart of the privileged moment in *Marius*
itself, where it is once again identified with the priority to
be gained from "a denial of habitual impressions" (*M*,
105). Hence "the individual is to himself the measure of all
things, and to rely on the exclusive certainty to himself of
his own impressions" (*M*, 109) becomes Marius's rule.
Here "direct sensation" is the only proper and "reassuring"
pathway to truth, for it is "the little point of this present
moment [that] alone really is, between a past which has
just ceased to be and a future which may never come" (*M*,
114), a "life of realized consciousness in the present"
(*M*, 123).

But "wholly concrete" (*R*, 150) and "special" (*R*, 66)
as the moment may be in Pater, for Woolf its literary location is always to be placed elsewhere. Thus it is, for
example, DeQuincey, she says, who gives us "descriptions
of states of mind in which . . . time is miraculously pro-
longed and space miraculously expanded" (*CE* I, 171),
echoing, with the safety of a swerve and perhaps with the
satisfaction of finding a source for Pater himself,[82] the
celebrated charge in the "Conclusion" to *The Renaissance*
that "our one chance lies in expanding that interval, in
getting as many pulsations as possible into the given time"
(*R*, 238). Indeed, in 1918 Woolf titles the review of
a negligible book "Moments of Vision" in order to formu-
late, through the cover of her author, an explicitly Paterian
project: "to catch and enclose certain moments which
break off from the mass, in which . . . things come together
in a combination of inexplicable significance, to arrest
those thoughts which . . . are almost menacing with meaning" (*CW*, 75). And yet never is this desire to "squeeze the

82. For anticipations of Pater in DeQuincey, see DeLaura, *Hebrew and
Hellene*, p. 334, n. 7.

moment," as she puts it as late as 1939 (*AWD*, 314), to be acknowledged as a repetition of Pater's "moment of vision" (*PP*, 158), habitually dislocated as it is, now in those "moments of astonishing intensity" assigned to Meredith (*CE* I, 235), now in "the impression of the moment" (*CE* I, 98) assigned to Sterne.[83]

We may find a clue to the reason for this habitual denial of Pater's authority so far as the moment is concerned by noting that "into the moment," as Woolf puts it in the essay so entitled, "steals self-assertion" (*CE* II, 295). Stealing is the proper word for it, and self-assertion its proper aim, since, like the "immediate vision" that Pater discovers belatedly in the Greeks, the moment represents autochthony—autogenesis—for Woolf, too. In Pater's bolder words, "the special moment" means "all that belongs only" to the individual (*R,* 66), and hence celebrates the self's ability to subdue the world to its own purposes, to be whole and self-possessed, concrete and original— to create itself out of itself.

Thus Woolf's need to repress the discovery of such a master trope in Pater takes us far beyond the political factors at work in the denial of his influence. It leads us instead to the paradoxical realization that the Paterian charge "to know one's own impression as it really is" is itself subject to repression as the exact price of putting its exhortation into practice. After all, to take Pater's moment to heart means to sever it from the anteriority of any influence—any parentage—whatsoever, and so to glory in the illusion of being self-begotten in an " 'Ideal Now.' "[84] Carrying as it does the injunction to see directly, without

83. For a catalogue of the moment in Woolf, especially in the fiction, see Beja, *Epiphany in the Modern Novel,* pp. 112 ff.

84. What Holroyd calls "the unforgivable Sin of Parentage" provides another Apostolic analogue (*Lytton Strachey,* I, 247).

the corrupting mediacy of a history—"first-hand truth seized," as Woolf describes the prize in a 1918 review (*CW*, 80)—the value of the moment is to be found in the access it seems to provide to purely personal truth and power. Thus the moment gives one the "advantage" for which Woolf is nostalgic, "the advantage of having no past," as she puts it in the opening sentence of a 1920 review in which she notes, "perhaps wrongly," "the advantages of having been born three or four centuries ago," when "consciousness … . was not impeded at every point by the knowledge of what had been said in that book, or painted on that canvas" (*CW*, 113).

Hence Woolf's characteristic polemical assertion that the modern present constitutes a radical separation from the past in life and literature alike in "How It Strikes A Contemporary":

> We are sharply cut off from our predecessors. A shift in the scale—the sudden slip of masses held in position for ages—has shaken the fabric from top to bottom, alienated us from the past and made us perhaps too vividly conscious of the present. . . . No age can have been more rich than ours in writers determined to give expression to the differences which separate them from the past and not to the resemblances which connect them with it. [*CE* II, 157–58]

Indeed, the celebrated and wholly preposterous claim in "Mr. Bennett and Mrs. Brown" that "in or about December, 1910, human character changed" (*CE* I, 320) is probably the modernist Woolf's most representative assertion. Of course, the dangers avoided by the "advantage" to be had from such a claim are made clear enough at the start of a review written as early as 1909:

A great book, like a great nature, may have dis-
astrous effects upon other people. It robs them of
their character and substitutes its own. [*CE* III, 127]

With one's own impression as the thing to realize distinctly, to save from the tarnish of influence, "the advantage of having no past" is both a wishful way to repossess
the character that has been lost and in its own right an
even severer injunction than the Paterian one which under-
lies and inspires it, and which it is designed to cover and
protect, even from the disciple. The truth of one's own impression, in other words, requires a necessary blindness to
all that threatens its autonomy and self-sufficiency—
"glasses we wear, though we cannot see them," says Woolf
apropos of seeing Shelley "plainly, as he was" (*CE* IV, 21).
Hence in "On Re-reading Novels" we find the characteristically wishful and assertive modernist pronouncement,
founded on little more than the "right" of the "new":
"The late-comer," writes Woolf of James's relation to
Richardson, "improves upon the pioneers" (*CE* II, 128).
The "right" of the "new," however, is to be understood no
longer in terms of a literary revolution but in terms of the
rearguard and compensatory necessities involved in establishing a literary identity of one's own.

Hence Woolf's greatest anxiety about Pater has little to
do with sexism, sexuality, or even Leslie Stephen. It lies in
the infuriating knowledge that she had inherited modernism rather than created it herself. That the usurper—or at
least so he seemed in belated retrospect—was a man from
Oxford only added salt to the real indignity. How to refine
the precursor out of existence, how to absorb him in a
vision even stronger and more encompassing than his own?
To see Woolf's eventual triumph over Pater we shall have
to explore her indebtedness to him first.

2

The Chemistry of the Crystal

That Pater is remembered best for his mannerisms as a stylist suggests not only how lightly we take his powers as a theoretician of art and culture, but also how little serious attention we tend to afford a writer's, particularly a critic's, fundamental materials—his personal brand of language, his distinctive rhetoric and vocabulary, and the distinctive kinds of knowledge they combine to produce. In order to disengage the Paterian thread from the fabric of Woolf's criticism in a specific way, of course, we shall in any case need an inventory of Pater's characteristic figures. By means of a catalogue of the recurrent tropes at work in his prose both early and late, we can in fact isolate some of the significant units in his eminently peculiar and recognizable rhetoric, and so try to gauge on the level of language itself just how precise the contours of his vision may be, especially if there is still some need to countermand Eliot's judgment that Pater is "incapable of sustained reasoning."[1] That Pater's vision is discordant at key moments in its itinerary will concern us only later on, although to begin by taking at his exact word even the customary Pater, the Pater we already know, will prepare us for the task ahead.

1. T. S. Eliot, "Arnold and Pater," in *Selected Essays*, rev. ed. (London: Faber and Faber, 1951), p. 440.

Expressiveness, of course, is the manifest focus of Pater's vision of art, and with it comes an attendant concern for the extent to which the work reveals what is peculiar or particular to the temperament or personality of the artist who has made it. In fact, "all knowledge," says Pater in *Plato and Platonism,* is to be understood on the model of "knowing a *person*" (*PP,* 129), much as, in *Gaston,* even Bruno's "abstract theory" becomes a "visible person talking with you" (*GL,* 155). Following from such a focus is Pater's sense of perfect art as an ideal kind of "integrity" or "unity with one's self" (*R,* 185), as he calls it in the portrait of Winckelmann, in which the artist's "every thought and feeling," like Giorgione's, is "twin-born with its sensible analogue or symbol" (*R,* 138). In fact, the "profound expressiveness" (*R,* 71) that characterizes the ideal work may be ascribed to the "magnetic" (*R,* 116) quality by which thought and feeling on the one hand, and the artist's medium or material on the other, are drawn together in such a way as to grant their union an almost natural status.[2]

To this rather traditional notion of fusing form and content into the ideal transparency of a perfect work of art, however, Pater adds his own special variation. The celebrated "gemlike flame" (*R,* 236) signifies not only the successful arrest of the privileged moment in all its apparent immediacy; it also signifies a particular kind of artistic competence that solders manner and matter together by means of what is really a prescriptive regimen that establishes for Pater a normative and synchronic measure of achievement for the history of art as a whole, and that functions as a principle of evaluation for Pater the practical critic.

2. See Ian Fletcher, *Walter Pater* (London: Longmans, Green, 1959), pp. 33 ff.

In the "Preface" to *The Renaissance,* Pater's project of critical self-definition is already formulated as a desire "to disengage" (*R,* x) the "active principle" (*R,* xi) of "genius" or aesthetic "virtue" (*R,* x) from its particular historical manifestations so as to examine it for its timeless components or constituent parts—for its "elementary particles" (*A,* 20) or "golden pieces" (*A,* 42), as Pater will call them in *Appreciations.* "Few artists," he writes, "not Goethe or Byron even, work quite cleanly, casting off all *débris,* and leaving us only what the heat of their imagination has wholly fused and transformed" (*R,* x–xi). The figure of the "chemist" (*R,* x) earlier in the "Preface" suggests that what Pater really has in mind here is a kind of chemical process (he even uses the surprising word "formula" at the start of the "Preface" [*R,* vii], retaining it as late as the 1892 essay on Raphael [*MS,* 39]) by which the force of genius is, quite literally, the "heat" (*R,* xi) by which "all impurities," as he says of Giorgione, are "burnt out of it, and no taint, no floating particle of anything but its own proper elements allowed to subsist within it" (*R,* 153). Thus the artist's "form" or "mode of handling" his subject "should penetrate every part of the matter" (*R,* 135), just as matter or "motive" should "saturate" and be "identical with" form (*R,* 206). Hence the celebrated opinion that "all art constantly aspires towards the condition of music" (*R,* 135), since in music alone is "the constant effort of art" to "obliterate" or interfuse the distinction between "matter" and "form" (*R,* 135) already realized by the medium itself.

It is, then, the "gemlike flame" that is the agent of this process of "refinement" (*R,* 203) by which all that is alien to the work—all "residue" (*R,* 85), or "surplusage" (*A,* 19), as Pater will call it in *Appreciations*—is fired out or burnt away. With its sadomasochistic implications inform-

ing a view of the artist here as an exemplary sufferer or
martyr who must "sacrifice . . . a thousand possible sympathies" (*M*, 216) in his pursuit of the perfect work, the
figure of the chastening flame is at the center of Pater's
notion of *ascesis,* that renunciative and self-restraining
discipline by which an artist like Leonardo reaches "perfection . . . through a series of disgusts" (*R*, 103). Thus the
"ideal art, in which the thought does not outstrip or lie
beyond the proper range of its sensible embodiment," is
the product of a "happy limit" (*R*, 206) or "narrowing"
(*M*, 216) imposed by genius upon itself.

Virtually all of Pater's historical heroes practice this
regimen of self-curtailment (it is the imaginary heroes, by
contrast, who are usually found in ruins), whether it is the
classicist Winckelmann, the anonymous creators of Greek
sculpture, perhaps above all Flaubert, the focus of the
essay on "Style." Here the apparently "natural economy"
that allows the exemplary Flaubert to search out an almost
"pre-existent" attraction between "a relative, somewhere in
the world of thought, and its correlative"—anticipating but
also reversing Eliot in advance—"somewhere in the world
of language" (*A*, 30) is really the product of a hard-won
"self-restraint, a skilful economy of means" rather than
a natural one, *"ascesis"* (*A*, 17). Such an artistic program
requires that "every component element" in any art "will
have undergone exact trial" (*A*, 18), and that the artist
" 'may be known,' " says Pater in a citation from Schiller,
" 'by what he *omits*' " (*A*, 18).

As a constant standard of evaluation, Pater's "formula"
can be used to account for an artist's shortcomings as well
as for his successes. Thus Pater measures the imperfections
in Wordsworth as a deviation from the familiar norm that
otherwise signifies the poet's strength: "When the really
poetical motive worked at all," says Pater, "it united . . . the
word and the idea; each, in the imaginative flame, becom-

ing inseparably one with the other, by that fusion of matter and form, which is the characteristic of the highest poetical expression" (A, 58). Had "the writer himself" also "purged away" the "alien element" or "residue" that is nonetheless to be found elsewhere in his poetry—that which is merely "conventional, derivative, inexpressive" (A, 42)—then the imperfections in his work would have been entirely consumed, leaving Wordworth's achievement far cleaner than it is. Indeed, even the distinction between classic and romantic formulated in the "Postscript" to *Appreciations* tends to vanish when the romantic artist manages, "by the very vividness and heat of [his] conception," to "purge away . . . all that is not . . . appropriate to it," eventually achieving a "form" which "becomes classical in its turn" (A, 258). By "refinement," then, Pater means a rather precise kind of artistic combustion or "alchemy" (R, 114; GS, 111; A, 247) by which manner and matter, form and content, coalesce into the willed perfection of an ideal work of art, or indeed, an ideal personality like Thomas Browne's, which earns Browne the measure of a "high and noble piece of chemistry" (A, 152).

The chemical metaphor even extends to Pater's notion of the structure of the perfect work, which is habitually described, in another celebrated figure, as a "crystal" (R, xi) whose symmetry and proportion bespeak "the perfect identification of matter and form" (R, 142) of which it is the product. Among the figure's variants are to be included gems like the "diamond," with which Pater represents the perfection of "Platonic aesthetics" (PP, 282), and the quality of luminous whiteness attributed to such perfect aesthetic structures by the Paterian representations which denote them. Thus a "white light" seems to be "cast up" on Botticelli's madonnas (R, 57), much as the "white flame" of Isabella's emotion "leaps" into her "white spirit" in *Measure for Measure* without spoiling, in an almost over-

determined use of the figure, her "cloistral whiteness" at
the start of the play (*A,* 178). In such moments the artist's
"power of refraction, selecting, transforming, recombining
the images it transmits" to "realise" a "situation" has been
tried to such a degree that even "in a chill and empty
atmosphere"—whether Shakespeare's courtroom or Botticelli's "wan," "abject," and even "cheerless" spirituality
(*R,* 56-57)—he will "define," as always, "the focus where
rays, in themselves pale and impotent, unite and begin to
burn" (*R,* 213-14).

Like the moment, the ideal of the crystal, too, emerges
at the very start of Pater's career in the 1864 "Diaphaneitè." Here the characteristic "blending and interpenetration" (*MS,* 250) of the perfect work of art is already
figured as, or embodied in, the "clear crystal nature"
(*MS,* 253) of genius in all its historical manifestations,
present as it is in "the eternal outline of the antique" (*MS,*
251) as well as in modern luminaries like Goethe (*MS,*
254) or Carlyle (*MS,* 253).

This crystalline art and the fusion of which it is the
product—that interpenetration wherein "the term . . . becomes, in a manner, what it signifies" (*A,* 22)—remain the
constant ideal and evaluative standard in Pater's work as
a whole, and may be traced through it accordingly. Thus,
in *Marius,* for example, where religion is above all else an
exercise in aesthetic perfection,[3] even the proper worship
of Isis is "itself a flame, of power to consume the whole
material of existence in clear light and heat, with no
smoldering residue" (*M,* 90). Indeed, in *Marius* the discipline of *ascesis* and the chemical figures that describe it
are applied to life in all its variety. Hence the " 'labor of
the file' " (*M,* 80), which enriches the artistic work proper

---

3. I have bracketed the familiar debate as to whether Pater seriously
(re)turns to religion late in his career in favor of emphasizing the consistency
of his rhetoric early and late.

"by far more than the weight of precious metal it removed" (*M*, 81, 67), is also to be found in the "military hardness, or *ascesis*" (*M*, 140) of a Roman officer like Cornelius, whose craft of "selection" and "refusal" (*M*, 191) accounts as well for the composure and "freshness" (*M*, 192) of his personal demeanor and transmits to Marius himself "the clear, cold corrective, which the fever of his present life demanded" (*M*, 192) during his first years in Rome.

Indeed, there is no sphere of existence that cannot be viewed through, and elucidated by, the interrelated figures of fusion and *ascesis*, denoting as they do the necessary preconditions for the production of perfect work in art and life alike. Even the "exquisite conscience" (*M*, 205) of Stoic morality, says Pater, is a "mode of comeliness" (*M*, 202) or "purely aesthetic beauty" (*M*, 204), a product as it is of the same "management" (*M*, 203) that would erect in the sphere of social government an ideal polity whose aesthetic perfection also resembles the New Jerusalem implicit in the "scrupulous . . . love" (*M*, 287) of Marius's aesthetic Christianity. Christ himself conforms to the pattern of Paterian virtue, too, the image as he is of one who gives up or renounces "the greatest gifts" (*M*, 312) according to the same renunciative pattern that distinguishes all of Pater's successful artists and aesthetic personalities. Even Falsehood, according to Lucian in the "Conversation Not Imaginary" late in the novel, reflects the structure of Christ's perfection since, like Christianity, Stoicism, and art, falsehood, too, is "conscious of no alloy within" (*M*, 331). Hence Pater leaves us with the provocative paradox that perfect Falsehood is the result of its being, as it were, true to itself.

The ideal of fusion also goes by the name of "fitness" in *Marius* (*M*, 136) as well as in *Plato and Platonism* (*PP*, 36, 254). In both cases the term manifestly refers to the way in which fusion, in an almost literal kind of way, represents a perfect match or fit between sensibility and whatever plastic medium it chooses in order to express itself, whether Marius's "daintily pliant sentences" (*M*, 136), "the fine arts" of Greece and "the art of discipline" in "the lives" of its citizens (*PP*, 36), even the " 'seamless' unity" of "the City of the Perfect" itself, Plato's Republic (*PP*, 255). Moreover, "aesthetic fitness" (*PP*, 268) carries with it a latent reverberation or murmur of significant religious meaning as well. If the term denotes a uniform kind of aesthetic harmony in both Greek polytheism and primitive Christianity, it also connotes a more specific kind of Protestant morality and perfection suggested not only by the implicit identity between Marius's quest and the quest for "A paradise within thee, happier far," but also by his feeling that the proper choice of philosophy and conduct in life is a sign for what Pater calls "instinctive election" (*M*, 200). *Ascesis* allows of a more specifically Christian reading in this context, too, certainly in the sense of the trial that Pater's artist-heroes must undergo in a manner reminiscent of questing Protestant pilgrims like Spenser's, Milton's, or Bunyan's, although also of the Catholic kind that Pater himself was drawn to by identifying, with qualifications to be sure, the renunciative discipline of both the artist and the polity of Lacedaemon with "the monasticism of the Middle Ages" (*PP*, 233), and by describing Marius's "close watching of his soul" as "a foresight of monasticism itself in the prophetic future" (*M*, 239). From this point of view, even the figure of the flame carries with it the specifically Christian variant of the " 'divine spark' " (*A*, 155) in the essay on Browne.

Moreover, the figure of fitness also stands for its own fitness as a figure, capable as it is of sounding a number of meanings or references at once without perceptible residue or surplusage. That the various levels or layers of life gathered under the tropes of fitness and *ascesis*—art, morality, politics, conduct, religion—share the same structure of articulation in Pater's rhetoric suggests that Pater's own work, in its apparent textural consistency from early to late, possesses as crystalline and transparent a structure as do the various isomorphic contexts it describes. Indeed, Pater's obvious delight in pagan polytheism, together with his virtual polymorphous perversity in the realm of the senses, suggests an equivalent delight in the polyphony of contexts to which his chemical rhetoric refers.

Of course, the figure of the artist as industrious and industrial (in both cases, read Victorian) chemist recalls, too, what is for Pater the paradigmatic beginning of art in the "perfectly accomplished metal-work" of early Greek sculpture (*GS*, 232). The precise link here is the figure of Hephaestus, "the god of fire," who becomes at this period in Greek life "representative of one only" of the "aspects" of fire, "its function, namely, in regard to early art" (*GS*, 219). The god "becomes," in short, "the patron of smiths, bent with his labour at the forge, as people had seen such real workers" (*GS*, 219). This is a notion of the modern artist that reappears, of course, in the Paterian Stephen of Joyce's *Portrait*, who will, in the celebrated words, "forge in the smithy of [his] soul the uncreated conscience of [his] race," and so render the Paterian artist an exemplary ironworker as well as a hieratic visionary. Indeed, metallurgy is the most persuasive historical source and model Pater has for the chemical fusion of medium and sensibility, and it provides his rhetoric with a working link to the genius the Greeks apparently had for "joining the parts together, with more perfect unity and smoothness of surface" (*GS*, 232).

Early Greek art, then, is "the art of soldering" ("coupled" as it is here with "the name of Glaucus of Chios," it recalls, too, the "*Yeux Glauques*" fashioned by the ham-

mer work of Pound's "medallions" in the *Mauberley*
sequence), and it is for Pater the first kind of art to "perfect . . . artistic effect with economy of labour" (*GS*, 232).
Most important, however, is that the successful laying of
the foundations of art here in the ironworker's forge is
followed directly by the birth of personality itself in Greek
art and culture (*GS*, 242), prepared for as it is in the stage
of the smith, and remaining the buried model for artistic
production in subsequent ages (*GS*, 264). Indeed, even the
figure of temperament itself may be read with an accent
on the tempering or combusting of hard metal or steel,
much as it may also be read with an accent on the tempering of a musical intrument in order to insure the sweetness
of its harmonies.

In addition to the chemical figure of the crystal, of
course, Pater also uses the figure of the house or dwelling
to generate a second vocabulary with which to describe the
well-wrought work of art and the well-wrought personality.
Carrying almost as much Protestant resonance as the ideal
of fitness and the necessity of trial,[4] the recurrent figure
of the house gathers under itself a set of images that range
from the Bunyanesque *"House Beautiful"* (*R*, 26; *A*, 60,
241), "which the creative minds of all generations—the
artists and those who have treated life in the spirit of art—
are always building together, for the refreshment of the
human spirit" (*A*, 241), to the rather humbler but equivalent one of the "house" of his "thoughts" that Marius
wishes to put in order (*M*, 251). Here, too, we should include the Château of Deux-manoirs in which Gaston passes
his childhood and which is the "visible record of all the
accumulated sense of human existence among its occu-

4. See, for example, the religious resonance of the fit structure in Pater's
opening citation from Browne in his essay in *Appreciations* (*A*, 126), and in
the "House of Bethany" in "The Child in the House" (*MS*, 195).

pants" (*GL,* 3); the cathedral at Chartres to which Gaston journeys in youth and which begins to suggest that Pater's unfinished romance is in fact organized by its buildings; and, indeed, the cathedral that structures "Apollo in Picardy," as well as those that give their names to "Vézelay" and "Notre-Dame d'Amiens."

Like the chemical crystal, the figure of the house or dwelling—"the airy building of the brain," as Pater puts it in his essay on Wordsworth (*A,* 45)—is a cipher for a notion of cultural achievement whose derivation is to be understood in the murmuring Freudian sense implied by Pater's occasional proleptic use of the terms "sublimation,"[5] "sublimes" (*R,* 204), and "sublimates" (*MS,* 83) as synonyms for the activity of *ascesis* itself. As a product of the fierce antinatural discipline required of genius on both the level of individual achievement and the level of civilization as a whole, both ciphers for culture, crystal and dwelling alike, bespeak the denial of instinct embodied in the "girding of the loins in youth" (*R,* xiii) which characterizes all of Pater's successful culture workers and which is precisely what is lacking among those dreamier members of his imaginary contingent who fail to achieve what is expected of their youthful promise.

Pater's use of the figure of the house is especially evident in the abundant species of "intellectual structure" (*A,* 215) to be found in his work: the "sanctuary" of Florentine painting (*R,* 102); the "literary architecture" presented in "Style" (*A,* 23) and in the portrait of Browne (*A,* 127); the "edifice" and "theoretic building" of Plato's philosophy (*PP,* 7, 202); the religious house of Cecilia in *Marius;* the village church in the imaginary portrait "Denys

5. The term appears in "Aesthetic Poetry," not included in the Library Edition of *Appreciations* (see *Selected Writings of Walter Pater,* ed. Bloom, p. 190).

L'Auxerrois"; even the "wall" and "chamber" of personality and mind that emerge in the "Conclusion" to *The Renaissance* (*R*, 235). Indeed, Pater uses the figure to describe the structure of the individual as often as he uses it to describe the various cultural edifices of which the individual forms a part. Hence it provides the overarching metaphor of the personal "habitation," "material shrine," or "house of thought" (*MS*, 178, 184) into which Florian Deleal fashions himself in "The Child in the House," as well as the rich image for thought as a whole of "the house within" in *Plato and Platonism*, with "its many chambers, its memories and associations, upon its inscribed and pictured walls" (*PP*, 120).

Included, too, is the activity of "building," whether Florian's "brain-building" in "The Child in the House" (*MS*, 173); the "word-building" that Marius learns from the rhetoricians (*M*, 80); or the building of the cathedral in "Denys" (*IP*, 55). Of crystalline genius itself, Pater calls it the "basement type" of cultural life as a whole in "Diaphaneitè" (*MS*, 254), rendering the figure a foundation in its own turn for the house of Pater's own thought insofar as his work aspires to be an expression of the virtues and requirements of civilization, too.

Moreover, much in the same way that Pater can judge Wordsworth negatively by the measure of fusion and fitness, so can he also use the figure of the house to picture genius in ruins. Here one recalls in particular those decayed and dilapidated houses in the imaginary portraits, where Pater's protagonists are often at as much of a loss to repair themselves as the figures with which they coincide. Hence the "desolate house" (*IP*, 113) in which Sebastian van Storck loses his unfulfilled life; the "burnt or overthrown" grange (*IP*, 119) in which the unhappy Duke Carl perishes with his bride-to-be; the sturdy but nonetheless

"irregular . . . ground-plan" of Gaston's hereditary château
(*GL*, 2); even the neglected and half-ruined family mausoleum which Marius, in an almost graphic psychoanalysis,
must rebuild in order to complete and compose the unfinished business of his life.

With the figure of the house or dwelling, too, comes the
early feeling and the later desire, so important to Marius,
to Florian, and to Emerald Uthwart all alike, for "a peculiar
ideal of home" (*M*, 17). Tangled in a matrix of associations
that links a pagan spirit of place or sense of "local sancti-
ties" (*A*, 50) with a Wordsworthian one, the Paterian ideal
of "home" is a plea for a sense of ground or attachment to
a "visible locality and abiding-place, the walls and towers
of which" a character like Marius "might really trace and
tell" (*M*, 207–08). Indeed, in *Gaston*, "those who kept up
the central tradition of their house" feel always bound to
"the visible spot, where the memory of their kindred was
liveliest and most exact" (*GL*, 4).

From this desire for ground follows another of Pater's
characteristic tropes for aesthetic competence and production, although it is one that begins to threaten the unity of
the Paterian ideal we have seen so far. This third way of
talking about art lies in a vocabulary of the natural
whose most recurrent figure is that of flowers, especially
the rose that W. H. Mallock took as a pejorative emblem
for Pater's achievement as a whole, and with whose image
Wilde opens *The Picture of Dorian Gray*.

In Pater's first book, the entire "mythology of the
Italian Renaissance" is figured as a "new" and "strange
flower" (*R*, 47) in the sketch of Pico. Within the period
itself, collective achievements like the poetry of the Pleiad
constitute a "special flower," too (*R*, 167), just as individual works like Du Bellay's *Regrets* are called "pale
flowers" (*R*, 173) in their own right. Indeed, cultural con-

ditions themselves are gathered under the trope of "sacred soil" (*R*, 190) in the portrait of Winckelmann, thus providing a ground or field of understanding for both Michelangelo's "blossoming" (*R*, 73) and Leonardo's "strange blossoms and fruits hitherto unknown" (*R*, 117).

In *Appreciations*, these tropes of the natural are to be found at work with the same consistency, with Coleridge's organicism functioning as a kind of touchstone for figures like the "flowers" of Rossetti's "poetry" (*A*, 210) or "the sudden blossoming" (*A*, 87) of Coleridge's own genius. Even the high discipline of conduct in the Lacedaemon of *Plato and Platonism* is a "perfect flower" (*PP*, 225), just as the Republic itself is envisioned as a "perfect flower" (*PP*, 260) in its own right, both of them examples of the late blossoming of "seeds" dropped by the "flower" of earlier philosophers like Pythagoras (*PP*, 66). In *Marius*, of course, the abundance of flowers of all kinds in the pageantry of Marius's native religion bespeaks its "spontaneous force" (*M*, 3) and remains a sign for the "undiminished freshness" (*M*, 20) of youthful impressionability throughout the novel. In young manhood, Marius "was always as fresh as the flowers he wore" (*M*, 104), while, even as he progresses in years, his sensibility remains fresh enough to be figured as "his . . . Epicurean rose-garden" (*M*, 210).

Such an alliance between these figures of nature and "direct sensation" (*M*, 114) is perfectly apt here, since Pater wishes to use his tropes as a means of identifying the crystalline perfection of genius with the "transparency," as he puts it in "Diaphaneitè," "of nature" itself (*MS*, 251). To match the idea or matter of a work or a personality with its perfect sensible embodiment means making "the term . . . what it signifies" and so constituting a full and transparent sign in which the idea and its sensible vehicle become fit or fused in "a veritable counterfeit of nature" itself (*GS*, 282); "painted glass," as Pater puts it in *Gaston*, "mimicking the clearness of the open sky" (*GL*, 6).

Indeed, art and culture seen as "natural objects" coincide in Pater's mythology with those periods of history in which subjectivity itself is paramount, whether in "the natural objects of the . . . Pointed style" (*MS*, 119) of the Gothic cathedral, whose recapturing of nature and of freshness gives it a precedence for Pater over the Romanesque style which it supersedes in the late cathedral pieces included in *Miscellaneous Studies;* or, indeed, in the supposed original for all the renaissances in history, the civilization of Greece, "springing as if straight from the soil" (*GS*, 154). Hence Gaston's notion of "modernity"—of renaissance—is the same as Pater's: "for a poetry, as veritable, as intimately near, as corporeal, as the new faces of the hour, the flowers of the actual season" (*GL*, 52). It is formalized best by Bruno, the "vigour" of whose "doctrine" is "like some hardy growth out of the very heart of nature" (*GL*, 141).

Accompanying these kinds of figures and their attendant vision of man's genius as a product of nature is a theology of the work of art as "half-sacred" (*A*, 75), as Pater puts it in the essay on Coleridge in *Appreciations,* and which puts us only a step away from the Religion of Art of the 1890s. More important, however, is that the notion of art as a sacred object carries with it a vestige, retrieved in Pater's pagan Wordsworth, of the "natural or half-natural objects" that constitute the "relics" of early Greek religion (*GS*, 239) in which the "visible idol" was "conceived" as "the actual dwelling-place of a god" (*GS*, 240). Much, then, as the modern notion of the artist as ironworker can be linked to the beginnings of Greek sculpture, so the modern and quasi-religious notion of the artist's voice speaking through his work can be linked in turn to the "sacred presence" (*GS,* 240) of a god in a pagan artifact or a particular spot of ground, and linked in *Gaston,* in a monotheistic and less persuasive revision, to "the indwelling spirit" (*GL,* 152) apprehended by Bruno in life as a whole.

It is these natural qualities that constitute the transcendent mode of discourse to which the Paterian artist aspires, a privileged style of language which is undissociated and which carries with it both an ideal and an understanding of art that Frank Kermode has characterized as a veritable "physical presence"—in Joyce's Catholic terms, as the word made flesh.[6] For Pater himself, of course, such an aesthetic ideal remains Greek in its constant attempt to regain those "Homeric conditions," as he calls them in *Plato,* under which "experience was intuition, and life a continuous surprise." Here, too, "every object," like the object created by modern art, is "unique," and "all knowledge" a knowledge of "the concrete and the particular, face to face," in another Christian echo or anticipation, "delightfully" (*PP,* 156).

Such natural transparence and presence, then, are the chief properties of genius's "eternal outline" as early as "Diaphaneitè" and as late as *Plato,* where "the eternal outline" of all perfect achievement is asserted to be "a definition of it which can by no supposition become a definition of anything else" (*PP,* 111). The work of art, in other words, is an object for which no substitutions are possible, an object, as we are accustomed to seeing it, that is original and unique. It is, of course, precisely this kind of modern—and Greek—originality that is signified by the privileged moment's ideal of "immediate vision" and the autochthony it bestows upon its beholder, although it is also autochthony that is signified by the figure of the gem-

6. Frank Kermode, *Romantic Image* (rpt. New York: Vintage, 1957), pp. 50, 53.

like flame itself, at least in the Promethean profile of fire adduced by Bachelard, for example, who places together "under the name of the Prometheus complex all those tendencies which impel us to know as much as our fathers, more than our fathers, as much as our teachers, more than our teachers."[7] Hence the gemlike flame and the autogenesis with which it is linked represent, too, the wishful priority of modernity itself, engaged as it always is, in all its renaissances, in an attempt to achieve "the advantage of having no past."

Given Pater's quest for the personality of the artist as it shows forth in his work, it is hardly unusual that he seeks the form of perfection in a language of "organic wholeness," as he calls it in his essay on Lamb (*A*, 116). What remains disturbing, however, is the degree to which the crystalline consistency of Pater's own vision is put into question by the presence of this language of nature within a constellation of figures that is, as we have seen, otherwise ruled by a language whose vocabulary is concerned with the willful discipline of culture. Is the artist an almost passive or unconscious flowering or growth in a natural rhythm of human history? Or is he a Flaubertian martyr of *ascesis,* the product of a rigorous discipline of repression and eventual sublimation, an emblem for civilization itself? Having constructed a language that bespeaks the conquest of nature by means of *ascesis* and its attendant achievements of fitness and the home or abode of sensibility, Pater also wishes to naturalize his account of culture by speaking of it through this second or covering language of organicism and natural growth. His remark in "Style" that "the house" an artist "has built is rather a body he has informed" (*A*, 24) focuses and magnifies this discontinuity by showing us how Pater's rhetoric wishes to

7. Gaston Bachelard, *The Psychoanalysis of Fire,* trans. Alan C. M. Ross (Boston: Beacon, 1964), p. 12.

ground its originating principle of expressiveness in the soil
of a nature that is itself subdued or repressed by the very
exercise of the powers it is supposed to signify.

Such a difficulty in making continuous or coincident
the figures of chemical fusion and *ascesis* with those of
flowers, blossoms, and other kinds of natural growth suggests that there is a "residue" or "surplusage" in Pater's
transparent vision after all. We can even locate a set of
hybrid figures in which Pater means either to ignore or to
reconcile this discontinuity by using both figural languages
in tandem, as though their presuppositions were coterminous. In *Marius,* for example, the votive rites to Isis
include the display of gold and silver ornaments simultaneously with "real fruit and flowers" (*M,* 88), an equivo-
cating double image like the "gem or flower" (*PP,* 157),
"flower or crystal" (*PP,* 214) with which Pater means to
figure alike the object of philosophical discourse and comely
manners in *Plato.* Both examples suggest the kind of discontinuous assumptions that are particularly manifest in a
similar but extended cluster of figures in *Plato* meant to
describe the Pythagorean elements in Plato himself:

> Ancient, half-obliterated inscriptions on the mental
> walls, the mental tablet, seeds of knowledge to come,
> shed by some flower of it long ago, it was in an earlier
> period of time they had been laid up in him, to blos-
> som again now, so kindly, so firmly! [*PP,* 66]

Much as *ascesis* and the doctrine of fitness fall under the
machinery of culture rather than under the rhythms of
nature, so the "inscriptions" on "the mental tablet" here
require an implicit understanding of the history of philosophy as a history of writing, and an understanding of the
history of culture in turn as an edifice or construction.
Such presuppositions, of course, are far different from the
ones that emerge in the second group of figures at work in

the passage, and that tacitly require us to translate the cultural categories of writing and building into the natural ones of "seeds," "flower," and "blossom." Indeed, in the essay on Lamb the same discontinuous tropes are to be found as well, with "men's life as a whole" described at one moment as an "organic wholeness" and, at another, as "the whole mechanism of humanity" (A, 115–16).

The trick is to resolve these two ways of talking, but the difficulties are formidable. How can a single model for culture accommodate the requirements of sublimation on the one hand and those of organic presence on the other? How can the artist as smith be reconciled with the artist as natural or hieratic visionary? How, in short, can self-expression be identified with self-curtailment?

We can at least see our way to a tentative resolution by noting, as Pater's gardenly figures should have suggested already, that the language of the natural is, after all, really a language of cultivation. Marius's "undiminished freshness" may well be represented by the figures of "seeds," "blossoms," and so on, although with the caveat that these are but elements in his "Epicurean rose-garden," in that circumscribed plot of a paradise within by which, for Pater at least, nature is already begotten by nurture. Moreover, cultivation is also a polite word for colonization, and suggests the achievement of sensibility to be similar to the annexation of territory in an imperialist line of reasoning that turns out to be a natural part of industrialization itself, at least in the Victorian context that gives the metaphor its contours.

Where nature is, there nurture already was, we might say of the organic in Pater. Nature appears only as representation, that is, in figures so blunt—"blossoms," "seeds," and so on—that they call attention to themselves as figures even as Pater himself reminds us, albeit with nostalgia for the illusion of a prelapsarian age of presence, that "experience, which has gradually saddened the earth's colours for us, stiffened its motions, withdrawn from it some blithe and debonair presence, has quite changed the character of the science of nature, as we understand it" (A, 76). To be sure, Pater here goes on to valorize "the suspicion of a mind latent in nature" (A, 76), although it is of the Hegelian kind whose focus is properly that of culture in Pater's own sense of the term, with nature clearly reduced to a metaphor, perhaps in evidence of that very dissociation lamented by Pater in his modernist myth of a lost golden age of presence and immediacy.

Such a formulation nonetheless maintains the irreducibility of the opposition between nature and culture, with the supposed "freshness" of Pater's heroes and their work coexisting uneasily with their status as exemplary sufferers. Indeed, the tension is in some ways a classically Victorian one between science and religion, reason and affection, which Pater reinterprets and brings to bear as tropes on questions of art and culture in his attempt to achieve a higher level of argument capable of resolving contradiction, or at least of dismissing some of the factors that contribute to it. With the chemistry of the crystal suggesting that theological organicism is one of Pater's least persuasive dialects, the language of nature remains largely a covering language in his texts, a language that tries to substitute for the renunciative labor of culture the appearance of spontaneous growth and visionary power in order to recompense the artist for his toil by granting him the conviction that he has found his way to something divine.

But before pursuing the consequences of this discontinuity—before unraveling the unity of Pater's ideal—let us turn again to Virginia Woolf in order to trace the Paterian thread that is so apparent there.

3

"Incandescence"

Having isolated some of Pater's characteristic figures, let us see to what extent they are present in Virginia Woolf's criticism as well. Like Pater, Woolf wishes critics "to declare the standard" (*CW*, 158) they have in mind when judging and analyzing books and their writers. If we want to ask what that standard is in Woolf's essays, early and late alike, we shall quickly find that it is, like Pater's, to be discovered in the way she talks about writing, and that its vocabulary of judgment and analysis bears an astonishing resemblance to Pater's own.

In her 1919 essay on "Reading," for example, Woolf asks what kind of book "matches . . . the morning hours," when the mind is particularly awake and eager for something more than "half-closed eyes and gliding voyages." To such a question she answers with a cluster of figures whose components are by now familiar to us: "We want something that has been shaped and clarified," she writes, "cut to catch the light, hard as gem or rock with the seal of human experience in it, and yet sheltering as in a clear gem the flame which burns now so high and now sinks so low in our own hearts" (*CE* II, 26). All the characteristics that Woolf's elaborate conceit assigns here to the praiseworthy text—its shape and clarity; its "hard," gemlike perfection; its nurturing, above all, of "the flame" which bespeaks the alliance between the inspiration in the writer's imagination and its appreciation in the reader's—are, of course, the same as those we have seen guiding Pater's own notion of the qualities to be found in the best art.

Moreover, following such an announcement of Paterian principles, however casual or implicit they may seem to be, Woolf turns almost immediately to one of Pater's favorite writers, Thomas Browne, and soon enough presents us with an assessment of Browne's literary values in terms of his being, "among a variety of other things, one of the first of our writers to be definitely himself" (CE II, 28). With expressiveness as the reigning critical principle in Pater as well, Woolf's judgment coincides rather directly with Pater's own assessment of Browne's writing as the "exact expression of his mind," with "the charm of an absolute sincerity" (A, 126) compensating for whatever "loose-ness" (A, 125) such subjectivity may appear to cause in the formal product that is its sensible vehicle. It is precisely Browne's subjectivity that Woolf praises, too— "Browne brings in the whole question . . . of knowing one's author," she concludes, deriving from his work the principle that "in whatever is written down is the form of a human being" (CE II, 29)—and it is Browne's sincerity that produces in its own turn the formal perfection such expressiveness seems at first to have foreclosed.

This identification of "absolute sincerity" with formal perfection, for Woolf as for Pater, lies, of course, in the degree of fitness with which a writer's style expresses his personality or temperament, with each defining the other in a movement that becomes for Woolf a principal critical theme. Thus, in a swerve like those by which she assigns the moment to Conrad, Hardy, and DeQuincey, Woolf points to Max Beerbohm as the figure who "has brought personality into literature . . . so consciously" that "we only know that the spirit of personality permeates every word that he writes." Swerve or not, Beerbohm's "personality" shows through in his work because his "triumph" is the Paterian "triumph of style" (*CE* II, 46). Indeed, "what we call style," says Woolf in "Phases of Fiction," is that discipline by which "the sentence shrinks and wraps itself firmly round the meaning" (*CE* II, 89). "Style may carry with it, especially in prose, so much personality that it keeps us within the range of that personality" (*CE* II, 92).

Fittingly enough, in fact, it is to Janet Case that Woolf writes in 1925 to say that "the better a thing is expressed, the more completely it is thought" (*Letters* III, 201). "I don't see how you can enjoy technique apart from the matter," she goes on, evidently in an attempt to counter what seem to be Case's expected objections to aestheticism in the vulgar sense: "But dont [*sic*], I beg of you, father on me that doctrine of yours about the way things are written mattering and not the things: how can you accuse me of believing that? I don't believe you can possibly separate expression from thought in an imaginative work" (*Letters* III, 201).

In order to describe how such fitness is attained—and how it is bungled or mismanaged, too, as the case may be— Woolf has frequent recourse throughout her criticism not only to a notion of "style" as "personality," but also, as we shall see at length soon enough, to the chemistry of the crystal. If, for example, Sidney's prose is suspect in "The Elizabethan Lumber Room" because it is "unable to grasp a thought closely and firmly, or to adapt itself flexibly and exactly to the chops and changes of the mind" (*CE* I, 50), Sterne's prose, by contrast, is praised because it meets the very standard by which Sidney fails: "No writing seems to flow more exactly into the very folds and creases of the individual mind, to express its changing moods, to answer its lightest whim and impulse, and yet the result is perfectly precise and composed" (*CE* I, 96). Indeed, with

Gibbon in particular, "the fusion was complete; matter
and manner became one" (*CE* I, 116).

The classic and enduring question for Woolf, of course,
is the question of what form or "design," as she puts it in
"Modern Fiction," can "resemble the vision in our minds,"
what method is right to express "what we wish to express"
(*CE* II, 105, 108), with the free expression of temperament the ruling standard in her very conception of writing.
This implicitly Paterian notion of composition is so habitual with Woolf that she even uses it to report her thoughts
in the relatively candid medium of *A Writer's Diary*. In
1918, for example, she finds Byron's genius to reside in his
"method," which is "a discovery by itself. It's what one
has looked for in vain—an elastic shape which will hold
whatever you choose to put into it. Thus he could write
out his mood as it came to him; he could say whatever
came into his head" (*AWD*, 3).

Hence Woolf's inclination to speak of aesthetic production as something natural in the case of genius, the elastic
style to which Mary Carmichael aspires in *A Room of
One's Own* being the consummate expression of such
a notion of art as an almost spontaneous growth: "It
feasted," says Woolf of Carmichael's prose when it is successful, "like a plant newly stood in the air" (*ROO*, 139).
In 1919 she even imagines the form of the diary itself as
a chemically self-perfecting one in which the "drifting
material of life" will have of its own accord "sorted itself
and refined itself and coalesced, as such deposits mysteri-
ously do, into a mould, transparent enough to reflect the
light of our life, and yet steady, tranquil compounds with
the aloofness of a work of art" (*AWD*, 13–14).

By the 1920s, however, the necessity of an active, rather
than an automatic or given, *ascesis* begins to emerge as

well: "you must put it all in before you can leave out" (*AWD*, 35), writes Woolf in 1921. In 1928, as she starts work on *The Waves* (then entitled *The Moths*), putting "it all in" and leaving the residue "out" start to become mutually interdependent, with the perfection of art identified, as in Pater, with the luminosity of the moment itself:

> The idea has come to me that what I want now to do is to saturate every atom. I mean to eliminate all waste, deadness, superfluity: to give the moment whole; whatever it includes. Say that the moment is a combination of thought; sensation; the voice of the sea. Waste, deadness, come from the inclusion of things that don't belong to the moment; this appalling narrative business of the realist: getting on from lunch to dinner: it is false, unreal, merely conventional. Why admit anything to literature that is not poetry—by which I mean saturated? Is that not my grudge against novelists? that they select nothing? The poets succeeding by simplifying: practically everything is left out. I want to put practically everything in: yet to saturate. That is what I want to do in *The Moths.* It must include nonsense, fact, sordidity: but made transparent. [*AWD*, 139]

Here the chemical metaphor is one of perfect saturation, with its basic unit, as in "Modern Fiction," the "atom" that had by now come to define more specifically Pater's notion of the "elementary particle." Despite the scientific language, however, Woolf's notion of saturation is one which still stands as a plea for an art that will rival or seem to be a part of nature itself, and, like Pater, she will sometimes magnify the discontinuity between *ascesis* and the naturalness of art in paradoxical figures for composition

like the "house," in another Paterian borrowing, which
"the oyster starts or the snail to secrete . . . for itself" in
the 1928 "Introduction" to *Mrs. Dalloway*.[1]

By the 1930s, Woolf is in full possession not only of
what she thinks is the right method for her fiction, but
also of a vocabulary with which to describe it adequately:
"I begin to see what I had in my mind," she writes of her
work on *The Waves*, "and want to begin cutting out masses
of irrelevance and clearing, sharpening and making the
good phrases shine" (*AWD*, 159). Expressiveness and
ascesis begin to approach their sought-for identity here,
with the ideal of perfect fitness or fusion informing her
further ruminations on the novel some six months later:
"a saturated unchopped completeness; changes of scene, of
mind, of person, done without spilling a drop. . . . it is
this writing that gives me my proportions" (*AWD*, 164).
Hence when *The Waves* is finished, she is able to write:
"I think I am about to embody at last the exact shapes my
brain holds" (*AWD*, 176). In fact, the method she has discovered here persists as an ideal throughout the 'thirties:
"I have to some extent forced myself to break every
mould and find a fresh form of being, that is of expression,
for everything I feel or think. So that when it is working
I get the sense of being fully energised—nothing stunted"
(*AWD*, 220).

Even the writer-hero who emerges in Woolf's *Diary*
during the difficult period that saw the composition of
The Years turns out to be none other than Pater's hero
Flaubert, who alone is fit enough to be "so tortured by
writing as I am," says Woolf, and with whose heroism she
identifies herself directly despite Pater's mediation in

1. See the Modern Library edition of *Mrs. Dalloway* (New York, 1928),
p. viii. The question of Woolf's naturalizing figures will be taken up more fully
in chapter 5, together with her extensive use of the figure of the house.

establishing him as a consummate martyr of *ascesis:* "reading Flaubert's letters"—those same letters quoted at length in "Style"—"I hear my own voice cry out Oh art! Patience: find him consoling, admonishing." Why? Because "I must get this book [*The Years*] quietly, strongly, daringly into shape. . . . envelop the whole in a medium" (*AWD*, 269–70).

If we turn next to the earliest of Woolf's essays to be collected, we shall find a particularly high density of Paterian figures in her reviews of 1904–10, although they establish less an early verbal apprenticeship that is later to be abandoned than they do a precedent and a pattern for the way she will talk about art throughout her career. In her first published essay,[2] in fact, her premise is that the Brontës' home at Haworth "expresses the Brontës" and that "the Brontës express Haworth," with the figure of the house an overt cipher, as it is of course in Pater himself, for the temperament of the artists with which it is identified. In fact, "they fit," says Woolf in an anticipation of the "Introduction" to *Mrs. Dalloway*, "like a snail to its shell" (*BP*, 166).

In a 1908 review of Sarah Bernhardt's memoirs, a literary subject negligible enough to allow the young Woolf to indulge in a statement of critical doctrine, the Paterian accent is so explicit that the essay's peroration, including Bernhardt's role in it as an exemplary aesthetic personality, is a virtual parody of Pater's peroration in the "Conclusion" to *The Renaissance:*

Are we not each in truth the centre of innumerable rays which so strike upon one figure only, and is it

2. Kirkpatrick (*A Bibliography of Virginia Woolf,* p. 97) lists one earlier essay, a review of William Dean Howells, published in *The Guardian* a week before "Haworth, November 1904," even though the piece on the Brontës is generally, and understandably, taken to be Woolf's first (see *BP*, 166, n. 1).

not our business to flash them straight and completely back again, and never suffer a single shaft to
blunt itself on the far side of us? Sarah Bernhardt at
least, by reason of some such concentration, will
sparkle for many generations a sinister and enigmatic message; but still she will sparkle, while the rest
of us—is the prophecy too arrogant?—lie dissipated
among the floods. [BP, 207]

In 1909 the emphatic focus of an essay on Elizabeth is
the queen's "temperament" (BP, 174), while in Woolf's
single article on music, published earlier that year as "Impressions at Bayreuth," stance and figure alike are drawn
so patently from Pater that we can only suggest the theme
of music to be the cause for so overt a set of borrowings.
With Parsifal her manifest subject, "the Grail," writes
Woolf, "seems to burn through all superincumbences"
and "one is fired with emotion"; "the stubborn matter"
of Wagner's "art dissolves in his fingers, and he shapes it
as he chooses":

> Parsifal seems poured out in a smooth stream at
> white heat; its shape is solid and entire. How much of
> the singular atmosphere which surrounds the opera in
> one's mind springs from other sources than the music
> itself it would be hard to say. It is the only work
> which has no incongruous associations. [BP, 19–20]

In short, says Woolf, "how fused our impressions are with
elements which we may not attempt to separate" (BP, 22).

As is usual, too, Woolf's Paterian standards are also used
to make negative or partial judgments. Thus Emerson's
"early pages," says Woolf in a 1910 review which may
justify the Case position Woolf resists in 1925, "are
written to the echo of great prose long before he could fit

words that gave his meaning into the rhythm" (*BP*, 68). Later on, however, "his sentences are made up of hard fragments each of which has been matched separately with the vision in his head" (*BP*, 70), "the result," says Woolf, "not only of ignoring so much, but of such concentration upon a few things" (*BP*, 71).

With *ascesis* or "concentration" central to a writer's fitness, Woolf's "irritation" with "the methods of mid-Victorian novelists" in a 1910 essay on Mrs. Gaskell is the direct result of her judgment that what the Victorians lack is precisely such a discipline of restraint and selection: "Able by nature to spin sentence after sentence melodiously"—here at least Case's objections are once again neutralized—"they seem to have left out nothing that they knew how to say. Our ambition, on the other hand, is to put in nothing that need not be there" (*BP*, 138). "A further deficiency," she adds, as if to make her own critical origins almost egregiously clear, "is that they lack 'personality' " (*BP*, 138).

There are, to be sure, two moments in Woolf's later criticism in which Pater is actually singled out for praise, even though these are the only generous—and genuine—insights into his work to be found anywhere in her writing, exceptions that may prove the rule of repression. Both examples come in reviews of new anthologies of English nonfiction, the first in the 1920 essay entitled "English Prose." Here a paragraph is devoted to a sympathetic, albeit curious, appreciation of Pater's achievement, with the surprised, and perhaps feigned, delight Woolf claims to feel at returning to him ("Can he possibly be what he once seemed?") implying that he was once read with care despite the pretence now that he is forgotten (*BP*, 15). Indeed, Pater's particular value for Woolf here derives from his ability to body forth the kind of tangled thoughts and feelings that surround his name in her own imagination, since he is not only "the writer who from words made blue and gold and green; marble, brick, the wax petals of flowers; warmth too and scent"; but, above all, the writer who made "the mind trace . . . subtle winding paths and surprise . . . recondite secrets" (*BP*, 15). Nonetheless, she withdraws from lengthier praise since she claims any such tribute will be insufficient. "If one cannot praise fitly," she decides, accenting a term whose usage may or may not be witting here, "it is better to be silent" (*BP*, 15).

In the companion piece to "English Prose," "The Modern Essay," published two years later in 1922, Woolf is far more lucid in analyzing Pater's achievement than she is in the earlier article, showing a familiarity with his work in both the figures she uses to describe it and in her evident sympathy for its critical project which is astonishing given her claim in 1920 that she had all but forgotten what Pater's writing was like. "There is no room for the impurities of literature in an essay," she says in an allusion to the tedious detail the novelist is obliged to give his reader in telling a story. No, "the essay must be pure—pure like water or pure like wine, but pure from dullness, deadness, and," above all, from "deposits of extraneous matter" (*CE* II, 43). Of all the writers represented in the collection under scrutiny here, Woolf singles out Pater as the one who "best achieves this arduous task, because before setting out to write his essay"—the one anthologized in the volume under review is the prose-poem on Leonardo—"he has somehow contrived to get his material fused" (*CE* II, 43). Not only has Woolf discerned those key Paterian notions of fusion and fitness at work in Pater's own writerly practice; she even demonstrates them—perhaps almost tautologically—by echoing or mirroring the very vocabulary in which they are worked out: "Only here, in the essay, where the bounds are so strict and facts have to be used in their nakedness, the true writer like Walter Pater makes these limitations yield their own quality," which is, of course, none other than the customary reward of *ascesis*, "shape and intensity" (*CE* II, 43).

Lest these figures and their filiation seem only incidental to Woolf's criticism, however, let us trace their course throughout her essays early and late to see to what extent they persist and to what extent they contribute to the design of her criticism as a whole. We can find out by paying particular attention to the way in which—to the terms by which—Woolf reads and evaluates all varieties of writers, whether classic or contemporary, foreign or domestic, male or female.

If, for example, we turn to the Brontës again, we find that both are "self-limited," according to Woolf, because "their impressions are close packed and strongly stamped between their narrow walls. Nothing issues from their minds which has not been marked with their own impress" (*CE* I, 187). This strong stamp of personality, figured in a secondary Paterian echo as aspects of a house ("walls"), is in fact the precise result of such narrowness and the discipline or *ascesis* that informs it. By means of "labour and the most obstinate integrity, by thinking every thought until it has subdued words to itself," the Brontës have "forged for themselves a prose which takes the mould of their minds entire" (*CE* I, 187). The "red and fitful glow of the heart's fire which illumines [Charlotte's] page" (*CE* I, 187) is, in the familiar pattern or paradox, the purgative energy that subdues her art to perfection at the same time that it is its hard-won product.

Thus Turgenev, too, "has gone through a long struggle of elimination" in order "to gain a simplicity so complex" (*CE* I, 248), much in the same way that, for all artists, as

Woolf puts it in "The Narrow Bridge of Art," "it seems true that some renunciation is inevitable" (*CE* II, 227). Hence the lengthy and positive resonance of "narrowness" throughout Woolf's criticism, a figure that insists on "the limitation," as she puts it in an essay on Oliver Goldsmith, that has "its advantages." Goldsmith is capable of giving "all his mind to the story," says Woolf, because "he knew precisely what to leave out." Hence "all is clear, related, and uncrowded" (*CE* I, 110).

The dynamics of artistic production for Woolf also extend to an overt notion of the perfect work as the transparent or crystalline product of a chemical process of labor. In the famous polemic against H. G. Wells in "Modern Fiction," for example, Woolf figures his shortcomings as "the fatal alloy in his genius" (*CE* II, 104), much as even Browne's idiosyncrasies are judged in "The Elizabethan Lumber Room" as "impurities which hereafter stain literature" (*CE* I, 53) despite the fact that they constitute the essence of his sincerity in "Reading." In both cases, the "alloy" or "impurities" remain because they have not been burned away by what Woolf calls the "fire" and "flame" of the intellectual "hearth" in her essay on Whitman (*CE* IV, 51).

Indeed, what is "unfused" or "unwrought" in a piece of writing (*CE* I, 166) is described in "Phases of Fiction" as a "surplus" (*CE* II, 88). Such a perspective accounts for an unexpected judgment which gives priority here to Dickens over George Eliot, since, in the latter, a "surplus" in her method of characterization "remains over" to "cloud and darken her page," while in Dickens himself such "surplus" has, by contrast, "been used up" (*CE* II, 88).

Thus a proper fitness between matter and manner produces the "crystallized phrases" of Meredith (*CE* I, 224) or the "crystal" images of Coleridge's lyrics (*CE* III, 221).

Moreover, such fitness is the result of that saving narrow-ness, say, in Peacock, which gives his "people . . . one idio-syncrasy apiece" and which in turn "crystallizes them into sharp separate characters" (*CE* II, 90). It can even allow "a sediment of good sense" in Goldsmith's poetry to "crystallize . . . itself into epigram" (*CE* I, 112). And be-cause Defoe has "at the outset limited his scope and con-fined his ambitions" (*CE* I, 67) according to a regimen of *ascesis,* he is capable of producing "masterpieces—books, that is, where the vision is clear" (*CE* I, 71), where all is "saturated with the truth of his own universe" and "no . . . discrepancy . . . allowed to intrude" (*CE* II, 59).

Ruskin, too, is "full of fire" (*CE* I, 206), and the best product of his genius, says Woolf, is the "unalloyed good" of *Praeterita* (*CE* I, 207). "There he has ceased to preach or to teach or to scourge"—he has purged away whatever surplus there may be in his other work—with the result that "his mood is . . . perfectly clear." His simplicity, in another Paterian flourish, is "the flower of perfect skill. The words lie like a transparent veil upon his meaning" (*CE* I, 207). Hence the *Praeterita* earns the Paterian quality of fitness and its attendant virtues of transparency and naturalness.

Meredith's work provides Woolf with a particularly fertile series of judgments to be made and discriminations rendered, once again according to the Paterian standards that we can see at work in her evaluation and analysis of all varieties of writing. At his best, Meredith "fires the cold scepticism out of us and makes the world glow in lucid transparency before our eyes" (*CE* I, 228). And yet the "uncompromising flame" (*CE* I, 234) of his genius—that "flare of fiery intensity" (*CE* I, 231)—sometimes leaves its work of purgation unfinished, especially "when philoso-phy is not consumed in a novel" (*CE* I, 230). Thus there is often a surplus or residue—something "unconsumed" by the "flame"—which we can see, says Woolf, when Meredith's writing "contains elements that do not fuse harmoniously" (*CE* I, 231).

The work of George Moore, allied as it is more traditionally with Pater's achievement than Woolf's own, is evaluated with an abundance of Paterian figures, too, as Woolf tries to discriminate its evident shortcomings from its successes by means of the customary standards. Although Moore's judgments, she writes, are often "ill-balanced, childish, and egotistical," the value of challenging them "lies not so much in the accuracy of each blow as in the heat it engenders, the sense it kindles that the matter of George Moore and his works is of the highest importance" (*CE* I, 338). Nonetheless, the "heat" of Moore's own imagination is unable to kindle itself to real perfection since there are "too many incompatible elements"—too many disparate atoms not properly fused—"to concentrate into the diamond," that gemlike variety of crystal, "of a great artist" (*CE* I, 339).

As for the Henry James that Virginia had been given to read as a youngster, it now grows more perfect through the Paterian lens. With a slight variation in the chemical process, and with points of contact with Pater's buildings and flowers, too, Woolf figures James's work in an almost overdetermined cluster of the familiar figures:

> When, therefore, almost perceptibly at a given moment, late in the story, something yields, something is overcome, something dark and dense grows in splendour, it is as if the beacon flamed bright on the hilltop; as if before our eyes the crown of long-deferred completion and culmination swung slowly into place. Not columns but pages, and not pages but chapters, might be filled with comment and attempted

analysis of this late and mighty flowering, this vin-
dication, this crowded gathering together and superb
welding into shape of all the separate strands, alien
instincts, irreconcilable desires of the twofold nature.
For, as we dimly perceive, here at last two warring
forces have coalesced; here, by a prodigious effort of
concentration, the field of human activity is brought
into fresh focus. [*CE* I, 283]

The flame of James's "beacon" reveals at once a kind of
literary architecture ("columns," "shapes") and a "mighty
flowering," with both figures standing as ciphers, as they
do in Pater, for a craft of fusion ("gathering together,"
"forces . . . coalesced") that is the product of a "prodigious" *ascesis* or "concentration." Here the process takes
the form of an applied or industrial chemistry ("welding")
reminiscent of Greek metallurgy and proleptic of Lily
Briscoe's "bolts of iron" in *To the Lighthouse* (*TL*, 264).
Indeed, the figure is so laden with meanings that it even
forces a mixed metaphor—one symptom of the over-
determination at work here—when it becomes the agent
by which "the separate strands" in James's "twofold
nature" are woven together in an image "irreconcilable"
with the letter of "welding" if not with its spirit.[3]

For her contemporaries Woolf uses the same vocabu-
laries of evaluation and analysis. Her essay on Forster's
fiction, for example, is a combination of praise and criticism, both rendered by means of the familiar tropes. Certain points in his novels become "irradiated," "saturated

3. The "fabric" that overlays Lily's "iron" mutters with the same irrecon-
cilability (*TL*, 264). It should be noted, too, that, unlike Pound or Joyce,
a modernist like Lawrence, more enamored of naturalizing myths than most of
his contemporaries, continues to resist valorizing chemical or industrial figures
for art, especially in his negative portrait of the industrial and aesthetic artist
Loerke in *Women in Love*, modeled, ironically enough, on the Bloomsbury
figure of painter Mark Gertler.

with light," says Woolf, and here "the fire of truth flames" (*CE* I, 346). At such moments Forster's work "becomes, or should become, luminously transparent" (*CE* I, 347), but because of surplus—once again, such residue is to be blamed on the realist's lamentable duty to include meto- nymic detail—the various strands or elements of Forster's novels "lack fusion" (*CE* I, 348). Only in a late book like *A Passage to India* does a "saturation" that is "thorough" emerge at all (*CE* I, 351). Here—to follow the Paterian thread(s) to another set of characteristic figures for imagi- native production—Forster has "relaxed" his "cares" about "his guests and . . . his house" (*CE* I, 350), no longer "a careful hostess," as he is in his earlier fiction, "who is anxious to introduce, to explain, to warn her guests of a step here, of a draught there" (*CE* I, 350). Hence the figure of the well-made house and its attendant graces can be made to turn back on itself, too, with Woolf's renegade use of the figure signifying, here at least, the apparent insincerity of the Victorian novelistic conventions from which Forster has only lately freed himself.

With Lawrence, Woolf's analysis is so replete with Paterian figures that she succeeds in demonstrating, how- ever inadvertently, the degree to which Lawrence himself is particulary transparent or accessible through Pater, as with James before. To be sure, Woolf's assessment of Lawrence's work in a retrospective essay written a year after his death, in 1931, is sometimes negative, although the evaluation proceeds in the customary way, and with the customary vocabulary. "The magnet that tries to draw together the different particles" of which *Sons and Lovers*, for example, is composed, says Woolf, is "the incandescent body," although she tries to take the body's instability as a source of value to be a sign for some larger absence in

Lawrence, reflected in Paul Morel's unsatisfied "desire for something withheld" (*CE* I, 354). Nonetheless, Woolf virtually talks herself into liking Lawrence the more she describes him in her Paterian terms, not only by casting Paul as a failed imaginary hero, but especially by refining "the incandescent body" itself into "this beauty glowing in the flesh, this intense and burning light" (*CE* I, 354).

Woolf's hesitation about praising Lawrence without qualification, of course, is doubtless bound up with her anxiety about his strength as a contemporary with whom she has much in common. The anxiety is particularly evident in her deceptive claim in the retrospective essay that, until his death, Lawrence "was known to her almost solely by reputation and scarcely at all by experience" (*CE* I, 352). Eleven years earlier, of course, Woolf had reviewed *The Lost Girl* in an essay containing the same objections to Lawrence's work voiced in the 1931 piece, and had articulated them by means of the same rhetoric, too. As in *Sons and Lovers,* "sex" in *The Lost Girl* "was the magnet to which the myriad of separate details would adhere" (*CW,* 159) but in fact do not, even though "incandescence" is still to be found in the "single phrase which we may liken to a glow or to a transparency" (*CW,* 160). The real standard at work in such judgments may be seen in Woolf's overarching criticism of Lawrence at the close of the 1931 essay for wishing "everything" in a novel like *Sons and Lovers* to have a "use," to have "a meaning." Nothing for Lawrence is, with a sneer, "an end in itself" (*CE* I, 355), for he is not "interested in literature as literature" (*CE* I, 355). After all, as "Mr. Bennett and Mrs. Brown" will attest, a work of fiction, argues Woolf, should be "complete in itself," "self-contained" (*CE* I, 327). What really goads her, though, is the modernity in Lawrence she feels

obliged to praise, however reluctantly, since it bestows
upon him an undeniable kind of priority:

> he echoes nobody, continues no tradition, is unaware
> of the past, of the present save as it affects the future.
> As a writer, this lack of tradition affects him im-
> mensely. The thought plumps directly into his mind;
> up spurt the sentences as round, as hard, as direct
> as water thrown out in all directions by the impact
> of a stone. [*CE* I, 355]

Still, the aesthetic critic is able to interpose a caveat once
again at the end of the judgment, and so keep the rival at
bay on the grounds, finally, of his imperfection: "One feels
that not a single word has been chosen for its beauty, or for
its effect upon the architect of the sentence" (*CE* I, 355).

As with Lawrence, Joyce, too, is subject to ambivalent
treatment in Woolf's criticism, an ambivalence also determined by her anxiety about a rivalry, although one that
is clearly more acute than the rivalry with Lawrence himself. "I reflected," she writes in her diary in 1920, "how
what I'm doing is probably being better done by Mr. Joyce.
Then I began to wonder," she adds humorously, "what it
is that I am doing" (*AWD,* 28). There is, of course, no essay
devoted exclusively to Joyce, and, apart from her obvious
borrowings from his work in her fiction, particularly in the
way *Mrs. Dalloway* doubles *Ulysses* in organizational
principles, what we find most revealing is an implicit
recognition of their shared Paterian allegiances in "Modern
Fiction," where Joyce's achievement becomes an attempt
"to reveal the flickerings of that innermost flame which
flashes its messages through the brain" (*CE* II, 107). The
"messages" in question, of course, are as much literary
ones as they are existential, with the mediacy of Pater's
"flame" a sign not only for the "atoms" as they fall upon

the mind, but also, and perhaps even primarily, for the very establishment of such a project in Pater's precedent or example. Hence Woolf's attack on Joyce's "indecency" in "Mr. Bennett and Mrs. Brown" (*CE* I, 334) is to be read in tandem with her record of Eliot's opinion in *A Writer's Diary* that Joyce " 'is a purely literary writer,' " " 'founded upon Walter Pater with a dash of Newman' " (*AWD*, 50).[4]

Although Woolf shares at least as much with Proust as she does with Lawrence and Joyce,[5] in Proust's case the lingering anxiety gives way to sheer praise, doubtless because the difference in language separates the two writers enough to foreclose a rivalry as serious as those with the writers in her own tradition.[6] In any case, though, the praise for Proust is rendered in the same terms through which Lawrence and Joyce are read with reservations, and through which her appreciation for James has been refined as well. Having noted in "Phases of Fiction" that James's American birth will always constitute "an obstacle never perfectly assimilated" by the settings or the art of his novels, Woolf goes on to place Proust above James for being without such a shortcoming, although the sociological considerations supposedly invoked here are really an excuse for introducing the customary figuration of writing that gives her an abiding power over her contemporaries by confronting all of them with the self-contained unity of her own—and Pater's—critical imagination: "Proust, the product of the civilization which he describes, is so porous, so pliable, so perfectly receptive

4. See also *Diary* II, 202.
5. On Woolf and Proust, see Ruth Z. Temple, "Never Say 'I': *To the Lighthouse* as Vision and Confession," in Claire Sprague, ed., *Virginia Woolf: A Collection of Critical Essays* (Englewood Cliffs, N.J.: Prentice-Hall, 1971), pp. 90–100.
6. There was, however, some anxiety attached to reading Proust for the first time (see *Letters* II, 499).

that we realize him only as an envelope, thin but elastic, which stretches wider and wider and serves not to enforce a view but to enclose a world" (*CE* II, 83).

Particularly noteworthy here, of course, is the way in which the figure of the "envelope," so important in Woolf as a sign for a strong style in art and a strong personality in life, reveals its equivalence with the central Paterian figure of the diaphane—of transparency—itself. If, for example, in "Modern Fiction," life is described as a "semi-transparent envelope" (*CE* II, 106), it is the writer's paradoxical and ascetic task to "convey" this "spirit . . . with as little mixture of the alien and external as possible" (*CE* II, 106), and so in fact exchange a higher mimesis for the self-contained raptures of *aesthesis*. Hence in Proust, "the commonest object, such as the telephone, loses its simplicity, its solidity, and becomes" not only "a part of life" but also "transparent. The commonest actions, such as going up in an elevator or eating cake, instead of being discharged automatically, rake up in their progress a whole series of thoughts, sensations, ideas, memories which were apparently sleeping on the walls of the mind" (*CE* II, 83).

With the additional figure of "the walls of the mind" suggesting a second point of contact with Pater's rhetoric, Woolf's notion of Proust's strength as a writer lies in his ability not simply to link up the structures of existence but to render the imperfect materials of life into the luminous organization of a perfect fiction. And yet what is really being celebrated here, as elsewhere in Woolf's criticism, is not so much the virtues of her apparent critical subject as it is the whole and self-contained perfection of her own critical vision, borrowed as it may be from Pater, but nonetheless strong and consistent enough in her translation of it to serve as the signature and vehicle of her own personality by which she may fire out all that is alien to her, even in strong contemporaries, by assimilating it to the uniform character of her own sensibility.

Indeed, the Paterian stance embraces so wide a spectrum of contemporary literature for Woolf that it can even assimilate writers as different as Strachey and the American novelist Joseph Hergesheimer to its uniform vision. Thus an imaginative biographer like Strachey, says Woolf in "The Art of Biography," can achieve perfection thanks to "a necessary limitation" (*CE* IV, 225) imposed upon him by the requirements of the very form in which he works. Indeed, imaginative biography, she argues, welcomes that "richer unity" (*CE* IV, 226) by which the "granite-like solidity" of fact and the "rainbow-like intangibility" of personality come to be "weld[ed] " into "one seamless whole" (*CE* IV, 229) in "The New Biography," with the form's Paterian lineage (also) apparent in the figures by which Woolf describes it. Here an implicit masonry becomes a component of the Jamesian variant of "welding," with the fusion of the "seamless" its perfect and expected result.

Despite the vast difference in form and context, Hergesheimer's fiction is also judged by means of the customary vocabulary, at least in Woolf's surprisingly enthusiastic review of his first novel. Her notices of his subsequent books all register disappointment when compared to the first, which in retrospect appears to be more than anything else an excuse to put the Paterian machinery into motion, especially since her delight is confined almost entirely to the novel's form:

> The comparison with something hard, lustrous and concrete is not altogether fanciful. In recollection, the last sentence being read, the reader's impression of the book as a whole assumes something of the smooth solidity of a well-fashioned gem. When the

last sentence is finished nothing vague or super-
fluous is left to blur the outline; the substance is all
neatly packed into the form, rounded off, disposed
of, completed. The sense of conclusiveness is so satis-
factory, and also so rare, that we could enjoy it
separately from any feeling of pity or pleasure
aroused by the fortunes of the characters, as a blind
man might enjoy the shape of a stone though unable
to see its colour. [CW, 105]

The trope of the "hard, lustrous" gem, expressive of the
way "the substance is all neatly packed into the form," is
so emblematic a pattern of Paterian fitness that the passage
is almost as much an unconscious parody of the "Conclusion" to *The Renaissance* as the climax of the essay on
Sarah Bernhardt. Indeed, the chemistry of the crystal is so
much in Woolf's mind as she writes that even the elements
of Hergesheimer's plot—a Pennsylvania family's truculent
independence and solitude—are described through the customary figures of combustion: "There was something
unmalleable in their composition," says Woolf, "which
stayed unmelted in the common furnace" (*CW*, 105),
a "furnace" whose literal meaning here is the melting pot
of American social life.

Ironically enough, though, Hergesheimer's novel plays
directly to Woolf's fondness for the figures of "welding"
and ironworking, since the family whose history is chroni-
cled here actually owns "a great ironworks" (*CW*, 105),
and provides not only an inadvertent link between the
Paterian chemistry and the deidealizations to which it is
subject among Pater's modern heirs, but may also suggest
a reason for Woolf's attractions to Hergesheimer's novel in
the first place.

Even the work of a contemporary nearer to Woolf's
heart like Dorothy Richardson is scrutinized through the

Paterian lens, with the surprising result that Richardson's version of *ascesis*—the discipline with which the traditional apparatus of the novel is largely "cut out" (*CW*, 120)—ends up creating an unexpected problematic in the new kind of novel she has to some degree invented. "All these things are cast away," writes Woolf of the fate of novelistic conventions in *The Tunnel*, "and there is left, denuded, unsheltered, unbegun and unfinished, the consciousness of Miriam Henderson, the small sensitive lump of matter, half transparent and half opaque" (*CW*, 120). Clearly Richardson's success is only partial since her work is "unfinished" or unfused—only "half transparent"—causing Woolf to recall with nostalgia "the shapeliness of the old accepted forms" (*CW*, 122), and suggesting in turn her sympathy and respect for literary tradition despite her public stance as a literary revolutionary.

Nevertheless, what Richardson has "invented," or at least "developed and applied to her own uses," is significant in political terms: "a sentence," says Woolf in a review of one of Richardson's later novels, "which we might call the psychological sentence of the feminine gender. It is of a more elastic fibre than the old, capable of stretching to the extreme, of suspending the frailest particles, of enveloping the vaguest shapes" (*CW*, 124). Hence Richardson succeeds after all in meeting the Paterian standard on the level of the sentence (note especially the "particles"), although with considerable irony, since her very success in forging "the psychological sentence of the feminine gender" is one authorized, at least in Woolf's critical assessment of it, by a man who elsewhere in her work personifies the patriarchy itself. Bound as she is to the ideal of a style for women that will, like the Brontës', take "the mould of their minds entire," even the articulation of such an ideal binds her to the very type of authority it is designed to overthrow or circumvent.

It is, however, Woolf's very bondage to Pater that is also her means of escape. As it turns out, the ideal of fitness and fusion—the ideal expressiveness of a style in perfect accord with the temperament of its writer—is brought to its logical conclusion by Woolf's desire for fitness in the sphere of female letters. "Before a woman can write exactly as she wishes to write," says Woolf in "Women and Fiction," "there is the technical difficulty . . . that the very form of the sentence does not," in that key word, "fit her":

> It is a sentence made by men; it is too loose, too heavy, too pompous for a woman's use. Yet in a novel, . . . an ordinary and usual type of sentence has to be found to carry the reader on easily and naturally from one end of the book to the other. And this a woman must make for herself, altering and adapting the current sentence until she writes one that takes the natural shape of her thought without crushing or distorting it. [*CE* II, 145]

To succeed in forging a style for women that will realize the truth of their own impressions is to depose Pater, at least in principle, in the very act of following him.

Let us pursue the Paterian thread in Woolf's prose, then, to a text where we might expect to find it least, but where it is in fact of central importance—in *A Room of One's Own*. Here, of course, Woolf's indignation about the male-dominated universities and the power of "the professors" (*ROO*, 58) is more forcefully expressed than anywhere else in her work. What disturbs her above all is the fact that women writers may not proceed with their art in the same clear atmosphere in which male writers are privileged to work. Such a claim requires her to ask what such a clear and comfortable atmosphere may be; to ask, in short, the

Paterian question: "What conditions are necessary for the creation of works of art?" (*ROO*, 38).

Concerned as she is by the "drawbacks" (*ROO*, 59) of anger and resentment produced in women writers for centuries by "the rule of a patriarchy" (*ROO*, 50) in literature and politics alike, she looks forward to the day when such "fear and bitterness" (*ROO*, 59) will subside in the mind of the woman of letters and allow her "the greatest release of all," the "freedom to think of things in themselves" (*ROO*, 59). With this somewhat Arnoldean, or really Newmanesque, proposition comes another statement of what the happiest conditions for a writer's work may be, although the derivation of this second proposition is unmistakably specific:

> That building, for example, do I like it or not? Is that picture beautiful or not? Is that in my opinion a good book or a bad? [*ROO*, 59]

Woolf's remarks here are little more than a condensed, though unacknowledged, citation from the "Preface" to *The Renaissance*, where Pater defines "the aesthetic critic" (*R*, viii) in precisely the terms that Woolf has used above:

> What is this song or picture, this engaging personality presented in life or in a book, to *me*? What effect does it really produce on me? Does it give me pleasure? and if so, what sort or degree of pleasure? How is my nature modified by its presence, and under its influence? [*R*, viii]

Interestingly enough, Pater's last question is not included in Woolf's palimpsestic litany, as though its very utterance would betray the silent borrowing at work here or somehow serve to acknowledge its presence by broaching the question of influence too openly or directly. Indeed, it is "influence" itself that Woolf targets as the very type of the tyrannical force women must counter and resist, with even the terms by which the problem is articulated, chief among them the absence of Pater's final question, a graphic swerve from influence that enacts the precise strategy of resistance which influence itself recommends. What Woolf objects to specifically, of course, is that women writers cannot pursue an ideally clear and unimpeded path in writing because of the "attachment" (*ROO*, 63)—the suppressed Paterian word for it is "influence"—that requires them to worry, in anger, fear, and bitterness, about politics despite a commitment to the kind of pure art and aesthetic criticism enunciated, through Pater, in her description of the ideal activity of the writer cited above.

This ideal of writing is to be found above all in Shakespeare, whose plays, says Woolf in an echo of the ideal recommended in "Mr. Bennett and Mrs. Brown," are "complete by themselves" (*ROO*, 63), and whose imagination in producing them is, in the celebrated judgment, "incandescent," "freeing whole and entire the work that is in him" because there is "no obstacle in it, no foreign matter unconsumed" (*ROO*, 85). The reason, of course, lies in the fact that, for Shakespeare himself, unlike his hypothetical sister Judith, every "hardship or grievance was fired out of him and consumed," allowing his poetry to "flow . . . from him free and unimpeded" (*ROO*, 86). Shakespeare, in other words, is the perfect Paterian artist because the implicit flame of his genius has fired out all kinetic residue (hence the application of the term "incandescent" that we have seen with Lawrence at his least didactic) and made his work perfectly expressive of his already luminous temperament. "If ever a human being got his work expressed completely," says Woolf, "it was Shakespeare" (*ROO*, 86).

Such a Paterian stance informs Woolf's evaluation of Shakespeare throughout the book, and serves as the standard by which she reads and analyzes female letters in English in both its real and its imaginary history. Against the ideal of Shakespeare emerge Woolf's miniature portraits of women writers across the centuries. Imaginary heroines like the Elizabethan Judith Shakespeare and the modern Mary Carmichael have, as it turns out, the same difficulty in being "incandescent" because of their necessary "attachment" to "hardship" and "grievance"—to the influence of politics and anger—which in the male Shakespeare is "fired out" and "consumed," but which in women writers introduces a fatal alloy into their ability and even their desire "to think of things in themselves" and to produce works of art in their own turn "complete in themselves." Although a relatively early woman poet like Lady Winchilsea may have had "the fire" of imagination "hot within her" (*ROO*, 89), the fact remains that the minds of most women writers are still "disturbed by alien emotions like fear and hatred" (*ROO*, 87). "Traces of that disturbance" (*ROO*, 88) remain as a kind of residue in their work—in Margaret of Newcastle's, for example, as well as in Lady Winchilsea's—which the heat of a woman's imagination, fired as it is by politics as well as by imagination itself, apparently does not, cannot, burn off. In both Lady Winchilsea and Margaret of Newcastle "burnt the same passion for poetry and both are disfigured and deformed by the same causes" (*ROO*, 91-92). Due to the "cause" of women, then, the saving discipline of *ascesis* cannot, and in some sense should not, function as it does in great male writers like Shakespeare. "No one checked her," says Woolf of Margaret in a paradoxical statement of the effects on the female artist of the abundant checks imposed on her as a woman (*ROO*, 92).

Despite the persistence of the obvious political problems, by the nineteenth century Woolf finds women
writers to be generally fitter than their earlier counterparts. Like the Brontës in Woolf's essays, then, a novelist
like Jane Austen is to be found writing "without hate,
without bitterness, without fear, without protest, without
preaching. That," says Woolf, "was how Shakespeare
wrote" (ROO, 101–02). Hence Austen, unlike Lady
Winchilsea or Margaret of Newcastle, conforms to the
pattern of Paterian perfection because, like Shakespeare,
her mind "had consumed all impediments" (ROO, 102).
In an almost literal version of fitness, "her gift and her
circumstances matched each other completely," the result
largely of "the narrowness of life that was imposed upon
her" (ROO, 102) by her domestic circumstances and that,
by necessity, caused her to sharpen and focus her imagination by means of the limitations of a saving *ascesis*.

Once Woolf begins to discuss novelists, of course, she
cannot refrain from describing her evaluative standard for
the form as a whole, and, like Pater, she presents such
a standard as a backdrop against which her concrete analyses of particular writers may emerge. Woolf's notion of the
novel is a highly formalist one, as her essays have already
suggested, and like Pater she figures such imaginative production in terms of a literary architecture:

If one shuts one's eyes and thinks of the novel as
a whole, it would seem to be a creation owning a certain looking-glass likeness to life, though of course
with simplifications and distortions innumerable. At
any rate, it is a structure leaving a shape on the
mind's eye, built now in squares, now pagoda shaped,
now throwing out wings and arcades, now solidly
compact and domed like the Cathedral of Saint Sofia
at Constantinople. [ROO, 106–07]

Nonetheless, the "shape" or "structure" of the novel as it is handed down through generations of male writers is not necessarily the perfect one for women, since "the stride of a man's mind," like the shape of his fiction and the sentences from which it is built, is "too unlike her own" (*ROO*, 114). With "no common sentence ready for her use" (*ROO*, 114), the woman writer too often discovers that such forms and sentences are not "the right shape" (*ROO*, 121) for her, as in Mary Carmichael's imaginary novel, which Woolf reads with the feeling that "something tore, something scratched" (*ROO*, 121). Hence the work Mary Carmichael has to look forward to is to "have out her scissors and fit" the clothes of her art "to every hollow and angle" of her sensibility (*ROO*, 133). By means of such sartorial *ascesis*, she must seek, quite literally, a fitter method of writing the prose with which her "abundance of sensation" and "fineness of perception"—two evident Paterian imperatives for the artist and aesthetic critic alike —"could build up out of the fleeting and the personal the lasting edifice which remains," apparently like a wrestler, "unthrown" (*ROO*, 140).

Apart from five hundred a year and a room of her own, what Mary Carmichael will need most to achieve her aim, then, is a chastening "narrowness": "leave out half that she now puts in" (*ROO*, 142). The result will be, in the familiar Paterian ideal now appropriated by women, "the development by the average woman of a prose style completely expressive of her mind" (*ROO*, 143).

Indeed, as Woolf's vision in *A Room of One's Own* moves toward its penultimate ideal of androgyny in art, the perfection she has in view is a peculiar kind of focusing of sensibility itself, in which "a natural fusion" (*ROO*, 147) of the perspectives of both sexes takes the form of a "state of mind in which one could continue without effort because nothing is required to be held back" (*ROO*,

147). Such a utopian state of sensibility, in other words, represents so perfect a fitness or fusion that no *ascesis* will even be required, as in Woolf's Byron, since the mental instrument will work so cleanly, like a machine in space, that no residue will be produced at all. Hence the ideal of "the androgynous mind" that Woolf derives here from Coleridge is "resonant and porous," capable of transmitting "emotion without impediment," "naturally creative, incandescent and undivided" (*ROO,* 148).

Woolf's abiding ideal in art, then, is the "freedom" and "peace" (*ROO,* 157) of an imagination at one with itself; a state in which conflict and debate have ceased (*ROO,* 159–60) and in which the polemics of politics are defused so as to allow the imagination its proper stasis or "incandescence." Such an ideal constitutes an abiding desire for a purely formal harmony, disabused of kinesis, political or otherwise, and capable simply of seeing the world, as Woolf puts it in her peroration, "more intensely" (*ROO,* 166).

Hence the first stage in Woolf's latecomer improvement over the pioneer is enacted, for she overcomes Pater and satisfies him at the same time by transforming his injunction to full expressiveness and formal perfection into the basis of a new vision of female letters. Here, too, she handles the paternal precursor in much the same way she handles its original in the figure of her legal father, who is satisfied and vanquished in one and the same gesture by the moral criticism he both authorizes and suffers to defeat him. Moreover, this overcoming by going through or satisfying the precursor in feminist terms is already prepared for in Woolf's more plainly modernist enactment of the Paterian injunction to realize one's own impression as it really is, and so frees her to assert the truth and power—and the naturalness—of her own personality over all influence whatsoever.

These are, however, only partial victories, and still carry with them a residue of the very bondage they are meant to fire away, especially the telltale theft of master tropes like personality and the moment, and the way the chemistry of the crystal directs the central metaphors by which Woolf judges art and expresses its ideals. For a notion of how Woolf fully overcomes the burden of Pater's influence, we need to return to Pater first and unravel the threads we left hanging there.

4

"A Difference for the Sense"

Throughout our discussion we have seen both Pater and Woolf relying almost exclusively on a notion of art as an expression of character or personality, an assumption that seems to lie untroubled at the root of their surprisingly common visions of criticism and art alike. Indeed, for both writers the perfection of genius is to be figured as a fitness or fusion between the artist's temperament and the "sensible analogue"—in language, paint, manners, and so on—which embodies or expresses it. It is the fiery discipline of *ascesis* that produces this seamless fusion or chemical "incandescence," and that grants the crystalline productions of genius a transparence akin to the transparence of nature itself. Hence the work of art is unique insofar as it is perfectly expressive and rivals, or indeed joins, nature by virtue of the freshness and immediacy of both the artist's presence within it and the critic's appreciation and response. Like the luminous immediacy of the privileged moment, the transparence and presence of the work of art proper is, to all appearances at least, pure and absolute, with no residue or surplusage left over to mar its self-contained and crystalline perfection.

But even though Pater's notion of genius relies on an ideal of "absolute sincerity," we have also seen that his very notion of selfhood tends to be more uneasy than these manifest assumptions and working categories might lead us to believe. Despite its apparent status as an ontological given from which artistic work proceeds, selfhood for Pater is an object that personality crafts with "the labor of the file," as impersonally, in a curious irony, as it crafts words, paint, or sound. Less a natural object than a well-wrought vessel, Paterian selfhood is a problematic quantity, already the kind of thing it is supposed to produce. Where and how does Pater locate or situate this self that is at once the obvious center and the problematic assumption of his entire project? If we wish to investigate the status of the self in his work, let us turn first to his notion of the artist's subjectivity, since it is usually the artist who provides Pater with a model for the nature of temperament as a whole.

Although "expression" is the cornerstone of Pater's vision of the artist at work, there emerges beside it, even in the "temperamental" 1870s, another way of describing the nature of composition that is discordant or at odds with it. Greek sculpture, of course, is Pater's quintessential mode of art, and in *Greek Studies* it is the birth of Greek sculpture as we know it that signals the first full emergence of subjectivity in the customary sense (*GS,* 229, 233, 242) and that provides Pater with his "basement type" for all the renaissances in the later history of the West, even Prior St. Jean's in the 1893 "Apollo in Picardy." And yet in *The Renaissance* itself, the spirit of Greek sculpture appears to reside somewhere else, since its perfection, Pater argues there, is the result of its desire "to seek the type in the individual, to abstract and express only what is structural and permanent, to purge from the individual all that belongs only to him, all the accidents, the feelings and actions of the special moment" (*R,* 66). This kind of purgation is a far different version of *ascesis* from the one in which the individual searches out his own peculiarities so as to clarify them by finding their fit sensible analogues in a plastic medium. Indeed, in Greek sculpture the individual is robbed of precisely those qualities—his "feelings" and "the special moment" that embodies them—that define his uniqueness.

Of course, Pater seems to correct the impersonal vision of Greek art cited above by describing in "Luca Della Robbia" how Michelangelo overturns it by (re)introducing "intimate experiences" (*R,* 67) into sculpture and thereby retrieves what both the Greeks and the Middle Ages apparently lose in expressiveness. And yet this brief allegory of the birth of the individual in a Renaissance largely embodied by Michelangelo does not form as clear a distinction between two different kinds of art—one classical, medieval, and impersonal, the other modern and self-expressive—as it may seem to do. Indeed, in the full portrait of Michelangelo, Pater shows his genius to derive from its position as the "inheritor" (*R,* 92) of a series of earlier impulses in the history of painting and sculpture whose development remains "unbroken" and "continuous" (*R,* 91) despite the apparent revolution accomplished by Michelangelo himself. Here Pater relies on a definition of genius and historical periodization formulated in the book's "Preface," a definition in which genius like Michelangelo's comes to stand for a piece of history by virtue, not of its newness and originality, but of its status as a container of the "powers or forces" (*R,* viii) that it inherits from the past. The figure Pater uses to characterize the status of the individual artist here is the "receptacle" (*R,* x), a figure virtually synonymous with that of "the depositary" (*R,* 60) by which he describes a work of art proper like a Botticelli painting.

From this point of view, what is noteworthy about Michelangelo is not the "individuality and intensity of expression" (R, 67) of his work at all, since such originality or expressiveness "often is, and always seems," says Pater, "the effect of accident" (R, 67). Michelangelo himself is simply a perfect crystal designed (by whom, of course, it remains unclear) to catch the beams, rays, or powers of influence that devolve upon him. Thus artistic conception as a whole begins to resemble giving expression less to the merely individual than to what Pater calls the "independent traditional existence" (R, 91) of certain conceptions, myths, legends, and models which, taken together in a collective and historical way, constitute those aesthetic traditions in which the work of any particular artist necessarily comes into being and from which it takes its life.

Such a notion of art is also at work in the way Pater reads a particular series of paintings in *The Renaissance*. The "type of womanly beauty" (R, 115) to be found in Leonardo's paintings, for example, is an extended working instance of such an alternative perspective on the nature of art, since Leonardo's women

> are the clairvoyants, through whom, as through delicate instruments, one becomes aware of the subtler forces of nature, and the modes of their action, all that is magnetic in it, all those finer conditions wherein material things rise to that subtlety of operation which constitutes them spiritual, where only the final nerve and the keener touch can follow. It is as if in certain significant examples we actually saw those forces at their work on human flesh. Nervous, electric, faint always with some inexplicable faintness,

these people seem to be subject to exceptional conditions, to feel powers at work in the common air
unfelt by others, to become, as it were, the receptacle
of them, and pass them on to us in a chain of secret
influences. [*R*, 116]

Like Michelangelo, the subjects of Leonardo's portraits are
able "to feel powers at work in the common air unfelt by
others"; their distinction or individuality, like Michelangelo's or, presumably, like Leonardo's, too, is simply
the result of a heightened degree of receptivity rather
than a special or distinct kind of creative activity. What
Leonardo's pictures embody and make apparent to us are
precisely those "powers" and "influences" at work in all
of us—our "common air"—which art heightens and allows
us to see.

Moreover, that Pater wishes to characterize these
"forces" as those "of nature" as such represents the vestige
even here of that plea for presence and immediacy imputed
to art, and to culture at large, in the natural, covering
language we have already seen at work in his manifest
vision of the artist's labor as personal, expressive, and
creative. But such immediacy is, strictly speaking, impossible here, since the very way in which these "material
things"—these "forces of nature"—become visible to us at
all is by means of their transmutation into the language of
the painter, sculptor, writer, or musician. Indeed, the very
means by which these apparently ineffable forces of nature
"rise to that subtlety of operation which constitutes
them," in a vestigial theological figure akin to the language
of the natural, "spiritual," is by means of the various ways
they can be represented to the human imagination.

It is, in fact, just such a perspective that informs Pater's
famous description of the Mona Lisa, a figure whose power

is to be ascribed to its ability to contain or act as a vessel or receptacle for the powers and forces of history and nature alike. "All the thoughts and experience of the world have etched and moulded there" (*R, 125*), says Pater of the Mona Lisa's countenance, making "the fancy of a perpetual life" real again by "summing up in itself" (as "modern philosophy" teaches us, says Pater, to conceive of "humanity" and its products) "all modes of thought and life" (*R, 125*).

The power that Pater assigns to the Mona Lisa, of course, is the power of myth itself, and despite—or perhaps because of—"modern philosophy," her mythical power is to be understood in the same sense in which Pater understands myth among the Greeks. Like Dionysus, who is "a sacred representation or interpretation of the whole human experience" (*GS, 10*); or like Demeter and Persephone, who "came at last to represent" to the Greeks "in a certain number of sensibly realised images, all they knew, felt, or fancied, of the natural world about them" (*GS, 97*); so the Mona Lisa is a master trope or receptacle that gathers up and represents "the whole human experience" to a post-Renaissance man like Pater as powerfully and absorbingly as Dionysus or Demeter and Persephone represent it to the Greeks themselves.

In fact, we might even say that the Mona Lisa is for Pater the trope of tropes, the vessel of vessels, a representation of all the representations—"all modes of thought and life"—of which experience is constituted. Hence she is "older than the rocks among which she sits" (*R, 125*), since nature emerges only after, or as a result of, the various myths or representations by which it is accessible or apprehensible to us. Moreover, like Greek myth itself, the Mona Lisa also carries with it the suggestion that, like Demeter, it has "no single author" (*GS, 101*), and thereby reaffirms the impression Leonardo's picture already gives of "sweeping together ten thousand experiences" (*R*, 125) rather than of expressing the experience of a single individual like Leonardo alone.

With Giorgione, of course, Pater goes on to skew our notion of art as a direct expression of a particular individual by finding Giorgione's genius to reside at least as much in his "influence" as in his own proper achievement. After all, the two are really inseparable, since Giorgione's originality "becomes" to begin with "a sort of impersonation of Venice itself, its projected reflex or ideal, all that was intense or desirable in it crystallising about the memory [here the subject of Pater's sentence has silently shifted from Giorgione himself to his influence] of this wonderful young man" (*R*, 148). Thus the figure of the crystal returns, this time as a structure or receptacle capable of catching impulses that pass through it from without, instead of as a representation for an "absolute sincerity" that is purely personal and that derives from "within." Indeed, the very confusion as to what works are Giorgione's and what "rightly or wrongly attributed to him"—"the *Giorgionesque*," those "many copies . . . prized as his" (*R*, 148)—suggests that a work of art is not necessarily to be identified with or assigned to a particular individual at all, making what we call personality in art really a node of influence or containment, a structure that can branch out to include other individuals whose artistic subjectivity nonetheless falls entirely under Giorgione's own. The same notion of containment, it should be noted, is also adumbrated in the essay on Du Bellay, in which the school or "constellation" of the Pleiad (*R*, 159) is derived from Ronsard's "refining upon" (*R*, 158) the old "character of French literature" and a new "influx of Renaissance taste" (*R*, 158).

In the closing pages of the Winckelmann essay, Pater focuses and clarifies his argument by distinguishing it from an "old" notion of "necessity" in which a "mythological personage" stands "without us," as in Hardy's revival of such creatures in *The Dynasts,* and "with whom we can do warfare" (*R*, 231). No, these "forces" of which genius and its works are the receptacles are in fact the very lineaments of selfhood:

> It is rather a magic web woven through and through us, like that magnetic system of which modern science speaks, penetrating us with a network, subtler than our subtlest nerves, yet bearing in it the central forces of the world. [*R*, 231]

Hence the power of the individual is the power of the collectivity, his "subtlest nerves" not even subtle enough to coincide entirely with that "network" of influence—of customs, notions, myths, forms of art, of cultural competence as a whole—whose "magic web" carries in its circuits "the central forces of the world" and weaves itself through us, constituting temperament even as it breaks down the famous "wall of personality" (*R*, 235) of which another, solipsistic Pater speaks in the "Conclusion."

What is striking about the phenomenology of the privileged moment adduced in the "Conclusion" itself, however, is that the "elements" (*R*, 233) or "forces" of which this "magic web" is composed are "delicate fibres . . . present not in the human body alone: we detect them in places most remote from it" (*R*, 233). The very fabric of our existence, in other words, extends beyond us, apparently of a piece qualitatively with the world from which it is supposedly separated by that "thick wall of personality" (*R*, 235) which only seems to be the master figure in the "Conclusion" for the status of the individual's relation to

the world at large. Hence personality, even in its privileged
moments of perception, establishes itself by virtue of
forces that extend not only beyond it, but which even
begin to put into question the reality of subjects and objects themselves.

The passage and intersection of Pater's "elements" provide the locus of both individual being and discrete physical objects only insofar as these elements become particularly dense or clustered, with no inherent or qualitative
difference to be found between what we are accustomed
to calling self and world. Pater implies a boundary between
them, of course, but it is a virtual boundary rather than
a "thick" or qualitative one:

> Like the elements of which we are composed, the
> action of these forces extends beyond us: it rusts iron
> and ripens corn. Far out on every side of us those
> elements are broadcast, driven in many currents; and
> birth and gesture and death and the springing of
> violets from the grave are but a few out of ten thou-
> sand resultant combinations. That clear, perpetual
> outline of face and limb is but an image of ours,
> under which we group them—a design in a web, the
> actual threads of which pass out beyond it. [R, 234]

Indeed, phenomena are themselves all of a piece, with their
discrete and particular appearances—"birth," "gesture,"
"death," "violets"—simply a segmentation and naming
that language in its totalizing sense performs upon the universal flux in its raw, that is to say unperceived, state.
Whatever "clear, perpetual outline" we discern among
these currents, even if it is the very stuff by which the individual is recognized at the lowest threshold of identity
(the "outline of face and limb") is simply "a design in
a web" of such intersecting forces whose "actual threads"

pass well beyond whatever designs we may use to articulate even our physical lives.

Thus personality or temperament, the cornerstone of Pater's manifest vision of art and culture, turns out to be profoundly unstable as a category. What Pater has in mind here is by no means a nonexistent self (the discipline of *ascesis,* or self-making, sees to that), but rather a virtual and tentative self composed of the same stuff as the world from which it is apparently so completely separated. Hence "that continual vanishing away, that strange, perpetual weaving and unweaving of ourselves" (*R,* 236), which Pater claims, in a moment of willful blindness, to be the place at which "analysis leaves off" (*R,* 236). To make such a claim says more about Pater's desire to resist deindividuation than about the possibility or impossibility of its analysis—an analysis, as it turns out, that is not only possible but indeed central to the "Conclusion" as a whole.

Pater, of course, has subsumed this last discussion under the rubric of the "without" (*R,* 233). By the time he addresses himself to the "within," he has, of course, already put into question the distinction between them. The only differences between "within" and "without" are those of intensity—of quantity. In the "inward world of thought and feeling, the whirlpool is still more rapid, the flame more eager and devouring" (*R,* 234). Indeed, reflection itself corrects the impression that the experience of subjectivity is to be understood as "a flood of external objects, pressing upon us with a sharp and importunate reality, calling us out of ourselves in a thousand forms of action" (*R,* 234). This, of course, is to fashion false dichotomies, since the very terms "objects," "external," "upon," "out of," begin to lack a proper reference or context once the full consequences of Pater's deindividuating phenomenology become apparent. What we are left with in this meditation on what is "within" is in fact the same vision uttered in the discussion of what is "without," although here the loosening of the "object" into "a group of impressions" (R, 235) is carried out from the point of view of the subject rather than from the point of view that saw him before as an object. In both cases, of course, the result is to arrive upon the same ground, with self and world both constituted in the same terms and out of the same fabric.

Pater's blindness to all this, however, is nowhere more evident than in the famous "wall of personality" sequence of the "Conclusion," and suggests to how large an extent even his solipsism is part of an ideal or covering myth whose purpose, like that of the rhetoric of flowers, soil, and freshness, is to obscure or repress the deindividuating vision that lies tangled beneath it:

> Experience, already reduced to a group of impressions, is ringed round for each one of us by that thick wall of personality through which no real voice has ever pierced on its way to us, or from us to that which we can only conjecture to be without. [R, 235]

If experience is ringed round by personality, where is the "without" from which forces are supposedly to pass through it? Indeed, nothing at all is supposed to be able to pierce the individual ringed round in his "isolation" (R, 235), even though such a claim requires for its own coherence some notion of an inside and an outside clearly separated from one another. Pater's solipsism, in other words, is erected on a spatial metaphor whose truth he is here intent to deny even as he requires it in order to deny it. Such tension in the logic of Pater's rhetoric points, of course, to the larger and more apparent tension involved in his very attempt, overcompensatory as it is, to maintain the subject in the face of an analysis that has overturned or gone beyond it earlier in the "Conclusion."

Later on we find still another deception—a famous obfuscation: "With this sense of the splendour of our experience and of its awful brevity, gathering all we are into one desperate effort to see and touch, we shall hardly have time to make theories about the things we see and touch" (*R,* 237). But as we have seen, the very logic by which Pater allows himself his perorations, problematic as they may be, is the product of precisely such "theories about the things we see and touch." Moreover, the "sacrifice" that Pater says any such "theory or idea or system" (*R,* 237) requires us to make in the realm of experience itself amounts to a powerful defense of—really a plea for— the blindness such a remark recommends, since his real wish here is to negate or neutralize the problematic consequences which his own analysis has drawn about the very status of the self. Indeed, in the later editions of the "Conclusion," Pater's original candor in 1868 about the fact that the individual "los[es] even his personality," "even himself," remains suppressed when he restores much of the original text in the book's third and fourth editions.[1] Surely Pater's resistance here to his own secondary perspective represents a desire to maintain those visionary

---

1. The remarks occur in the "Conclusion" as it first appeared in the closing pages of Pater's anonymous article on William Morris in the *Westminster Review* 34: 311; quoted in Monsman (*Pater's Portraits,* pp. 121–22; *Walter Pater,* p. 56). The edition of *The Renaissance* included in the Library Edition is the fourth and most revised version (1893), but even here, of course, Pater's deindividuating argument is manifest (see Samuel Wright, *Bibliography of the Writings,* pp. 166 ff.; Monsman, *Walter Pater,* p. 70). Although Graham Hough has assured us that Pater does not put into question "the substantial existence of the self" (*The Last Romantics* [London: Duckworth, 1949], p. 141), it is difficult to overlook the fact that Pater himself endorses such a conclusion as early as 1868 and as late as 1893, and that much of his work, as the present chapter will attempt to show, sustains it.

idealities associated with the artist in his transcendent profile, even if the heroism of Pater's manifest stance gains
in glory by the contrast. Having brought "the individual"
to a precarious and "tragic" enough point in any case, the
logic that would jettison what remains of "personality" is
almost too lethal for Pater to bear, and he averts his eyes
from the deepest recesses of his vision here at its close.[2]

Given Pater's reluctance to inquire into this secondary
vision at greater length, it is left to us to ferret out its
terms.[3] With the shift in emphasis from self to world, we
ought to ask what the world is under Pater's deindividuating profile. If the "solidity" of subjects and objects alike
is the product of the "solidity with which language invests
them" (R, 235), we ought to pay particular attention to
Pater's notion of the world in terms of his notion of "language." Let us begin by turning again to the phenomenology
of the moment established at the start of the "Conclusion."

"What is the whole physical life in that moment," asks
Pater, "but a combination of natural elements to which
science gives their names?" (R, 233). Are the "names"
properly those belonging to "science" as a language, or
those belonging to, inherent in, the "elements" as such?
To the extent, of course, that these "natural elements" are

2. Monsman's apparently equal insistence in *Walter Pater* on Pater's "idea
of a personality as a fantastically complex palimpsest woven from the flux"
(p. 74) is finally in the service of a conciliatory attempt to resolve the solipsistic Pater and the deindividuating Pater by finding a link between them.
Though Monsman is willing to describe "Pater's real Self" as "an unseen core
of cultural relationships" (p. 174), his rhetoric retains the notion of a given
self that expands its sympathies and multiplies its identities; that "transcends
its limited condition" (p. 153). Even more, he wishes to identify "this gradual
expansion of the circle of the self" with the crystalline perfection of "the
diaphanous hero" (p. 173), an identification that surely conflates the two
contradictory and differential systems at work in Pater's own rhetoric.
3. Some of the present discussion's concerns are suggested in J. Hillis
Miller, "Walter Pater: A Partial Portrait," *Daedalus* 105 (Winter 1976): 97–113.

present to us at all, they are present, as it turns out, through the naming operations of "science" itself, with their proper—and *propre,* or genitive—field of reference belonging to the system which names and thereby constitutes them, rather than to the raw state from which scientific language rescues—or, more properly, shapes or fashions —the "physical" and the "natural" so as to make them discernible to us as such.

Of course, the emphasis on the "physical" at the start of the "Conclusion" is a symptom once again of Pater's desire to valorize the "natural" as such, as a category apart from what is nurture or culture. Nonetheless, the linguistic function assigned here to "science" suggests that our very perception of nature is already mediated by the necessity of naming—that naming and perception are virtually one and the same process, with the world itself a text or matrix of texts. Pater's ironic appeal to the language of science recalls, too, how far from nature the chemistry of the crystal has already placed both the aesthetic subject and the objects of his labor, with Pater's antithetical language of nature and ground itself largely composed of an ultimately denaturing rhetoric of cultivation.

Hence language for Pater means all the languages of life, from sensation and perception to philosophy, religion, and the arts. Its most elementary dialect is also the one to which Pater habitually appeals as a model for its more sophisticated permutations—the discrimination of light and shadow. As a principal mode of infantile and childhood perception, and as the underlying model for the mechanisms at work in painting as well, it provides Pater with a scheme by which he can gather all forms of art and perception—*aesthesis* in its full sense—under a single model, and a scheme from which the discriminations fundamental to all systems of culture can in turn be generated.

Pater's most microscopic account of childhood perception, of course, is to be found in "The Child in the House,"
where the discrimination of light and shadow plays a primary role in the process of "brain-building" (MS, 173)
that the sketch attempts to narrate. Here the basic level of
perception for the child Florian Deleal lies in his ability to
distinguish light from shade—"the singular brightness of
bright weather . . ., its singular darknesses" (MS, 176)—
a distinction that produces Florian's earliest notion of
experience (at least in the retrospect of memory) and that
remains the figural model for all his experience, emotional
and intellectual alike, in later years. It is, however, only
the mechanism by which light, shadow, and color become
available to the child that interests Pater, for it is clear that
the particular objects of perception involved are in themselves of no privileged importance in the process:

> For it is false to suppose that a child's sense of beauty
> is dependent on any choiceness or special fineness, in
> the objects which present themselves to it, though
> this indeed comes to be the rule with most of us in
> later life; earlier, in some degree, we see inwardly; and
> the child finds for itself, and with unstinted delight,
> a difference for the sense, in those whites and reds
> through the smoke on very homely buildings, and in
> the gold of the dandelions at the road-side, just beyond
> the houses, where not a handful of earth is virgin and
> untouched, in the lack of better ministries to its
> desire of beauty. [MS, 175]

The key thought here is "the child finds . . . a difference
for the sense"; "those whites and reds" are simply the
occasion or example by which the mechanism of perception is set into play. What the mechanism is, of course, is
the "difference" between the colors rather than the colors

themselves, the fact that each one is constituted in relation to the other. Notice, too, that it is apparently all shades of "whites and reds" that are here made available to the child by means of this single example, and that "whites and reds" are themselves no more than a particular refinement of the more elementary difference to be found between light and shadow. Moreover, this elementary difference is found to constitute the child's experience in other sensory realms, too, whether it is the difference between "storm or sunshine" (*MS,* 175), between nearness and distance (*MS,* 182), or between the pleasure of "presence" and the pain of "regret or desire" (*MS,* 186).

Difference as such, of course, precedes even its most elementary showing-forth in the difference between light and shadow. As the originary and originating condition for the child's very sense of the world, difference may even be the term for which Pater labors when he wonders aloud in the "Preface" to *The Renaissance* "under what conditions" one's impressions are "experienced" (*R,* ix), as he searches for an exact form of the "relative" (*R,* viii)—for the "powers or forces" that produce that "more or less" in things by which we judge them (*R,* ix), whether "in the study," indifferently, "of light, of morals," or "of number" (*R,* vii).

The rule of difference, however, is to be seen only in its effects, although its effects are to be seen everywhere, even in the way the angles and edges of the phenomenal world emerge to Florian's awareness:

> [He] began to note with deepening watchfulness . . . the phases of the seasons and of the growing or waning day, down even to the shadowy changes wrought on bare wall or ceiling—the light cast up from the snow, bringing out their darkest angles; the brown light in the cloud, which meant rain; that

almost too austere clearness, in the protracted light of
the lengthening day, before warm weather began, as
if it lingered but to make a severer workday, with the
school-books opened earlier and later; that beam of
June sunshine, at last, as he lay awake before the
time, a way of gold-dust across the darkness; all the
humming, the freshness, the perfume of the garden
seemed to lie upon it. [*MS*, 188]

The difference between light and dark is the central or
binding thread that unites all these objects of sense in
a common condition of emergence, and that even shapes
the world of affect and meaning—"lingered" / severer";
"protracted" / "lengthening"—that gets superimposed upon
these objects of sense by association with them.

We have already seen how sensation and its affects
emerge by means of such self-constituting differences in
the play, for example, of nearness and distance, and in the
emotions that accompany and duplicate their contrast.
What Pater wishes to impress upon us as Florian develops
further is the way in which the same model also constitutes the world of his intellect, whose structure is already
adumbrated in the structure of sensation, and which we
are already nearing in the passage cited above. Thus, once
Florian's intellect begins to grow, his philosophical interests are concerned with "the estimate of the proportion,"
or "difference," "of the sensuous and the ideal elements in
human knowledge" (*MS*, 186), while even his "desire of
physical beauty mingled itself early," says Pater, with "the
fear of death—the fear of death intensified by the desire of
beauty" (*MS*, 189–90), with each one growing more exact
in relation to the other.

Hence the play of difference marks out not only the
terrain of the external world, but also—and, incredibly

enough, really for the first time—the very space of Florian's inner life: "A place adumbrated itself in his thoughts," says Pater with more than a fanciful use of the topographical figure, since "this region" or territory "in his intellectual scheme all subsequent experience did but tend still further to realise and define" (*MS*, 194). Florian's self, in other words, is figured as a "place" or "house" because it signifies the settlement of a "region" or territory on the map or text of the world into which he has been born. Even "those sacred personalities" from the Bible who "housed themselves" in the "place" or "region" of Florian's youthful religious thoughts are welcome there by virtue of the difference they provide with "our every-day existence," as "a complementary strain or burden" (*MS*, 194) to it. Indeed, Pater likens this complementarity whereby Florian invests his inner life with a "warmth" (*MS*, 194) lacking in the world at large to an "intenser and more expressive light and shade, of human life and its familiar or exceptional incidents" (*MS*, 193), with even these last differential categories ("familiar"/"exceptional") simply a refinement of the difference which precedes and prepares for them in the more paradigmatic difference between "light and shade." As Florian grows, in other words, his increasing discrimination proceeds according to the same discovery of "difference" in all varieties of things, with the territory of thought and sensation mapped by the same process that maps the phenomenal world. Hence Pater's figure of the "tones of sentiment" which are "afterwards customary" (*MS*, 176) with Florian the adult carries with it a rather strict recollection of the tonal sensory model that fashions perception in childhood.

So Pater reverses our usual notion of language as an instrument or mere mode of access to a self-sufficient world "without" as well as to an organic self "within."

For Pater, self and world alike are present only as a matrix of differential and commonly held languages—in the "rhetoric of daily life" (*M,* 183), for example, or in the "language" articulated by the body's "affections" (*GS,* 255)—into which the subject emerges at his birth, and within which he constellates his peculiar temperament or identity by means of the choices he makes (or that make him) in mapping the region of sensation and reflection that he calls his own with greater and greater certainty as he grows older. From this point of view, language actually produces the world, with what we see really a product of the way vision itself is structured.

To be sure, this process is individualist or conventionally Paterian on the one hand, since the terms of the subject's capture are unique to him. Like the colors of Dante's brushes for Stephen in Joyce's *Portrait,* Florian's "red hawthorn" (*MS,* 185–86) provides an original sense of "red" for him only, while others gain an equivalent sense of "red" through associations unique only to them. On the other hand, though, the process is also part of the "common air," since Florian fashions both the world and the space of his own reflection from the "elements" that are provided him, not by nature as such, but by the lexicon of cultural differences—of pertinent perceptions—which he inherits at his birth. That his late arrival in the world disallows him the privilege of being "autochthonous" or self-begotten goes, of course, without saying.

It is the self's capture, then, that makes it a "receptacle" or "depositary" like Michelangelo or like a Botticelli painting. Indeed, Pater's definition of "a great picture" in the essay on Giorgione bears a striking resemblance to the way a "place adumbrated itself" in Florian's "thoughts":

In its primary aspect, a great picture has no more definite message for us than an accidental play of sun-

light and shadow for a few moments on the wall or
floor: is itself, in truth, a space of such fallen light,
caught as the colours are in an Eastern carpet. . . .
[R, 133]

Like sensation and perception, painting, too, is constructed out of the difference or play "of sunlight and
shadow," constituting a "space" that is "caught" much as
the "region" of Florian's selfhood or inner life is a "place"
that comes to be "adumbrated" out of differences, too;
hence Pater's claim that the "true pictorial quality" is that
"which lies between" (R, 132). Like the quality of percep-
tive and sensory experience, the originary quality of painting is also to be found in the difference that lies between
the elements that constitute it, that in fact constitutes
those elements themselves. If a great picture has no more
definite message for us than an accidental play of sunlight
and shadow, it is because the only "message" legitimately
operative in it is the message of the message itself—how
what is visible or perceptible achieves recognition at all by
means of difference.

Difference even organizes Pater's notion of painting and
sculpture throughout *The Renaissance.* In Michelangelo its
economy is perhaps clearest, with his "creation of life" in
sculpture "coming always as relief or recovery, and always
in strong contrast with the rough-hewn mass in which it is
kindled" (R, 76). As in Pater's contention that the triumph of fifteenth-century Tuscan sculpture is the triumph
of "low relief" (R, 64), here "relief or recovery" are to be
read first as physical or visual items, meaning as they do
the very emergence of Michelangelo's sculptured figures as
"contrast" or "relief," with the spectator almost literally
re-covering the figure as a harmonious whole once the eye
has grasped, however automatically, the logic of its "relief" illusionism.

At this point we may restore the thematic qualities of "relief" and "recovery" to Pater's interpretation by noting how they emerge as exponents of the sculpture's formal conditions. Indeed, the same can be said of the higher-order thematizations that emerge from the primary visible qualities of Tuscan sculpture, too, where the "depression of surface" that characterizes "low relief" becomes "a pathetic suggestion of the wasting and etherealisation of death" (*R*, 64). In this way even the primary play of light and shadow in a Botticelli painting may be said to contain a semantic layer to the eye of the aesthetic critic, "with his consciousness," says Pater of himself through a shifter manifestly assigned to Botticelli, "of the shadow upon it of the great things from which it shrinks" (*R*, 60).

Thus the difference of "relief"—the equivalent in sculpture of "light and shadow" in painting—produces semantic or thematic differences, too, much as it produces them in the later, intellectualizing stages of childhood. Even the thematic oppositions to be found in Michelangelo are simply the finer gradations to be adduced from "relief" and "contrast" themselves—the "frost and fire" (*R*, 87) to be found in the imagery of his sonnets, for example, or the "indignation or sorrow" (*R*, 81) to be read in the "distress" and "sweetness" (*R*, 85) of his life.

Indeed, difference generates the very periodicity of art and cultural history that Pater wishes to demonstrate in his mapping of the notion of "the Renaissance" itself. "Many-sided but yet united" (*R*, 2), the Renaissance is united because of its many sides, brought into existence as it is by means of the differences that constitute it. Thus it is the moral and historical "opposition into which Abelard is thrown" (*R*, 7) or the "morsels of a different quality" (*R*, 22) in *Aucassin* that produce by their differences the very movement to be designated here, with Pico's "union of contrasts" (R, 48) emblematic of the differential structure of the Renaissance as a whole. Pater even uses light and shade as both model and metaphor for its more elaborated permutations, describing as he does all of French culture, for example, as "in itself neither deeper nor more permanent than a chance effect of light" (R, 158), or describing the rhythms of both Hellenism and medievalism by means of the figures of "light" and "colour" (R, 190).

In fact, in the Winckelmann essay the figure of light and shadow designates the way all the arts function, "painting, music, and poetry" alike: "through their gradations of shade, their exquisite intervals"—the tokens of the type of difference in the visual and the sonic respectively—"they project in an external form that which is most inward in passion or sentiment" (R, 211). Implicit here is not so much a disjunction between "inward" and "external" as the continuities that bridge or identify them. Indeed, in "Winckelmann," the figure of light and shadow is used and reused in different and more refined combinations, whether as the "white light" of Greek sculpture or the "refraction" (R, 213) of images within it, or even as the "rays" of inspiration or the "relief" of a Browning poem brought to Pater's mind by the Greeks (R, 214).

And much as the early sensory differences of childhood provide the basis for those later intellectual differences that emerge as the child builds up a "house of thought," so the visual arts set up a model of difference to account for the functions at work in nonvisual discourses like literature, philosophy, and religion. In *Appreciations,* a volume devoted entirely to literature, Pater figures verbal art in the same way that he has figured the visual arts in *The Renaissance* and sensation and perception in "The Child in the House." Thus, in the Coleridge essay, the truth the critic is after is "the truth of . . . relations," of "a world of fine gradations" (*A*, 67–68). To prove it Pater goes on to discuss Coleridge's view of culture as a "series of refining shades" (*A*, 78), figurally retracing the structure of verbal semantics back to a formal visual model in exact contrast to the way he derives the semantic from the visual in *The Renaissance.* Even Shakespeare can be described in terms of difference, with his "strongly contrasted characters" (*A*, 174) subject in turn to a description in terms of "the subtle interchange of light and shade" (*A*, 174). The apparent formalism of difference can also generate thematic categories like love: "Love," says Pater of Rossetti in the suppressed essay on "Aesthetic Poetry," is "defined by the absence of the beloved,"[4] suggesting a differential structure for desire akin to the one Florian inherits when he learns the difference between "near" and "distant."

To trace the design of difference in philosophy and religion leads us next to *Marius,* where Pater is particularly explicit about his "active principle," at least in its effects. In describing Marius's desire for "the actually aesthetic charm of a cold austerity of mind," for example, Pater adds, "as if the kinship of that to the clearness of physical light were something more than a figure of speech" (*M*, 102). It is, after all, also the figure of mind itself, at least insofar as the differences that constitute thought are to be understood according to the same model that constitutes the visible in the visual arts and in perception. That difference rules philosophy as well as painting, sculpture, and perception is in fact made clear by the way Marius organizes his intellectual dilemmas. Troubled by his Cyrenaicism, Marius figures its shortcomings in terms of poorly articulated differences in painting: "The spectacle of their fierce

4. *Selected Writings of Walter Pater,* ed. Bloom, p. 192.

. . . tenacious hold on their own narrow apprehension,"
says Pater of the Cyrenaics, "makes one think of a picture
with no relief, no soft shadows nor breadth of space, or of
a drama"—extending the model of difference into literature once again—"without proportionate repose" (M, 218).
Indeed, Marius here adjudges his present need by noting its
difference from its own ideal, one which is itself based on
a factor of difference or proportion, "an economy of the
moments of life" (M, 218). This latter ideal, however, is
not sufficient in practice because the "narrow apprehension" of its teachers fails to generate the striking contrasts
necessary for such an "economy" of "moments" to be as
strong or as meaningful as Marius wishes it to be. Indeed,
all of philosophical speculation, says Pater, is structured by
difference: "Chance: or Providence! Chance: or Wisdom
. . . those are the 'fenced opposites' of the speculative
dilemma" (M, 238).

What is satisfying for Marius in Christianity, then, is its
ability "to harmonize contrasts" (M, 293) rather than to
reduce them, as his earlier epicureanism has ironically
done. By means of an economy of "juxtaposition,"
Marius's version of Christianity "beget[s] thereby a unique
effect of freshness, a grave yet wholesome beauty" (M,
293), balancing as it does the "two contrasted aspects" of
"the character of Christ" (M, 296)—"asceticism" and "culture" (M, 297)—in a religion that understands their mutual
necessity well before doctrinal debates later force the
church to have to choose between the two by making the
contrast too harsh (M, 297).

One of the most important thrusts of difference in
Marius, however, is to resolve the troublesome opposition
between spirit and flesh, and with it all those tiresome
oppositions between "absolute principles" that vex Pater
in an essay like "Coleridge" (A, 103). Marius's quest may

even be defined as an attempt to find a discourse, an
aesthetic form or new mode of reasoning, that will unite or
make continuous the traditional discontinuities that assail
him on all levels of experience—spirit and flesh, subject
and object, idealism and materialism, diffidence and sympathy, theory and practice, synchrony and diachrony,
passivity and activity. Hence the book's project is to
try to demonstrate its subtitle—*His Sensations and Ideas*—
as a continuity or continuum rather than as a conflict
or tension.

Though always approaching a ground of interdepen-
dence as Pater handles them, these inherited distinctions
nonetheless organize Marius's experience well enough in
his early years. Even as primal an event as the death of
Marius's mother, says Pater, "turned seriousness of feeling
into a matter of the intelligence" (*M,* 35). With the help of
puns, Pater here demonstrates how well the inherited categories of "feeling" and "intelligence" can accommodate
and direct Marius's loss by elevating it into a fit object of
contemplation. Indeed, "seriousness" of "feeling"—of
heart and flesh—actually transforms "feeling" into a question for the "intelligence," even though the "intelligence"
will nonetheless carry with it a trace of the question's
origin in "feeling" because it will still remain "a matter"
—something material or sensory—for the "intelligence"
to work upon.

The latent connections to be found between "feeling"
or "matter" on the one hand and "seriousness" or "intelligence" on the other are adumbrated only a little more
plainly a chapter later when Marius discovers the combined
power and suppleness of the rhetoric of Cornelius Fronto:
"What words he had found for conveying, with a single
touch," says Pater, "the sense of textures, colors, incidents!" (*M,* 46). Hence Fronto's language finds a means of
"conveying" all variety of the real without calling atten-

tion to the distance between what is actually sensory and the highly embellished rhetoric that expresses it, again with a pun, by means of its own kind of "touch."

In Heraclitus, Marius finds himself a step closer to an outright resolution of these inherited dichotomies, although once again it is deferred in favor of an indirect approach to the problem: "In this 'perpetual flux' of things and of souls," writes Pater, "there was, as Heraclitus conceived, a continuance, if not of their material or spiritual elements, yet of orderly intelligible relationships, like the harmony of musical notes, wrought out in and through the series of their mutations" (M, 107). Here a direct "continuance" of the qualities of the "material" and "spiritual" is bracketed, and in its place emerges a model for the motions of both real and ideal worlds based on a notion of "relationships" conceived on the order of musical harmonies, a sphere in which the supposed distinction between the ideality of form and the reality of matter is already refined out of existence.

What the exact or "concrete" nature of this resolution may be, however, is not yet forthcoming, even though, thanks to Heraclitus, Marius has already conceived it in terms of pure "relationships." With his "New Cyrenaicism," of course, Marius decides that all "the products of the imagination must themselves be held to present the most perfect forms of life," with "life" now coming to include, as Pater puts it, "spirit and matter alike" (M, 122). What the mode of vision is that will produce such a unified gaze, however, is still unclear to Marius, once again despite the proximity here, too, of the "study of music" which "would conduct one to an exquisite appreciation of all the finer traits of nature and of man" (M, 122).

With his acquaintance with Cecilia, however, comes Marius's first fully articulated notion of what it is he wishes to discover and what the terms of that discovery

have to be. In an elaborate paragraph based on the conceit
of Cecilia's house—Pater's familiar cipher for a harmonious
"intellectual structure"—Marius begins at last to desire
what Pater's own analyses have already produced, although
perhaps unknowingly. Distancing himself from his own
utterance by assigning the entire paragraph to "that
mystical" and unidentifiable "German writer quoted once
before," Pater praises Cecilia because " 'at last, in the entire expressiveness of what is outward, there is for her, to
speak properly, between outward and inward, no longer any
distinction at all' " (*M*, 273–74). This recognition is "the
critical turning-point" in Marius's "days" (*M*, 275), and as
such is a "critical turning-point" in Pater's own disposition
toward what the "Conclusion" to *The Renaissance* and
even parts of the later essay on "Style" have to tell us
about the isolated and imprisoned status of the self in art
and experience alike. In *Marius*, as in "The Child in the
House" and in the deindividuating sequences of his criticism, Pater wishes to overcome not only the opposition
between ideal and real, but also the opposition between
"outward and inward" which is the originating and overarching dichotomy at the root of his manifest critical
project to celebrate "the individual in his isolation" and to
certify for the literature of the future the independent
and enduring value of "one's own impression."

But even if such an overcoming is the grail or object of
Marius's quest, its exact definition continues to elude
Marius and Pater alike, even at the book's close. Although
the definition is already present in the mechanism of difference adduced seven years earlier in "The Child in the
House," it is clear that, in any direct notional way, the
concept is unavailable to Pater as such, and will have to be
derived independently, and with some difficulty, in *Marius*
itself. What is striking about difference in "The Child in the

House," of course, is that it provides Pater with a unit of signification applicable at once to the life of the senses and the life of the mind. Ideas and sensations, in other words, are continuous there because both emerge by virtue of the same differential model.

In *Marius,* however, the definition is approached in wholly different terms, couched as it is as a reinterpretation of the notion of "the holy vessel" or "sacred object" of truth itself (*M,* 328). In the translated dialogue entitled "A Conversation Not Imaginary," Marius listens as Lucian submits the category of "the lost object" (of which the grail is both type and token here) to a thorough interrogation, and from his questioning emerges the new form of reasoning for which Marius has labored:

> —And we too, Lucian! if we have found the holy vessel in possession of the Stoics, shall no longer have need to search other philosophers, having attained that we were seeking. Why trouble ourselves further?
> —No need, if something had indeed been found, and you knew it to be that lost thing: if, at the least, you could recognize the sacred object when you saw it. But truly, as the matter now stands, not two persons only have entered the temple, one or the other of whom must needs have taken the golden cup, but a whole crowd of persons. And then, it is not clear what the lost object really is—cup, or flagon, or diadem; for one of the priests avers this, another that; they are not even in agreement as to its material: some will have it to be of brass, others of silver, or gold. It thus becomes necessary to search the garments of all persons who have entered the temple, if the lost vessel is to be recovered. And if you find a golden cup on the first of them, it will still be

necessary to proceed in searching the garments of the others; for it is not certain that this cup really belonged to the temple. Might there not be many such golden vessels?—No! we must go on to every one of them, placing all that we find in the midst together, and then make our guess which of all those things may fairly be supposed to be the property of the god. For, again, this circumstance adds greatly to our difficulty, that without exception every one searched is found to have something upon him—cup, or flagon, or diadem, of brass, of silver, of gold: and still, all the while, it is not ascertained which of all these is the sacred thing. And you must still hesitate to pronounce any one of them guilty of the sacrilege—those objects may be their own lawful property: one cause of all this obscurity being, as I think, that there was no inscription on the lost cup, if cup it was. Had the name of the god, or even that of the donor, been upon it, at least we should have had less trouble, and having detected the inscription, should have ceased to trouble any one else by our search. [*M*, 328–29]

The key moment comes when Lucian declares that "there was no inscription on the lost cup, if cup it was." Thus it is impossible on two counts to tell which object among the many collected is the sacred or privileged one. Indeed, it is fast becoming clear that there is no such thing as a privileged object at all. What structures the quest initially, however, is the desire that there be such a vessel, complete with an inscription distinguishing it from all the other objects on display, and thereby making it recognizable as itself, by itself, unequivocally and under all circumstances, no matter how many other objects may surround it.

But what is put in question here, of course, is the very possibility of the existence of such a single, unique object of truth in either art or experience. The lack of an inscription means that the wishful object is wanting precisely those inherent properties that would signify it as uniquely itself; the single object, in other words, turns out to bear no inscription at all. Even more, the permanent lack of an inscription suggests that there is no such thing as an inherent property to be found in any object whatsoever.

It is at this point that the very terms of the search are either to be reinterpreted or the search itself abandoned. Lucian himself seems to be ambivalent about which alternative to take. Even though he fails to throw up his hands and abandon the quest altogether, neither is he particularly forthcoming about what new terms in the search for inscriptions are latent in the old. Thus there is a kind of snap or break in the text when, on rereading the passage for its secondary logic, we reach the phrase "the property of the god." Clearly there is some emerging logic at work here, although what its terms may be are obviously not to be sought in the dialogue's manifest inconclusiveness. "The property of the god," that which the original inscription was to communicate like a proper name inscribed on the object as the mark of its possession, still seems to be the aim of the search. But if no objects carry inscriptions and so possess no inherent sign to identify them as the property of any owner whatsoever, how can any object have the property of "property" at all?

Hence Lucian's contention that by "placing all that we find in the midst together" we may "guess which of all those things may fairly be supposed to be the property of the god." Despite the obfuscating and cavalier word "guess," what is struggling for expression here is a new sort of taxonomic logic, a logic by which we would neither pursue an empty quest nor abandon questing altogether, but which would allow us instead to rethink our very manner of searching from the start. Only with "all that we find" before us can we begin, says Lucian, because the secret is not to be found in one vessel or another, but, as Marius's musical model has already suggested, in the "relationships" to be discovered among them. Only by weighing the similarities and differences to be discovered among the various objects can one define or "inscribe" any one of them. Even to the extent that each has already been designated or inscribed—as "brass" or "silver," "cup" or "flagon"— each has already been submitted to a logic of difference in the means used both to produce it and to recognize it once it is in circulation as a cultural object. Thus, like individuality itself, the notion of uniqueness is also subject to dislocation since all objects are constituted by means of their relation to other objects in a matrix of differential relations common to a culture in which, by tacit agreement, "silver" is not "brass," "cup" is not "flagon," and "I" is not "you."

There is, moreover, a temporal aspect to the situation as well, and it becomes explicit once we consider how differential "relationships" get made. If the taxonomic principle to be learned from Lucian's exercise is to operate at all, it operates in time, at least in the temporality in which the various lines of relation unfold to the observer's eye. Giving a particular object a meaning—inscribing it—means that the observer is (now) seeing it at least a second time. Otherwise, it cannot have been submitted to the comparisons and contrasts which alone act to situate it and thus to inscribe it according to Pater's "relative" mechanism of meaning.

Indeed, what difference now suggests is that a "residue" or "surplusage" is not so much an excess to be burnt away by the culture-worker as it is the very condition that allows his work to unfold. In fact, Pater's entire theory of signification rests on an assumption of residue, which undercuts not only the ideal of crystalline fusion, but also that of the integrity of the moment. If signification through difference is to exist at all, there must remain some residue, something left behind—deposited like a precipitate in the mind—which will function as a mnemonic trace to allow consciousness a way of recognizing its double or repetition when it is encountered (again). The process is also capable of (indeed, seems to require) working backwards. If the mind encounters something new but finds it nonetheless familiar or uncanny, it is because the present has allowed access to a memory trace that has remained inoperative or inactive until the moment its double or repetition arrives to key it off.

With these necessities in mind, Pater deidealizes Marius's consummate epiphany even as he establishes it, situating both the " 'Ideal Now' " and Marius's "very self" within the temporality which both attempt to deny:

> In this peculiar and privileged hour, his bodily frame, as he could recognize, although just then, in the whole sum of its capacities, so entirely possessed by him—Nay! actually his very self—was yet determined by a far-reaching system of material forces external to it, a thousand combining currents from earth and sky. Its seemingly active powers of apprehension were, in fact, but susceptibilities to influence. The perfection of its capacity might be said to depend on its passive surrender, as of a leaf on the wind, to the motions of the great stream of physical energy without it. And might not the intellectual frame also, still more intimately himself as in truth it

was, after the analogy of the bodily life, be a moment
only, an impulse or series of impulses, a single process, in an intellectual or spiritual system external to
it, diffused through all   time and place—that great
stream of spiritual energy, of which his own imperfect thoughts, yesterday or to-day, would be but the
remote, and therefore imperfect pulsations? [M, 255]

Pater assumes an equivalence here between the "privileged
hour" and Marius's "very self" insofar as Marius achieves
his present clarity and integrity by means of his epiphany.
Both ideals, however, are subject to depurification once
Pater brings their common components to light. Despite
Marius's almost literal self-possession, the proper determi-
nants of the moment that allows him to bring his life into
focus are nonetheless "external" both to it and to the
"very self" that receives it. One wonders, then, where and
what this "self" is that is not coincident with the "forces"
or "currents" that constitute it—whose own center, as it
were, is outside the structure it seems to define. Indeed,
this is the paradox of Romantic inspiration itself, by which
the ecstasis of composition transports the writing subject
out of himself, decentering him much as psychoanalysis
does at the very moment of his self-realization.

Like the "self," moreover, this privileged interval of
luminosity and transparence is also situated within the
vortex of "influence" into which Marius has emerged at
birth, and which makes of his new and immediate vision in
the present something belated and already prepared for.
Even what we call perception is always belated, too, with
(re)cognition erected on a factor of difference which
defers or delays the immediacy and presence of the object
it supposedly beholds by making all vision reminiscence.
Marius's "hour" of transparent vision, then, can never
be as crystalline and as pure as Pater's ideal would have

it, founded as it is on the very residue it supposedly burns away.

Hence the moment is neither privileged nor unique because it comes to exist thanks to what Pater calls in the late essay on Pascal the "under-texture" (*MS,* 84) of cultural life as a whole. Even hierophany, Pater argues, carries with it a trace or residue, an under-text, of something already known, of something of which the immediate and revelatory vision in the present is but a double or repetition. Indeed, Pater introduces the term "under-texture" in connection with Pascal's indebtedness to Montaigne, and shows how the "under-texture" of "Montaigne's very phrases" in Pascal's own or proper text is not simply an echo, but what he refers to, with considerable wit, as the way Pascal "re-echoes Montaigne" (*MS,* 84). Thus Pater also takes away from the precursor what he takes away from the belated disciple, thereby rendering even the supposed original of Pascal's text in Montaigne itself a palimpsest or repetition of something already articulated.

Indeed, Pater lays bare the necessities implicit here in a succinct sentence: "Yet those very moments," he writes of the conviction of free will and its attendant ideals of self-possession and epiphany, "on reflexion, on second thoughts, present themselves again, as but links in a chain, in an all-embracing network of chains" (*MS,* 70). Less a late questioning of early ideals than a clarification of what has been hidden from the start,[5] the statement is

5. Although DeLaura's *Hebrew and Hellene in Victorian England* (pp. 277–78) and Monsman's *Pater's Portraits* (pp. 81, 152) also claim that Pater moves beyond the individual, their shared contention is a developmental one that follows the career of Pater's manifest sympathies. Moreover, their notion of what looms beyond the self is also a transcendent and theological one. By contrast, the attempt here is to demonstrate, however ironically, the consistency of Pater's discordant vision throughout his work, and to substitute for a notion of shifts in opinion, reconciliation, or transcendence a notion of theory and practice, ideals and necessity, in the language of Pater's texts early and late.

cautionary because it adumbrates the very mechanism that
brings the moment into being. Discrimination itself is possible only if there is a trail (a "chain," to use Pater's balancing contemporary term for the "portrait") of elements
or experience along or against which any moment or
object in the present can be matched or distinguished.
Without these operations, of course, no object or moment
can even be recognized as such.

If the logic of the "under-texture" is overtly but ab-
stractly put in "Pascal," it is put directly in terms of
personality in the portrait of Emerald Uthwart. Here the
necessity of the "under-texture" emerges once again, with
the hypothetical Lockean figure for the young Emerald as
a "plain tablet, for the influences of place to inscribe"
(*MS*, 207) quickly supplanted by the alternative figure of
a surface already inscribed even when Emerald is a child:
"He sits in the schoolroom," writes Pater, "at the heavy
old desks, carved this way and that, crowded as an old
churchyard with forgotten names" (*MS*, 207). As a me-
tonymy for education or acculturation, the figure of the
desk carved with the forgotten names of the dead (Joyce
rewrites the scene when Stephen discovers the word
"foetus" inscribed on a desk in his father's old schoolroom
at Cork) suggests that even in the relatively fresh moments
of youth one is already inserted in a predetermined order,
and that any act of composition, any utterance whatsoever, is really a belated and palimpsestic one.

Pater goes so far as to gather even the flesh under the
figure of the inscription. The very "physiognomy" of
Emerald's "race," he writes, is "ennobled . . . as if by the
writing, the signature, there, of a grave intelligence, by
grave information" (*MS*, 221). Having encountered the
figures of "the dead" and of writing earlier in the portrait,
we can see that Pater puns considerably on "grave,"
identifying the buried past with engraving or inscription as

though to provide a graphic counterpart, like the graves of Marius's ancestors, for this notion of an under-text beneath the visible text or surface of the present. Indeed, Pater provides us only a few sentences later on with the following summary of Emerald's situation and a definition of the residue or under-texture by whose right he takes his very existence: "The somewhat unmeaningly handsome facial type of the Uthwarts, moulded to a mere animal or physical perfection through wholesome centuries, is breathed on now, informed, by the touches, traces, complex influences from past and present a thousandfold, crossing each other in this late century, and yet at unity in the simple law of the system to which he is now subject" (*MS*, 221).

With residue necessary to perception, personality, and even the privileged moment, let us follow Pater as he specifies the exact nature of such residue or under-texture in the case of the artist. Although this is largely the burden of the essays collected in *Appreciations,* particularly "Style," the deindividuating vision we have already seen in *The Renaissance* prepares us for this later excursus and, indeed, prefigures it in rather exact ways. For not only does *The Renaissance* already take Pater beyond the subject and beyond the original or unique work of art—it also shows us Pater "unravelling" the moment's "subtlest threads" (*R*, 212) even as he erects it as an ideal. Thus, "to discriminate that moment," he writes in "Winckelmann," one must locate it within a "cobweb of allusions" (*R*, 215) or, in the visual variant, locate "a single moment of passion" by means of "relief" (*R*, 214) or difference. Indeed, in the Giorgione essay, the "brief and wholly concrete moment" is accounted for explicitly by the fact that "all the interests and effects of a long history, have condensed themselves, and . . . seem to absorb past and future in an intense consciousness of the present" (*R,* 150), even if the "present" is always condemned to repeat the past and to surrender to the temporality it wishes to abjure in the " 'Ideal Now.' "

In *Appreciations* itself, Pater addresses the problem of under-texture directly in terms of literature and writing, articulating in elaborate detail the conditions of the writer's medium and deidealizing both the circumstances under which he labors and the text he produces. First, however, the ideals themselves must be voiced afresh, and Pater gives them their fullest expression in the discussion of Flaubert in "Style." Here Pater begins with the usual categories and ends by raising once again the problem of inner and outer in his attempt to describe the means by which a writer like Flaubert "says to the reader,—I want you to see precisely what I see" (*A,* 31). Although this project is apparently to be accomplished according to that original Paterian ideal whereby the artist attempts "the word's adjustment to its meaning" in accordance with the familiar injunction "to know yourself, to have ascertained your own sense exactly" (*A,* 31), what arises in the analysis itself overturns the very terms by which it is introduced:

> Into the mind sensitive to "form," a flood of random sounds, colours, incidents, is ever penetrating from the world without, to become, by sympathetic selection, a part of its very structure, and, in turn, the visible vesture and expression of that other world it sees so steadily within, nay, already with a partial conformity thereto, to be refined, enlarged, corrected, at a hundred points. . . . [*A,* 31]

Beginning with the traditional topography of the "flood" of sensations that penetrates "the mind" from "the world without," Pater's language quickly abolishes these boundaries by claiming that external phenomena "become, by sympathetic selection, a part of [the mind's] very structure." Even more, having become such a part of the mind, they also become, "in turn, the visible vesture and expression of that other world it sees so steadily within."

What is "within," in other words, is to be expressed only by virtue of what is "without" it, with the externality of language and the internality of what it expresses becoming virtually identical with one another. This is less a seamless fusion, of course, than it is a replacement or redefinition of the inner by the outer, or, really, the establishment of what is "within" by means of what is "without." In the words of Flaubert cited earlier by Pater, " 'the idea only exists by virtue of the form' " it takes (*A*, 30), with "form" in Flaubert's case the form of language proper. Like the inscribed desk at which Emerald learns to write, the world of the individual comes into being "already with a partial conformity" to the world "without" him because its languages provide him with the very elements by which his world "within" will come to be constituted. This movement of "becoming" is always "already" prepared for, too, since the very materials of individuality are, ironically, insured by virtue of their public or common existence even before one's birth.

This under-texture in life and art alike is what Pater calls in the Wordsworth essay in *Appreciations* "the network of man and nature . . . pervaded by a common, universal life" (*A*, 56). By no means a mystical or theological doctrine, such "a common, universal life" imposes particular but unusual conditions on the self in the essay on Coleridge, where man, says Pater, is "not . . . simple and isolated; for the mind of the race, the character of the age, sway him this way or that through the medium of language and current ideas," with "remote laws of inheritance, the vibra-

tion of long-past acts reaching him in the midst of the new
order of things in which he lives" (*A, 67*).

Thus, even Wordsworth's poetry has "a power not altogether his own" (*A, 41*), a fact that may be accounted
for by Pater's description of "the religion of men of
letters" in the essay on Lamb as a "religion" that "lives,
in the main retrospectively, in a system of received sentiments and beliefs; received, like those great things of literature and art, in the first instance, on the authority of
a long tradition, in the course of which they have linked
themselves in a thousand complex ways to the conditions
of human life" (*A, 120*). Thus, with a pun, "such form of
religion becomes the solemn background on which the
nearer and more exciting objects" of Lamb's own "immediate experience relieve themselves" (*A, 120–21*), that is
to say, against which background they stand out in "relief." "The composite experience of all the ages is part of
each one of us," says Pater in "Aesthetic Poetry,"[6] and it
is against this "composite experience" or "solemn background" that our lives and work come into being by means
of their differences from it.

If we return now to "Style," Pater's argument about
literary labor should be abundantly clear:

> The literary artist is of necessity a scholar, and in
> what he proposes to do will have in mind, first of all,
> the scholar and the scholarly conscience—the male
> conscience in this matter, as we must think it, under
> a system of education which still to so large an extent
> limits real scholarship to men. In his self-criticism, he
> supposes always that sort of reader who will go (full
> of eyes) warily, considerately, though without con-
> sideration for him, over the ground which the female

6. *Selected Writings of Walter Pater,* ed. Bloom, p. 196.

conscience traverses so lightly, so amiably. For the material in which he works is no more a creation of his own than the sculptor's marble. Product of a myriad various minds and contending tongues, compact of obscure and minute association, a language has its own abundant and often recondite laws, in the habitual and summary recognition of which scholarship consists. A writer, full of a matter he is before all things anxious to express, may think of those laws, the limitations of vocabulary, structure, and the like, as a restriction, but if a real artist will find in them an opportunity. His punctilious observance of the proprieties of his medium will diffuse through all he writes a general air of sensibility, or refined usage. *Exclusiones debitae naturae*—the exclusions, or rejections, which nature demands. . . . We might say that the art of the scholar is summed up in the observance of those rejections demanded by the nature of his medium, the material he must use. [*A,* 12–13]

Thus it is the way the writer chooses his words from the vast lexicon of expression available to him that bestows upon him whatever originality, or lack of it, his work will carry. Indeed, what is really original about the writer's work are the rejections he makes from a common storehouse of tropes, subjects, narrative and poetic structures, and so on. Thus *ascesis* itself turns on a factor of difference, with what is left out not only what is rejected but also what is taken for granted in the under-texture. Indeed, *ascesis* may thereby indicate by particular absence those influences from which the writer swerves away in his attempt to voice what is uniquely his own, what is proper only to him, even if such literary property is to be won only through the absence of other such properties. Here

Pater's figure of the "network of chains" in the essay on Pascal takes on the additional connotation of bondage or imprisonment to those earlier literary achievements from which a given strong writer's work proceeds by means of its difference from them. This is "the burden of precedent," in the words of *Marius,* "laid upon every artist" (*M,* 82). In fact, the only really operative temporal factor in Pater's work as a whole is this differential process of rearrangement and suppression that a given writer, like a given personality, will belatedly perform upon his influences.

Thus Pater's desire to characterize such a process of rejection with the phrase "in the strictest sense original" (*A,* 15) constitutes little more than a plea for the pure qualities of unique and expressive selfhood and authorship that the terms of his analysis have once again dispersed, with literary composition resembling instead a movement away from that faithful translation or transcription of Plato which Pater here describes, with the figure of the palimpsest or literal under-text, as the following of "a drawing under tracing-paper" (*A,* 15).

There is probably no more graphic an example of this kind of rearrangement and partial burial of what is unavoidably inherited than Marius's rearrangement and reburial of the bones of his ancestors. Indeed, this penultimate moment in which he attempts to relieve the "burden of forms" imposed upon him by the "system of symbolic usages" (*M,* 3) in which he has been brought up only makes explicit Pater's narrative strategy throughout the book. For, like Marius's thoughts even during the religious services of his youth, Pater's text is to be found simultaneously "moving backwards" as well as "forwards" (*M,* 6), both on the level of its own telling and in the various concrete allusions it uses in the process. Thus Marius's youthful visit to the temple of Aesculapius, for example, is "understood" only "afterwards in retrospect," by means of a later vision which allows him to remember the way the temple's "splendor . . . dawned upon him on that morning of his first visit" (*M*, 33). Indeed, this early "recognition" can be recognized or remembered only because it "operated afterwards" (*M*, 33), and is seen as "now acquired" in that past moment only by means of later knowledge brought to bear on it in retrospect.

By means of "the prophetic future" (*M*, 239), then, the temporal dimension of Lucian's taxonomic exercise finds a more radical example than we have yet seen, and shows us how even this early "moment" in Marius's life comes into being by means of future experiences that allow its supposed freshness to be recalled. This rearrangement of past by future, of early by late, is, of course, the only way the past is present to us at all, and Pater exploits the strategic resources of the process in the way he establishes his vision of Marius's Rome through the allusions available to him from subsequent history. Thus Flavian's rhetoric, for example, "had caught," in the late Roman Empire, "the rhyming cadence . . . of the medieval Latin" (*M*, 94). So, too, we find Pater comparing the religion of Marius's youth to "the German enthusiasts . . . of our own century" (*M*, 39), or comparing "Roman Euphuism" to "the Euphuism of the Elizabethan age" as well as to "the modern French romanticists" (*M*, 81).

A full list of such "usages" in *Marius* would be a long one, and our few examples should be sufficient to show how Marius's later rearrangement and reburial of those early dead in his family doubles the very manner in which Pater tells his story. What is to be learned from Marius's action seems to lie in the assertion that such a modification or rewriting of the past is the price of strength and composure in the present. Like Marius or like Rome itself, we come to exist upon a "vast substruction . . . line upon line of successive ages of builders" (*M,* 143), "layer upon layer of dead things and people" (*M,* 164), with Woolf's designation of Pater as archaeologist in "Slater's Pins" a compelling interpretation of the Pater who emerges in the book she once read before bed. Like Cecilia's house, the "House Beautiful" of culture through the ages is made up of "the remains of older art, here arranged and harmonized" (*M,* 276) by those who come afterward.

Thus Pater's discussion earlier in "Style" of why the writer transcribes not "fact, but . . . his sense of it" (*A,* 9–10) rests far less on a vulgar impressionism than on a notion of the writer as a historian or scholar who, "amid the records of the past, . . . after his own sense, modifies" (*A,* 9). In "Style," in fact, Pater's notion of the more or less palimpsestic nature of all texts—of the under-text(s) in any given text—makes him particularly attentive to the figures or rhetoric in which any text inheres and through which its filiations may best, and almost literally, be traced. Figures are the "elementary particles" of all language, and the strong writer, in "realis[ing]" the "colour and light and shade" in them, "will not treat coloured glass as if it were clear." "While half the world is using figure unconsciously," says Pater, the writer "will be fully aware . . . of all that latent figurative texture in speech" as a whole (*A,* 20). This is another way of saying what Pater's notion of the world as a complex of languages or "names" has already suggested—that what appears to be the merely instrumental status of language as a mode of access to a self-sufficient world "without" is really a self-contained system of figures whose own laws constitute the world it seems only to refer to. For Pater, we think through our rhetoric, through our under-texture—after all, it is "part" of our "very structure"—or, rather, our rhetoric, to modify Coleridge's phrase, thinks for us.

Thus it is in this universe of language that we can also locate the tensions in Pater's own rhetoric, for its contradictions issue not, of course, from a confused vision, but from "the metaphor," as Pater puts it, "that is mixed in all our speech" (A, 20). The very use of language, argues Pater, is what traps us in semantic discordance, since "figure . . . is rarely content to die to thought precisely at the right moment, but will inevitably linger awhile, stirring a long 'brainwave' behind it of perhaps quite alien associations" (A, 18). This, however, is only evidence of the tangled threads with which the under-texture is put together, and, to mix a metaphor, is also the reason that the desired harmonies of Pater's musical model for art can always become sour or discordant depending on the closeness of the reading they receive.

Strictly speaking, moreover, if there is no originality, neither is there literary theft, at least according to the claim in the essay on Coleridge that, in Heine's words, " 'there can be no plagiarism' " (A, 75). While Heine's remark is meant to apply to philosophy, it is clear that the principle is equally true for literature.

Moreover, the belatedness of all writing is what accounts for Pater's fondness for what is pale, decadent, refined, like the "fainter and more spectral" qualities of Pre-Raphaelite verse as it compares to the High Romanticism of which it is the "delicate" and "second flowering."[7] All writing in fact is likewise a "second flowering" or palimpsest since, like the Pre-Raphaelites in relation to Romanticism proper, it is always "an afterthought."[8] Here, too, "spectral" suggests not only the ghostly presence of the

7. Ibid., p. 190.
8. Ibid.

dead, preserved fossil-like in any (later) text the way
Shakespeare, for example, "incorporate[s]" "the relics of
other men's poetry" in *Measure for Measure* (*A,* 182); it
also suggests the way in which a text locates itself on the
spectrum of tradition by means of its own "refraction" or
regradation of the forces or currents that pass through it.
Indeed, in the "Postscript," Pater must characterize all
art the way he characterizes classicism itself, as "the working out of refinements of manner on some authorised
matter" (*A,* 259-60) rather than—or really as "a supplement and a correction" to (*A,* 249)—what he calls in his
Romantic or individualist profile "the exercise of original
imagination" (*A,* 259).

Thus the search for what is original—whether the organic
self, the unique work of art, or the epiphanic moment—is
always to be situated within a residual "cobweb of allusions," a "system of symbolic usages" behind or before
which a single and immediately apprehensible "sacred
object" of truth is impossible to find. Pater, of course, has
his own myth of origins and originality in the Greeks,
although his argument in *Plato and Platonism* that Plato,
too, is a latecomer tends to put his own originary myth
into question, to recognize it as a myth and no more. Indeed, with *Plato,* the deidealizing necessities we have
traced in the present chapter finally usurp the focus of
Pater's argument almost completely, balancing or correcting the emphasis on ideals in *The Renaissance* and so
largely framing his career, as Knoepflmacher and DeLaura
suggest, between an early solipsism and a later sympathy.

"It is hardly an exaggeration," writes Pater at the start
of his study, "to say that in Plato, in spite of his wonderful savour of literary freshness, there is nothing absolutely
new" (*PP,* 8). The reasons are by now familiar ones: "as
in many other very original products of human genius, the

seemingly new is old also, a palimpsest," in one keyword, "a tapestry" in another, "of which the actual threads have served before, or like the animal frame itself, every particle of which has already lived and died many times over" (*PP*, 8). Indeed, with this reassessment of where the qualities of genius reside comes the emphasis instead on rearrangement as the mark of what we call originality: "the *form*," says Pater of Plato, "is new. But then, in the creation of philosophical literature, as in all other products of art, *form*, in the full signification of that word, is everything, and the mere matter is nothing" (*PP*, 8).

In tracing Plato's own filiations in Pythagoras, Heraclitus, and Parmenides, Pater is equally cautious about claiming any absolute originality for the precursors, too, returning again and again to the contention that "the original" is more a logical necessity than a reality, and that "at both ends of experience," at its real beginning and end, "there is—nothing!" (*PP*, 35).

For Pater, in other words, life itself is to be identified completely with culture. Even religion and nature are tropes designed to cover or defer the "nothing" that precedes and follows what we call consciousness. And as tropes they are easily integrated into the vision by which Pater here overrides not only the Victorian conflicts between mechanism and organism, science and religion that are part of his own immediate "burden of forms," but also those even wider philosophical disputes that constitute the "burden of precedent" in tradition as a whole:

> For in truth we come into the world, each one of us, "not in nakedness," but by the natural course of organic development clothed far more completely than even Pythagoras supposed in a vesture of the past, nay, fatally shrouded, it might seem, in those laws or

tricks of heredity which we mistake for our volitions;
in the language which is more than one half of our
thoughts; in the moral and mental habits, the customs, the literature, the very houses, which we did
not make for ourselves; in the vesture of a past, which
is (so science would assure us) not ours, but of the
race, the species: that *Zeit-geist*, or abstract secular
process, in which, as we could have had no direct
consciousness of it, so we can pretend to no future
personal interest. It is humanity itself now—abstract
humanity—that figures as the transmigrating soul,
accumulating into its "colossal manhood" the experience of ages; making use of, and casting aside in its
march, the souls of countless individuals, as Pythagoras supposed the individual soul to cast aside again
and again its outworn body. [*PP*, 72–73]

Having situated any given individual within such an
unconscious and resolutely "secular process," Pater's
accent throughout the book remains one of "locating the
particular in the general, mediating between general and
particular, between our individual experience and the
common experience of our kind" (*PP*, 152). "There is," he
writes, "a general consciousness, a permanent common
sense, independent indeed of each one of us, but with
which we are, each one of us, in communication" (*PP*, 151).
Neither an Ideal Platonism nor a pantheistic or even scientific mysticism, this "permanent common sense" is to be
found in "those abstract or common notions" which all of
us share and which "come to the individual mind through
language, through common or general names . . . into which
one's individual experience, little by little, drop by drop,
conveys their full meaning or content" (*PP*, 151–52). Indeed, it is the commonalty of "language" that directs and

determines individual experience rather than the other way
around, with experience itself validating, perhaps tautologically, the truth that language teaches it. "From first to
last," says Pater, "our faculty of thinking is limited by our
command of speech" (*PP,* 142), which in turn commands
or speaks us.

Pater is absolutely explicit about it:

> Our common ideas, without which, in fact, we none
> of us could think at all, are not the consequence, not
> the products, but the cause of our reason in us: we
> do not make them; but they make us what we are, as
> reasonable beings. [*PP,* 168]

Thus the individual comes into being as a locus of the
intersections of the world's languages as they devolve upon
him from origins remote and ultimately untraceable. Much
as Plato has "diffused, divided, resolved, refracted, differ-
entiated" the "eternal Being, of Parmenides" (*PP,* 168), so
all of us latecomers refract and differentiate what we in-
herit, rearranging and re-placing it much as Marius rearranges and re-places the remains of his ancestors. Even
what we call perception is, as "The Child in the House"
has already shown us, less the way a stable self gains access
to the world than it is a function of how we are embedded
in the "permanent common sense":

> we, our souls, ourselves, are for ever imitating what
> we see and hear, the forms, the sounds which haunt
> our memories, our imagination. We imitate not only
> if we play a part on the stage but when we sit as specta-
> tors, while our thoughts follow the acting of another,
> when we read Homer and put ourselves, lightly,
> fluently, into the place of those he describes: we
> imitate unconsciously the line and colour of the walls

around us, the trees by the wayside, the animals we
pet or make use of, the very dress we wear. [*PP,* 272]

Thus Pater's quest for the "sacred object" of genius and
its works swerves from its ideals in favor of a secondary
vision that displaces and supplants them. The ideal project,
of course, is full coincidence—with oneself, with the text
written, and with the text read. Pater's own work, however, remains different from itself despite its celebration of
a natural expressiveness manifestly harmonious and serene.
His texts question their own assumptions and replace them
with others even as each of his projects pursues its own
aims and asserts its own values in the mutual interdepen-
dence or difference that constitutes each one in relation
to the other.

5

"The Common Life"

Let us return to *A Room of One's Own* to begin to see what other notions of art and personality exist side by side with those of fitness, incandescence, and *ascesis* that Woolf has drawn from Pater, and to see what alterations such a view may produce in our understanding of the way Woolf handles the "burden of precedent" she inherits from him. If the chemistry of the crystal has shown us how Pater enables Woolf to organize and define herself as a critic and to make her essays cohere in a common project and a consistent use of figure, Pater's secondary vision will eventually enable us to see how Woolf overcomes her discipleship by means of a theory of literature and culture that routs the precursor far more effectively than her assertion of modernist and feminist rights allows her to do. Such an overcoming, however, is always set in motion by the anxiety to be had by doubling or copying, even though the doubling in this secondary wave of Pater's influx is confined largely to stance alone rather than to stance and figure together. Nevertheless, there are certain strong figural coincidences here, too, where vision and trope again conjoin so forcefully that despite the many differences between our writers and the less idiosyncratic nature of the figures they deploy in their secondary profiles, we are again reminded of how much Woolf takes from Pater even when she may be least aware of it.

One of Woolf's chief difficulties in *A Room of One's Own* lies in the failure of her attempt to define women in any single way. Such a failure is necessary, as Woolf well knows, because her sex is a "queer, composite being" —at least in its customary representations—"an odd monster" (*ROO*, 66), not amenable to easy or categorical description despite the temptation to imagine women and men as distinct from the point of view of inherent qualities. Women must be defined, then, not in terms of some unitary essence or overridingly feminine characteristic, but in terms of the contradictory qualities they share along with everything else in life. Thus women can only be described, says Woolf, as a bundle or collection of qualities, as "a vessel in which all sorts of spirits and forces are coursing and flashing perpetually" (*ROO*, 66–67).

Although the "vessel" is not incompatible with certain traditional figures for femininity as an enclosure, Woolf claims no such special symbolic status for it here. In fact, so unprivileged is the figure of the "vessel" that she uses it indifferently to characterize the novel as well, with fiction's ability to capture the world's many "odd" properties earning it the description of "a more fitting receptacle" for the task than the poetic drama it supersedes as a form (*ROO*, 125).

The retention of the term "fitting," of course, is not the only Paterian resonance at work in this last figure, since, like Woolf's theft of the rhetorical questions Pater uses to define the aesthetic critic in the "Preface" to *The Renaissance,* the figure of the "receptacle" recurs there as well, and designates the space of character and art in the same terms by which Woolf designates them here.[1] But if

---

1. Even Woolf's "spirits and forces" partially double Pater's "powers or forces" in the "Preface" (*R*, viii).

"fitting" points back to Pater, it also points to its own inability as a figure to account for what the term "receptacle" accounts for, even if Woolf uses the two words as if their knowledges were coterminous. "Fitting," after all, carries with it the sense of an ideal coincidence between word and essence, between letter and personality, while the logic of the figure of the "receptacle," by contrast, lies in its ability to gather, as a container or captor, the many noncoincident qualities or "forces" that characterize women or the novel indifferently. In fact, the reason Woolf needs the terms "vessel" and "receptacle" in the first place is because the "odd" or "composite" nature of all things in life makes the notion of a "fitting" designation that will identify and glove some essence they may possess strictly impossible.

Noncoincident as the "spirits and forces" are that constitute women and the novel alike, what happens to Woolf's notion of art and character as "fitting" expressions of their creators? Different from themselves, novels and women can no longer be luminous and self-contained so long as art and personality are each to be judged as the signature of an imagination at one with itself. Even Woolf's famous celebration of the self's autonomy in "Modern Fiction" raises difficulties about the status of the self similar to those we have seen in Pater's equivalent celebration of "the individual in his isolation" in the "Conclusion" to *The Renaissance.* Inveighing against the familiar constraints of conventional plotting and storytelling because they force the novelist's view of life into standard patterns of meaning that do not do justice to the variety of individual experience, Woolf proposes as an alternative a modern fiction that proceeds from the novelist's own "utmost sincerity" (*CE* II, 107) and that takes for its subject "the quick of the mind" itself (*CE* II, 107).

But even though it is what is "innermost" in the individual mind that Woolf proposes as the modern novelist's proper subject, what is "innermost" and what is not emerge as the essay's central problem in the well-known passage that focuses on "an ordinary mind on an ordinary day":

> Life is not a series of gig-lamps symmetrically arranged; life is a luminous halo, a semi-transparent envelope surrounding us from the beginning of consciousness to the end. Is it not the task of the novelist to convey this varying, this unknown and uncircumscribed spirit, whatever aberration or complexity it may display, with as little mixture of the alien and external as possible? [*CE* II, 106]

As it turns out, there is much "aberration" and "complexity" here (including the borrowing from the early pages of *Heart of Darkness*), much that is "alien" to Woolf's vision in the very figures by which it is expressed. If "life is a luminous halo, a semi-transparent envelope surrounding us from the beginning of consciousness to the end," how can life also be an "uncircumscribed spirit"? Is not "life," in the first figure, that which surrounds or circumscribes us like an "envelope"? And is it not, in the second figure, precisely the opposite, that which is not circumscribed? (Is the qualifying "semi-" a suggestion of Woolf's desire to have it both ways?) And how else can the novelist "convey" life except by using the externality of language itself to do so? Indeed, where the "innermost" is to be found is now only a secondary problem within the larger one of where the self or "ordinary mind" is to be located in the first place. We may resolve the difficulties either by identifying "life" with subjective or solipsistic experience alone, and thereby read Woolf's "envelope" as Pater's "wall of personality"; or by reading "envelope" as a "vessel" or "receptacle" in which the self is mapped, enclosed, and contained. What we seem to lose in the second reading is the dimension of the "innermost"—the dimension of depth and radical separation of self from world—in favor of a notion of self as continuous in its materials with the world from which it is so often indistinguishable.

All this is only implicit in *A Room of One's Own*, however, at least until late in the book when Woolf confesses herself irritated with the obtrusiveness of personality itself as a factor in life and literature alike, particularly with the way the imperial ego is wielded in so much male writing. Although Woolf here assigns an inherent property to the masculine in violation of what the term "receptacle" has to teach her about essences, what disturbs her as she reads a novel by a hypothetical Mr. A is less a sexual characteristic than an epistemological one. Here she finds "a shadow" lying "across the page," "a straight dark bar, a shadow shaped something like the letter 'I,' '" which, in a graphic representation for a covering or repressive force, obscures "the landscape behind it" (*ROO*, 150). "One began to be tired of 'I' " (*ROO*, 150), Woolf concludes, despite her elevation of personality and expressiveness elsewhere in her criticism, even in this same book in which the ideal of incandescence seems to be absolutely paramount. Woolf's objection is cast specifically as an irritation with the falsity of the ego as a category, which seems to her an unreliable means by which to represent experience. Here, in fact, the "I" becomes as hypothetical—as alphabetical and as purely conventional—as the "A" with which she has designated the identity of her male author.

Of course, the repressive and purely conventional character of the "I" suggests that what is properly real lies in "the landscape behind it," with "character" itself to be interpreted literally, as a letter or a convention like the "I" which represents it. Indeed, in the essay "Street Haunting," written only a few months after *A Room of One's Own,* Woolf's irritation with the convention of the "I" is carried beyond mere opinionating into a critique of integral self-hood as a notion. Here she removes the "dark bar" of the "I" and allows us to see what is really at work in "the landscape behind it":

> Is the true self this which stands on the pavement in January, or that which bends over the balcony in June? Am I here, or am I there? Or is the true self neither this nor that, neither here nor there, but something so varied and wandering that it is only when we give the rein to its wishes and let it take its way unimpeded that we are indeed ourselves? Circumstances compel unity; for convenience sake a man must be a whole. The good citizen when he opens his door in the evening must be banker, golfer, husband, father; not a nomad wandering the desert, a mystic staring at the sky, a debauchee in the slums of San Francisco, a soldier heading a revolution, a pariah howling with scepticism and solitude. When he opens his door, he must run his fingers through his hair and put his umbrella in the stand like the rest. [*CE* IV, 161]

The quest for "anchorage in these thwarting currents of being" (*CE* IV, 161) is plainly a difficult one, as Woolf concludes from this unobscured view of the "wandering" images to be found behind the convention of character (many of Woolf's critics have also concluded as much).[2]

2. The precarious status of the self in Woolf is made especially clear in Naremore (*The World Without A Self*). See also Avrom Fleishman, *Virginia Woolf: A Critical Reading,* especially his discussion of *Jacob's Room* and *The Waves.*

Although a year earlier she speaks of a "real self" in *Orlando* (*O*, 282), there, too, she wittingly questions the self's natural reality in the passages that lead up to its efflorescence by casting it as an imperial convention—"the Captain self, the Key self" (*O*, 279)—with which Orlando simply yokes together the "great variety of selves" beating within her (*O*, 278).

Indeed, in the kaleidoscopic sketch "Evening Over Sussex," Woolf dramatizes the way "the self" as we know it "splits up" (*CE* II, 290) on those dreamy occasions when the mind slips half into unconsciousness, and proceeds to give us a series of "selves" holding "colloquy" (*CE* II, 291) with one another over the course of an automobile excursion. Talking to oneself soon becomes an occasion for watching the very integrity of the ego dissolve before one's eyes (the "remarks" of "a fourth self," for example, "are often entirely disconnected with what has been happening" [*CE* II, 291]), and eventually compels the narrator of the sketch to try to reconstitute her normal, daily identity much as the "good citizen" in "Street Haunting" feels compelled to do "when he opens his door." Woolf plays havoc with personal pronouns as the piece concludes: "I summoned them together," she says of herself and her "selves"; "we have got to be one self," she announces to them as their "Captain self," and returns to the "I" only after she has established her authority as the "she" "who preside[s] over the company" (*CE* II, 292).

One is left, of course, with the question not only of location but also of locution: who, after all, speaks under the customary rubric of the personal pronoun in a text with these kinds of circumstances? Like "Street Haunting," in other words, "Evening Over Sussex" dissolves the daily self back into its components and assures us that the

"I" is never coincident—never at one—with itself. Indeed, in "Evening Over Sussex," Woolf delivers her radical moral in an almost casual aside: "there was disappearance," she writes, "and the death of the individual" (*CE* II, 292).

With all these contingencies swarming around the question of individuality in her essays, it is not unusual that Woolf turns out to have reserved them for use in fashioning the strikingly collective vision of culture that emerges at the close of *A Room of One's Own.* From the point of view of art alone, Woolf's surprising contention is that "masterpieces are not single and solitary births" (*ROO,* 98), the "utmost sincerity" of modern fiction notwithstanding. No, "masterpieces," she argues, "are the outcome of many years of thinking in common, of thinking by the body of the people, so that the experience of the mass is behind the single voice" (*ROO,* 98). Hence the artist, like the self at large, is the "receptacle" of the "currents" of culture as a whole, and his work necessarily a reworking of the various texts that have preceded it.

Hence Woolf deidealizes the creative, or, to speak now more properly, the aesthetic subject, transforming the originality and isolation that otherwise characterize the artist into a vision of art and art history that emphasizes commonalty rather than uniqueness. Distinguishing between "writing as an art" and writing "as a method of self-expression" (*ROO,* 120), Woolf at last concludes that "books continue each other, in spite of our habit of judging them separately" (*ROO,* 120). Even Woolf's peroration on androgyny joins with this notion of the commonalty of artistic work when she interprets the figure of "fertilisation" in art as a means of insuring that a work can "grow in the minds of others" (*ROO,* 157). That is to say, if a book or painting is well made, it will enter the apparently natural universe of social and aesthetic intercourse in which we all live—that common discourse of traditions, customs, manners, myths, arts, and so on—and so take its place in that total life of culture in which both a text's production and its reading are to be situated.

Hence the book's ultimate climax, inserted within the feminist charge that women seek economic and spiritual freedom as the ransom of their liberation: "I am talking," says Woolf, "of the common life which is the real life and not of the little separate lives which we live as individuals" (ROO, 171). Indeed, our lives as individuals are realizable "not always in their relation to each other, but in relation to reality" (ROO, 171). Here "reality" is to be defined not as pure subjectivity or solipsism at all, but as that "common life" to be found not in any individual alone, nor in any individual at all, but in those "forces" and "currents" that bind the living and the dead together, and from which each of us is given the elements that constitute our individual being.

As a principle of art and social life alike, Woolf's formulation deindividualizes the subject even more radically, and certainly more overtly, than does Pater's, and plainly hails the self's participation in "the common life" as an occasion for rejoicing. Even the figure of Judith Shakespeare, the "dead poet" reborn at the book's close, is less a theological absurdity than a thoroughly secular truth about the enduring reality of "the common life" for men and women alike. "Shakespeare's sister," writes Woolf, "will put on the body which she has so often laid down" by "drawing her life from the lives of the unknown who were her forerunners, as her brother did before her" (ROO, 172). Thus, even though Woolf claims that women must "go alone" (ROO, 172) at the labor of writing, even they have models like Judith Shakespeare—or, indeed, like her brother—with whom they can "go" it in "common."

Just what the self is and how it is to be situated within "the common life" is revealed in the astonishing memoir, "A Sketch of the Past," written in 1939 and published only recently in the autobiographical collection, *Moments of Being*. The piece occupies a place in Woolf's work equivalent to "The Child in the House" in Pater's, since it presents us with a microscopic account of the way sensation and perception develop in childhood and with the most striking and summary model of selfhood to be found in all of Woolf's writing.

That Woolf writes about herself, of course, is particularly ironic, since this most self-evident of autobiographical exercises quickly becomes problematic in the extreme. To be sure, Woolf wants to surmount the usual "memoir writer's difficulties"—"leav[ing] out the person to whom things happened." Of course, the reason for the difficulties "is that it is so difficult to describe any human being" (*MB*, 65). Hence what the sketch is really about is the problem of human description itself, and what better way to address it than by trying to fix one's own sense of self, particularly in its beginnings.

There is, however, a difference between the beginning of the organism and the beginning of the self, and it is a difference that Woolf is anxious to insist upon as she looks back at her own infancy. Because the "past is much affected by the present moment" (*MB*, 75), she is cautious not to assign to childhood that adult sense of self in which we feel ourselves to be "sealed vessels afloat on what it is convenient to call reality" (*MB*, 122). No, what is remarkable about infancy is that a sense of self is rather late in developing. "I am hardly aware of myself," writes Woolf of her eighth year, "but only of the sensation. I am," she decides, "only the container of the feeling of ecstasy, of the feeling of rapture" (*MB*, 67).

Indeed, all that Woolf can recall of childhood with any certainty at all are those particularly memorable nodes of infantile experience that she calls "moments of being" (*MB,* 70). This, of course, is to reconstitute her own origins in Paterian terms, with the added irony that her very attempt to keep the past free from the influence of the present by recalling the purest moments she can is already a sign or taint of the precursor's prior visitation. That Pater thereby stands earlier than Woolf's own origins in the deferred action by which she reconstitutes them is, moreover, only to put into play Pater's own notion of how the past comes into being through the retrospect that follows and shapes it.

Even more, the very mechanism by which the past gets reconstituted here doubles Pater's own notion of the way the world emerges to the child. In the trajectory of retrospect, after all, Woolf's "moments" get remembered not as self-sufficient atoms of experience—not as memorable in themselves, but as moments in a series composed both of other such moments and the lack of them: "These separate moments of being," writes Woolf, "were however embedded in many more moments of non-being" (*MB,* 70). What makes things pertinent and memorable, in other words, is a mechanism of difference, not only between "moments of being" and "non-being," but also within the moment itself, whose differential complexion may be discerned in the way Woolf represents a moment of infantile rapture by describing "a baby, who can just distinguish a great blot of blue and purple on a black background" (*MB,* 79). Indeed, what makes the world as a whole pertinent to the young Woolf is a difference that constitutes her experience in every aspect of her emerging life—between "blue and purple on a black background," or, indeed, in the discovery of "the difference," as she puts it a few pages earlier,

"between despair and satisfaction" (*MB*, 71). Like Florian
and Marius, and like Stephen Dedalus, too, Woolf finds in
"difference," then, not only the rule by which sensation
emerges, but the rule that governs the emergence of significance on increasingly abstract and nonsensory levels of
experience as well.

What is established here is still not what Woolf is willing
to call a self, but rather a field of relations into which the
child is inserted. This field or structure of differences is
graphically represented as "a blue gummy veil" (*MB*, 66),
for example, in which the various shapes and sounds of
childhood "were caught" (*MB*, 66); although the "veil" is
not, of course, to be identified with the self proper, but
with the growing comprehensibility of the world against
and within which the self will eventually be plotted. It is,
writes Woolf, "as if I were passive . . . ; exposed to a whole
avalanche of meaning that had heaped itself up and discharged itself upon me, unprotected, with nothing to ward
it off" (*MB*, 78). It is the growing sense of an organization
to the "avalanche," however, that allows the child to discover that "one is living all the time in relation to certain
background rods or conceptions. Mine is that there is
a pattern hid behind"—or, more appropriately, within—
"the cotton wool" (*MB*, 73) that represents the fabric
of the world.

Of course, the world into which one emerges here is
already constituted, making the child's developing sense of
order not so much a purely subjective one as it is a shared
competence in recognizing "that which we all lived in common" (*MB*, 83). Such a notion of what is "lived in common"
corresponds to Woolf's feeling earlier in the sketch that
"things we have felt with great intensity have an existence
independent of our minds" (*MB*, 67). And what is "common" and "independent of our minds," of course, are

those various "rods and conceptions" that structure the "avalanche"—that make it "a pattern" or a "veil" rather than "non-being."

It is, of course, the mother who is a principal bearer or embodiment of these "rods and conceptions," although her privileged status is the result not so much of her biological priority as it is of her simple ability to dominate the field of "influence" (*MB*, 80), as Woolf calls it, which surrounds the child. "She was one of the invisible presences" —a privileged one, but only "one" of many—"who after all play so important a part in every life" (*MB*, 80). Indeed, this meditation on the role of the mother leads Woolf to a general statement about "influence" in life as a whole:

> This influence, by which I mean the consciousness of other groups impinging upon ourselves; public opinion; what other people say and think; all those magnets which attract us this way to be like that, or repel us the other and make us different from that; has never been analysed in any of those Lives which I so much enjoy reading, or very superficially.
>
> Yet it is by such invisible presences that the "subject of this memoir" is tugged this way and that every day of his life; it is they that keep him in position. [*MB*, 80]

Thus it is the "background" of "influence" into which the " 'subject' " emerges that puts her (or "him") in the "position" that will capture and determine her. Describing her "background" as late as 1900, Woolf even calls it "the machine into which we were inserted" (*MB*, 131), a figure that not only refines her earlier notion of life as a "pattern" alive with "magnets," but that also coincides with the implicit figure of a circuitry with which she represents her plunge into the past at the start of the sketch: "Instead of remembering here a scene and there a sound," she says, "I shall fit a plug into the wall; and listen in to the past" (*MB*, 67).

This "machine" of "influence" is itself described in Woolf's "shorthand" as "an extended surface" (*MB*, 83) on which one gets located or positioned as though on a circuit-board or map. Thus, too, the apparently fanciful way in which Woolf remembers her mother's description of her homemade newspaper—"it was about souls flying round and choosing bodies to be born into" (*MB*, 95)—is really a secular notion of metempsychosis like Pater's, or, indeed, like Joyce's in *Ulysses*, by which the life of a particular individual becomes a function of the contexts into which it is inserted. Even the Coleridgean figure by which Woolf describes her pleasure at her mother's reaction to the newspaper doubles the metempsychosis that is its apparent subject: "it was like being a violin and being played upon" (*MB*, 95), she says, thereby representing her own sensations as personal combinations in a common scale or register of which the "I," at least in childhood, is a passive expression.

Before proceeding to Woolf's understanding of how the self gets fully articulated on this map of influence, let us remark for a moment the way in which she derives from this notion of life as "an extended surface" her far more characteristic sense of life as a phenomenon of depth. "The past only comes back," she writes, "when the present runs so smoothly that it is like the sliding surface of a deep river. Then one sees through the surface to the depths" (*MB*, 98). Like Freud's geological metaphors or, indeed, like Pater's figure of the fossil, the figure of depth, particularly watery depth, serves Woolf as a more fitting means of representing the simultaneity of past and present than the more recalcitrant image of circuitry. How to represent her feeling that "strong emotion must leave its trace" (*MB*, 67) is easily solved by a figure like the following: "For the present when backed by the past is a thousand times deeper than the present when it presses so close that you can feel nothing else, when the film on the camera"—another surprisingly technological metaphor—"reaches only the eye" (*MB*, 98). Indeed, the figure of depth allows Woolf to reach something more than "the eye," that almost ultimate measure of truth for Pater himself, and one that Woolf can apparently supersede by means of her more powerful language of depth, even though the gain to be had from it, as we shall see later on, is not to be found in the greater epistemological value it may seem to possess.

If we return to the figure of the "extended surface," however, we can see Woolf's notion of how the self finally emerges with astonishing clarity. How does one get positioned on the map of common influence? Here is Woolf's version of the process:

> There was a small looking-glass in the hall at Talland House. It had, I remember, a ledge with a brush on it. By standing on tiptoe I could see my face in the glass. When I was six or seven perhaps, I got into the habit of looking at my face in the glass. But I only did this if I was sure that I was alone. [*MB*, 67–68]

What the young Woolf discovers in the mirror is precisely the "I" that is so elusive and difficult to achieve during these formative years of sensual chaos. The romance of the mirror, of course, is not a single event, but something that was a "habit," an event repeated more than once so as to assure Woolf of the enduring stability of the self she beholds at last. And yet the enduring "I" that emerges in the mirror is not, after all, oneself proper, but the image of oneself on a surface. Nonetheless, it is the image alone that must serve as one's proper self, unavailable as it is elsewhere, despite the permanent condition of alienation its specular terms build into the very fabric of identity. Thus it is the origin of the ego in the mirror that accounts for the noncoincidence of self with self that Woolf discerns in all her descriptions of identity, and that even literalizes or concretizes Pater's sense of self in *Marius* as that of the "companion" or " 'assistant' " (*M,* 256), the "some one else" whom Pater quixotically identifies as Marius's "own proper self" (*M,* 237–38).

There is, moreover, an additional factor at work in the specular origin of Woolf's sense of self. Having described her "habit" of looking at her face "in the glass," Woolf continues: "I was ashamed of it. A strong feeling of guilt seemed naturally attached to it. But why was this so?" (*MB,* 68). In an answer to her question, Woolf calls upon the "obvious reason" that she and Vanessa were "tomboys," and that "to have been found looking in the glass would have been against our tomboy code" (*MB,* 68). Her second reason, however, is far more resonant, relying as it does on the fact that she had "inherited a streak of the puritan, of the Clapham Sect" (*MB,* 68) from her father, and so finds the act of contemplating oneself to fall under all that his muscular and procreative morality forbade: a passive introspection that connotes the same fearfully nongenerative relation to life presented in "Slater's Pins," where contemplation is associated not only with homosexuality, but also with the linking term that lies silently between them—narcissism.

Hence the emergence of the "I" and narcissism seem, at least in the retrospect of memory, to be so dangerously close to one another that the anxiety attached to the latter tends to migrate or spill over onto the "I" itself to produce what Woolf calls her "looking-glass shame" (*MB*, 68). Whether the aetiology of this "shame" is to be sought in Woolf's "tomboy" escapades with Vanessa or, more likely, in what she refers to in the same passage as her shame and fear of her body, need not concern us here, memories of Gerald Duckworth's fondlings notwithstanding (*MB*, 69). Nor is it essential that we seek the origin of her "shame" in the paternal injunction, again apparent only in retrospect, that her "ecstasies and raptures" be patently "disconnected" from her "own body" (*MB*, 68).

In fact, the specular nature of the ego, particularly the way one's very sense of bodily integrity is established in the mirror, seems to satisfy Stephen's demand that pleasure be "disconnected" from the body proper, since even the physical self here becomes only an image, a sign of its own absence. At the same time, however, these imagistic conditions nonetheless reconstitute what lies behind Stephen's "puritan" anxiety about contemplating oneself in the first place, the Puritan prohibition against graven images.[3]

We may also trace the emergence of the ego as an image or representation from its other source in Woolf's earliest sense of herself as a "container." The figure of the "container" has two principal variants in the sketch, both of which naturalize the process they represent: the figure of the "grape" (is there a trace of Keats in it?) by which Woolf describes her infancy ("the feeling . . . of lying in a grape and seeing through a film of semi-transparent yellow" [*MB*, 65]); and the figure of the "membrane" ("The buzz, the croon, the smell, all seemed to press voluptuously against some membrane" [*MB*, 66]).

---

3. Pater himself teases the prohibition by suggesting the first full flush of Greek sculpture to reside in a *"period of graven images"* concerned above all with the making of idols (*GS*, 237).

What is interesting about this proleptic self as "grape"
or "membrane" is that it serves as much to defer sensation
as it does to absorb it, thereby establishing a difference
between self and world even as world and self are being
constituted differentially. Indeed, this "membrane"
(Freud uses the same term to describe the development of
the ego in his biological fable in *Beyond the Pleasure
Principle*)[4] defers the world by absorbing it, slowly form-
ing a barrier which becomes the ego proper and which
turns the world away even as it stores up its stimuli further
within in the form of a "trace" (*MB*, 67). "Later," says
Woolf, "we add to feelings" (*MB*, 67), suggesting "the
past" to be once again "much affected by the present
moment" from whose variable vantage point we constantly
reinterpret the "trace" and so constellate our past differently each time, much as Woolf herself does in the
various sketches of childhood to be found in *Moments of
Being* itself, each of which reconstitutes the same biographical time in a different way.

Another name for this turning away, of course, is the
word "trope" itself, whose root meaning is "a turn"—the
(defensive) substitution of a figure or representation for
something else that is absent. Here, of course, the establishment of the ego as a means of deferring or "troping"
the world joins up with Woolf's notion of a specular ego,
since both approaches to subjectivity lie in a common
understanding of the "I" as something that constitutes
itself as a representation only. Here, too, we should recall
Woolf's summary artist figure, Miss La Trobe in *Between
the Acts,* whose very name reflects what her culminating
moment of dramaturgy will set out in graphic terms: that

---

4. *The Standard Edition of the Complete Psychological Works of Sigmund
Freud,* ed. James Strachey (London: The Hogarth Press, 1953–66), XVIII, 27.

the world and the people in it are tropes or images constituted in a mirror.

If we need to be convinced that selfhood is not a given
in Woolf's work, let us turn to *Mrs. Dalloway* for as
thorough a meditation on the nature of self and identity as
there is in her fiction. Retiring to her bedroom after her
morning errands, Clarissa's reveries reach a kind of conclusion when she gazes into the mirror to examine her face:

> She pursed her lips when she looked in the glass. It
> was to give her face point. That was her self—pointed;
> dartlike; definite. That was her self when some
> effort, some call on her to be her self, drew the
> parts together, she alone knew how different, how
> incompatible and composed so for the world only
> into one centre, one diamond, one woman who sat
> in her drawing-room and made a meeting-point, a
> radiancy. . . . [*MD*, 57]

The sense of selfhood here is one of achievement or
accomplishment, the result of "some effort, some call on
her to be her self." That Woolf chooses to punctuate "herself" with two words instead of the usual one suggests
that the achievement of this "definite" quality of a self
"composed . . . into one centre" is the result, not of a sure
and natural process of development, but of a discipline and
curtailment that makes the "parts" given to Clarissa in
time past cohere and harmonize. Most important of all,
of course, is that Clarissa draws "the parts together" by
means of beholding her image in the looking-glass. Without
the mirror, Clarissa is "incompatible," "different" from
herself. With the mirror, she gains in her reflection what
she does not possess organically, a whole version of herself,
although an identity, to be sure, that is still "different"

from itself because the price of its wholeness is its constitution as the image of another.

Even apart from her mirror self, or as a reflection of it,
Clarissa's identity is already constituted in different ways by
the different tropes or images by which she is represented,
and by which she has learned to represent herself. The two
primary ones, of course, are "Clarissa" and "Mrs. Dalloway," with each proper name signifying a different cluster
of the various and incompatible "parts" that constitute
her "own" or "proper" self—under the rubric "Clarissa,"
for example, her memories of Bourton, her relationship
with Peter Walsh, her sexual fascination with other women,
and so on; under "Mrs. Dalloway," her marriage to Richard,
her daughter Elizabeth, her role as hostess, and so on.

Even more, Clarissa's "definite" self is figured here
under the name of a gem—a "diamond"—that sends us
back to that Paterian definition of selfhood whereby personality fashions itself into a crystal. Clarissa's diamond, of
course, is just such a crystal, and the "radiancy" of its
momentary perfection before the glass—the product of the
discipline Clarissa undergoes so as to "compose" this "one
centre" or central self—is a "meeting-point" like the one
that constitutes the "focus" of Paterian intensity, together
with the sacrifices such a single focus ("only") requires.
Thus, as "Mrs. Dalloway," she must forego much of what
falls under the trope "Clarissa," just as her momentary
returns throughout the day to the world of "Clarissa" require her to sacrifice the "thousand" other "sympathies"
that fall under her identity as "Mrs. Dalloway." From this
point of view, it is also her "self" that Clarissa sees when
she gazes at the old woman in the window across from her
bedroom late in the novel, an image of age, loneliness, and
approaching death that she fashions into a (self-)portrait
of dignity and repose.

What is lacking, or at least what is not given, is the "something central which permeated" (*MD*, 49) that is Clarissa's most celebrated lament. Although she thinks such an absence is peculiar to her alone, it is, of course, a common absence built into Woolf's very notion of character as an image alienated from the self it defines, as a distinctive mark or graphic symbol (to take character at its letter) like the "I" itself.

At the start of her noontime meditation, of course, Clarissa feels her identity ebb, "feeling herself suddenly shrivelled, aged, breastless, the grinding, blowing, flowering of the day, out of doors, out of the window, out of her body and brain which now failed" (*MD*, 48). The passing away of these "currents" of "influence" on whose "extended surface" one normally positions oneself makes Clarissa acutely aware of the "forces" of which her various selves are composed, the power they have to fill her becoming particularly apparent once they begin to pass out of and away from her to suggest the nothingness of death and the end of troping or illusion with which death is equivalent. It is, moreover, especially noteworthy that Woolf deploys the Paterian figure of the house to describe the ebb of Clarissa's sense of self ("out of doors, out of the window, out of her body and brain"), since it allows us to see how central the figure of the dwelling or manmade enclosure is to both writers' notion of selfhood as a fortified space of property. The stable "I," of course, is, if nothing else, a "capital" disposition of character, with its capital qualities suggesting a notion of selfhood as one, quite literally, of ownership or "property."[5]

5. Here, too, we may suggest the central position of the house not only in *Mrs. Dalloway*, but, as we shall see at some length later on, in almost all of Woolf's novels, particularly in *To the Lighthouse*, where the Ramsays' summer house is strongly fortified in Part I; in ruins, like Duke Carl's grange, in Part II;

A sense of self-dissolution, however, is not unusual with
Clarissa, and if it functions as an ebb or loss here, it also
functions as a positive joy or advantage elsewhere in the
novel. Indeed, the dissolution of her identity back into its
component and nonidentical "parts" is what gives her faith
in her ability to endure after death, at least if one is attentive to the shared or common nature of the circuits through
which selfhood is composed:

> somehow in the streets of London, on the ebb and
> flow of things, here, there, she survived, Peter sur-
> vived, lived in each other, she being part, she was
> positive, of the trees at home; of the house there,
> ugly, rambling all to bits and pieces as it was; part of
> people she had never met; being laid out like a mist
> between the people she knew best, who lifted her on
> their branches as she had seen the trees lift the mist,
> but it spread ever so far, her life, herself. [*MD*, 16] [6]

With "the house" or self "rambling all to bits and pieces"
here, the narrator foregrounds instead the common pathways by which its "parts" or "pieces" are orchestrated.

---

and in its reconstituted wholeness, like the tomb of Marius's ancestors, in
Part III. Indeed, the figure of the house has a remarkably consistent career in
Woolf's novels, beginning with the Villa San Gervasio and the hotel in *The
Voyage Out*, each of which represents a particular ideal of security for the
novel's questing heroine Rachel, and ending with the strong figure of Pointz
Hall in *Between the Acts*. In between, of course, there are the Hilberys' comic
fortress in *Night and Day;* the cottage, the Acropolis, and a series of inter-
mediary dwellings in *Jacob's Room;* the great and enduring house of Orlando
and his forbears in *Orlando;* and the Pargiter mansion in *The Years*, whose
own strength ebbs as the novel moves forward in time.

6. Clarissa's belief also bears an uncanny resemblance to Pater's argument
in the first essay he read to the Old Mortality (one that Woolf would almost
certainly never have known about), "Subjective Immortality." The "dead
man," says Pater there, "lives as it were in the memory of his friends" (quoted
in Monsman, *Walter Pater*, p. 31). The term, in quotation marks, appears in
Marius (*M*, 16).

The "branches," "trees," and "mist" are in fact only one set of images by which the narrator represents those currents of being that connect people throughout the novel, even people one "had never met."

Although the figures in this instance are organic ones, the novel also includes recurrent images like the binding "thread"[7] that almost literally tie or unite characters, events, and places throughout the story, and that designate not so much a natural unity to life[8] as they do a common life of tropes and conceptions shared by characters and narrators alike.[9] From this point of view, the anonymous old woman who sings Strauss at the underground station almost at the center of the novel[10] comes to represent the voice of the common life itself, with its anonymous murmurs trickling down from origins so remote that to fix them would be impossible. In many ways, too, the Tube woman is even a radical deidealization—a common-ing down—of a figure like Pater's Mona Lisa, with both figures representing the same force even if they are otherwise so different.

7. For a mapping of many of the novel's binding motifs, see J. Hillis Miller, "Virginia Woolf's All Souls' Day: The Omniscient Narrator in *Mrs. Dalloway*," in *The Shaken Realist: Essays in Modern Literature in Honor of Frederick J. Hoffman,* ed. Friedman and Vickery (Baton Rouge: Louisiana State University Press, 1970), pp. 100–27.

8. Even Naremore's notion of Woolf's movement beyond the individual is a notion of the common life as a biological or organic unity, particularly his focus on her undersea imagery.

9. This is true not only of the technical devices by which the narrator links her characters by means of the repetition, for example, of particular phrases, but also of the novel's very understanding of life as a whole as it is embodied in the text's figural schemes. See especially Reuben Brower, "Something Central Which Permeated: Virginia Woolf and *Mrs. Dalloway*," in *Fields of Light* (New York: Oxford University Press, 1951), pp. 123–37; and Allen McLaurin's notion, drawn from Charles Mauron's preface to Fry's translation of Mallarmé, of *Mrs. Dalloway* as a "symbolic keyboard" (*Virginia Woolf: The Echoes Enslaved* [Cambridge: Cambridge University Press, 1973], pp. 149 ff.).

10. See Miller ("Virginia Woolf's All Souls' Day"), pp. 114–15.

Indeed, Woolf's novel is itself designed to be such a vessel or container of the world's common languages. Although "no mathematical instrument . . . could register the vibration" of "common appeal" that the mystic car sends through the crowd early in the novel (*MD*, 29), Woolf's prose turns out to be just such a seismographic "machine" built to monitor such "vibration" as it echoes or resonates through the labyrinthine pathways of public and private association represented by the novel's figural apparatus, and which the novel also doubles as a set of resonant linguistic pathways in its own right.

These figures or, really, metalanguages, are often organic ones, and suggest a vision of life as a pattern of connections "drawn out" on "every leaf on the trees" (*MD*, 12). Among these naturalizing figures may be included the patterned and patterning figures of "smoke" (*MD*, 7, 39, 126); "mesh" (*MD*, 10); "mist" (*MD*, 16, 258); "veins" (*MD*, 31); "waves" (*MD*, 61, 87); "branches" (*MD*, 87, 88); "leaves" (*MD*, 87, 210); "leaf" (*MD*, 100, 172); "trees" (*MD*, 100, 103, 210); "twig" (*MD*, 100); "nerve fibres" (*MD*, 104); "entrails" (*MD*, 200)—all of them signifying the movement or "vibration" from "branch to branch" (*MD*, 221) of these networks of networks.[11]

The patterning power of Woolf's networks is to be seen even more clearly in those figures of manmade patterns that are woven through the narrative, too, particularly the figures of fabric and of houses, both of which represent system and display its operations at the same time. Hence the "pink gauze" that Sally Seton "seemed" to wear at

---

11. Raymond Williams notes that George Eliot's "favourite metaphor for society is a network: a 'tangled skein'; a 'tangled web,' " suggesting an additional source for Woolf's figures in another of her principal precursors, at least from the point of view of the tradition of the novel. See *Culture and Society, 1780–1950* (rpt. New York: Harper Torchbooks, 1966), p. 108.

Bourton (*MD*, 54) not only represents the pathways of psychic association by which Clarissa's memory of her is put into operation, but also serves as the token of the memory itself. Similarly, the "transparent muslins" (*MD*, 10) of the dancing and "laughing girls" in Clarissa's fantasy of courtly parties early in the novel not only double "the soft mesh" of the "morning air" in which the fantasy unfolds as Clarissa walks through the park, but also render it, in a cluster of puns, a "mesh" of threads which, "as the day wore on, would unwind" (*MD*, 10).

The master tropes in this rhetorical thread of fabrics are the figures of "silk" and "folds" connected with Clarissa's "sewing" (*MD*, 61), which as an activity doubles the narrator's own propensity for weaving and threading the world together, and which is doubled in turn by the way Septimus's wife Rezia "must stitch" (*MD*, 216) her "sewing" (*MD*, 220) in an attempt to repair her married life. Indeed, even "our soul," thinks Peter on his way to the Dalloways' party, is always "threading" (*MD*, 242) its way through the pathways or "gauze" of memory and association, even though in this last instance the narrator mixes her metaphors by using the figure of fabric in tandem with a vision of watery depth ("our soul . . . fishlike inhabits deep seas and plies among obscurities threading her way" [*MD*, 242]). Thus, too, Richard Dalloway feels his attachment to Lady Bruton sustain itself after lunch "as a single spider's thread . . . attaches itself to the point of a leaf" (*MD*, 172). Here we should also include the "screen" (*MD*, 141, 211) that lies over the world for Septimus, as well as the "fine tissue" and "fine net" of "service" that "spread round" (*MD*, 163) Lady Bruton and her house, and which also double "that fibre which was the ramrod" of Lady Bruton's "soul" (*MD*, 164). Among the figure's permutations are to be included the

figure of the "curtain" (*MD*, 191, 253, 256), the "tissue" of
life (*MD*, 194), and the "string" of attachment (*MD*, 192).

Under the figure of the house fall a series of figures for
structure, too, among them the "innumerable bedrooms"
of Buckingham Palace (*MD*, 31) through whose corridors
messages of all kinds can circulate, even those barroom
insults that "echoed strangely across the way in the ears of
girls buying white underlinen threaded with pure white
ribbon for their weddings" (*MD*, 29), with this last figure
doubling and tripling within itself the threading operations
it describes. The movement of Peter's mind is described in
terms of a house, too, "as if inside his brain by another
hand strings were pulled, shutters moved" (*MD*, 80), while
the "swing doors" (*MD*, 158) in Lady Bruton's house signify the same movement of "service" as the "tissue" or
"net" that also describes it (*MD*, 163) and that represents
the same space of social interaction as the "swing doors"
of the florist (*MD*, 21) or the unhinged spaces of the
Dalloways' house (*MD*, 7) where the party will take place.

The novel's most literal organizing figure as well as its
most Joycean one is to be found in the streets of London
themselves. In a phrase like "the traffic hummed in a circle"
(*MD*, 39), the synesthetic movement from the traffic's
noise to the visual pattern of the "circle" which such
sounds make here and elsewhere in the novel (especially in
the "circles" of Big Ben's chimes) is also a movement from
one representation of systematicity to another, with the
rings of the "circle" simply a more fleeting cipher for the
kind of networks more concretely embodied by the pattern of London streets that maps out common pathways
throughout the novel. Characters, in fact, are often positioned at a moment of crossing (*MD*, 8, 26, 123, 174) as
the narrator uses this rather literal metaphor of roads and
junctions to suggest those points at which circuits of in-

fluence intersect to produce the puns and the transformations that designate the crossing of figural systems and the
conjunction of characters by means of them.[12]

All these figures taken together draw nothing less than
a "map of the world" (*MD*, 222), with the narrator's
allusions to Greenwich (*MD*, 43, 155) grounding her figure
much as the streets of London ground her notion of junctions and pathways in the network of the common life.
The figure of the map and the territory it represents and
organizes is a particularly resonant one given the way the
novel's interest in political economy and imperialism under-
lies all the mataphors of exchange, psychical and commer-
cial alike, of which life in *Mrs. Dalloway* is composed. In
order to address the role of politics in the novel, however,
we should look first at Septimus Warren Smith.

Septimus's difficulty, of course, is his inability, unlike
Clarissa, to compose his "parts" into the "one centre" of
a "self." To Septimus, "one centre" is a "horror" (*MD*,
24-25). Without discipline—without *ascesis*—he admits
into his world virtually all of the sympathies or currents of
being that most of us filter, select, and harmonize through
a blindness or a deferral necessary for the proper establishment of an ego. Thus Septimus is always in dissolution
("he was not Septimus now" [*MD*, 37]), since he fails to
position himself in the flux of influence that buffets him
with its overdetermined abundance. He "was always stop-
ping in the middle, changing his mind; wanting to add
something; hearing something new" (*MD*, 212). Despite
his claim that "he could not feel" (*MD*, 132), what troubles
him is that he feels too much:

12. Side by side with such concrete representations of systems are exceedingly abstract ones, too, particularly the narrator's lengthy aside late in the
novel that purports to describe the movement of the clouds in the sky, but
which is really a model for the behavior of systems as such (*MD*, 209-10).

he could not read the language yet; but it was plain
enough, this beauty, this exquisite beauty, and tears
filled his eyes as he looked at the smoke words lan-
guishing and melting in the sky and bestowing upon
him in their inexhaustible charity and laughing good-
ness one shape after another of unimaginable beauty
and signalling their intention to provide him, for
nothing, for ever, for looking merely, with beauty,
more beauty! Tears ran down his cheeks. [*MD*, 34–35]

Septimus, then, fails to sustain or perfect any particular
reading of life and so remains a diffuse and hazy locus of
the forces or languages that course and collide in a semantic field not proportioned into what custom calls a self.
Indeed, Septimus's many possible self-conceptions are
described in a litany akin to the one in "Street Haunting":

the most exalted of mankind; the criminal who faced
his judges; the victim exposed on the heights; the
fugitive; the drowned sailor; the poet of the immortal
ode; the Lord who had gone from life to death; to
Septimus Warren Smith, who sat in the arm-chair
under the skylight staring at a photograph of Lady
Bradshaw in Court dress, muttering messages about
beauty. [*MD*, 147]

"Every power," says the narrator, "poured its treasures on
his head" (*MD*, 210), with "avalanche" the equivalent
term from "A Sketch of the Past." These "treasures," of
course, include the "diamond" of selfhood, but Septimus
must let the gem that is Clarissa's prize elude his grasp.

Thus Clarissa is Septimus's "double,"[13] as Woolf puts it
in the novel's preface, only insofar as she possesses what he
lacks—a mirror image or "double" to provide him with

---

13. "Introduction" to *Mrs. Dalloway*, p. vi.

a sense of self. To the extent that Septimus attempts any
such identification at all, of course, it is with Evans, the
officer blown to bits in the war, and an image not of
wholeness but of fragmentation, of the body in pieces.

What the coercion of the doctors Holmes and Bradshaw
adds to our notion of the selfhood Septimus cannot
achieve is that the mapping or coordination of a self is also
to be understood in political terms. For not only is the
"capital" character of the "I" reflected in the notion of
ownership or possession embodied in the bourgeois figure
of the secure house; it is also reflected in the way the
settlement and rule of a territorial ego is a manifestly
imperialist activity to be located in the "tropic gale" in
Clarissa's "breast" (*MD*, 71) or in the company of the
"assembly of powers" (*MD*, 68) that marshal Peter the
Indian Army officer's mature life.

Indeed, much as the "Captain self" is above all a "good
citizen" in "Street Haunting," Clarissa's youthful desire to
"found a society to abolish private property" (*MD*, 52)
gives way in later years to her capital propensities as Mrs.
Dalloway, wife of a Conservative member of Parliament
and a hostess who takes pleasure in "being part" of imperial society, especially "since her people were courtiers
once in the time of the Georges" (*MD*, 10). Moreover,
Septimus's job before the war was as clerk for "land and
estate agents," "valuers," in short, of property (*MD*, 130).
Now, of course, the very notion of property is foreign to
him, and it is the job of the doctors Holmes and Bradshaw
to reeducate him in the ways of capitalist territory.

The doctors, of course, are "dominators" (*MD*, 20),
with Bradshaw's identification with the maintenance of
civil order and prosperity made explicit in the novel (*MD*,
150–51). Even his colonized wife is described as "wedged
on a calm ocean, where only spice winds blow" (*MD*, 143),

a kind of prisoner on a British frigate cruising for the
"spice" or "treasure" of the Indies. Here, too, we should
recall that Lady Bruton's power over her friends is the
power of a "spectral grenadier" (*MD*, 271) who "had the
thought of Empire always at hand" (*MD*, 272), and that
Peter's career imperialism only makes explicit those
dominating aspects of his personality that caused Clarissa
not to marry him. Of course, Clarissa's marriage to Richard
makes her nonetheless dependent on the "deposit" (*MD*,
46) of his affection, a figure that also points to the marital
bank account and the wealth of the colonies which sustains its value, all brought together in a harmonic triad of
meaning. Now even the "diamond" of Clarissa's self carries
with it the additional meaning of South African riches.

Thus the "dominion" and "power" (*MD*, 153) which
Bradshaw possesses bespeaks the properties necessary to
the rule of the capital "I." If Septimus will not colonize
himself (as Doris Kilman has), then it will have to be done
for him. Thus he becomes a fugitive in an imperialist landscape: "Holmes and Bradshaw are on you. They scour the
desert. They fly screaming into the wilderness" (*MD*, 148);
"their packs scour the desert" (*MD*, 136). Much as the
"bayonets" of London "pinioned" evening to the sky
(*MD*, 243), so the doctors' imperial "powers" will pinion
Septimus into a proper space of self whether he likes
it or not.

Septimus, however, refuses the "knife" (*MD*, 224) as
the instrument of his suicide, and thereby refuses all the
weaponry of imperialism, whether the "bayonet" or,
indeed, the "blade" (*MD*, 62) that Peter habitually fondles
throughout the novel. Indeed, if strong selfhood is a secure
house, then the manner of Septimus's death—"He had
thrown himself from a window" (*MD*, 277)—is a perfect

sign for what it is he abjures. The "mangled" (*MD*, 225) Septimus literalizes the de-forming ebb of Clarissa's identity as a movement "out of doors, out of the window" in order to deliver himself up to those "voices of the dead" (*MD*, 219) who represent, not only to him but to all the characters in the novel, the common life itself.

Nor is Woolf's concern with the common life and the status of the self within it confined to *Mrs. Dalloway*. Her characteristic figures for system dominate the rhetorical texture of all her novels and frequently serve, as they do in *Mrs. Dalloway*, among the books' chief organizing devices. And though there is some increasing sympathy for technological metaphor and the more overt priority it gives to system over self as the fiction progresses, Woolf's characteristic use of figure is largely the same early and late.

As a quest for structure both formally and thematically, *The Voyage Out* (1915) is everywhere concerned with the discovery of "pattern" (*VO*, 247, 385, 456). The narrator even uses the word "system" to designate the world of English society that nurtures Rachel Vinrace (*VO*, 34) and to describe the "two separate systems of life" (*VO*, 268) to be found at the Villa San Gervasio and the tourist hotel at Santa Marina, the South American resort where the book's major action takes place.

Rachel, of course, is loath to accept the artificial rigor of the "humming . . . machine" (*VO*, 48) by which Richard Dalloway represents the world of imperial commerce and international politics. She prefers instead to find order and meaning in what seems to her, as it does to Terence Hewet, the natural pattern of the "creepers," for example, "which knotted tree to tree" (*VO*, 331) in their journey up the Amazon, and which inspires the organizing and pacifying figure of "the immense umbrella of green above" (*VO*, 331) associated with the protective fullness of their love for one another late in the novel.

It is Helen Ambrose's "embroidery" (*VO*, 30, 89, 245, 379) that is the novel's master metaphor for its various systems of connection, weaving together the book's apparently disjoined concerns and mediating between the young lovers' desire for natural order and those artificial or conventional systems of order represented by Dalloway's "complicated machine" (*VO*, 72). Chief among the novel's figures for natural design are, as in *Mrs. Dalloway*, those of "trees," whose unifying function lies in the way they "mobbed their heads together in a row" (*VO*, 104–05) and whose "branches" (*VO*, 204), like the evening "mist" (*VO*, 247) at Santa Marina, represent the "bridge" (*VO*, 332) and "the ties that bind" (*VO*, 230) that Rachel wants so desperately to find between people and between the conflicting elements of her experience.

Among the book's figures for artificial order, on the other hand, is the familiar one of the dwelling: the ship *Euphrosyne*; the hotel with its "bedrooms . . . all on the same pattern" (*VO*, 308); or even the figurative "building" that rises up in the minds of the hotel guests when they are "ennobled" (*VO*, 196) by an evening of music and dancing. Other such figures include the "invisible chalk-marks" (*VO*, 175) of social classification; even the "plaiting" of "straw" (*VO*, 348) by Indian women in the Amazon, which doubles the culturizing pattern the narrator has already found in the way "a mountain stream . . . plaited itself into strands" (*VO*, 104).

In both cases, of course, what is represented is that which is held "in common" (*VO*, 73)—even "dreams," says the narrator, "went from one brain to another" (*VO*, 55)—whether it is union on a deep biological level like "the bottom of the sea" (*VO*, 416) associated with Rachel's illness;[14] or collectivity understood in a social and cultural way instead and associated with images of a surface or a text, like the edition of Pindar which Ridley Ambrose is preparing (*VO*, 200) or the history of English literature being written by Miss Allan (*VO*, 118). Indeed, almost interchangeable with the figures of foliage in their organizing function during the Amazonian voyage are the figures of texts—"books or pieces of paper" (*VO*, 327). Moreover, when the sewing and reading resumes in the hotel lobby following Rachel's death (*VO*, 451), it is community that is restored in the face of Rachel's complaint that "her heat and discomfort had put a gulf between her world and the ordinary world which she could not bridge" (*VO*, 401).

Rachel's particular quest for "pattern," of course, is her quest for self. Her lack of identity at the start of the novel is even described in terms of a "lack of . . . definite outline" in her "face" (*VO*, 14), as though her face is as yet "unmarked" (*VO*, 20) by the letter of character. Indeed, Rachel's failure to build up a whole and integrated self is cast in the familiar terms of the looking-glass, too: "In the glass," says the narrator, "she wore an expression of tense melancholy, for she had come to the depressing conclusion . . . that her face was not the face she wanted, and in all probability never would be" (*VO*, 41).

Hence Rachel is, to switch now to the implicit figure of the map, not "pinned down" and so "shifted her position" with "a gesture of weariness"[15] that already points to the failure both of nerve and identity signified by her death. In fact, when illness finally strikes her, Hewet "seemed to

14. See especially Naremore, *World Without A Self*, pp. 5–59.
15. This in a passage among the many that Woolf added to the first American edition of the novel in 1920 ([New York: George H. Doran, 1920], p. 215).

hear the shiver of broken glass"—the sound of a breaking mirror perhaps—which "left him sitting in the open air" (*VO,* 400). It is, however, Rachel who is left to drift once illness begins to carry her away from the world and from the problem of identity completely. With the breaking of the mirror, she returns to the undifferentiated chaos and lack of illusion represented by death.

Night and Day (1919), of course, is equally concerned with the question of self and community—it is, after all, manifestly a novel of youthful rebellion—although it is far more candid than *The Voyage Out* is about the way individual experience is to be situated within a field of relations held in common, even if Woolf has yet to articulate a structure to the common life as clearly as she will later on. Hence Mary Datchet lives within a "network of nerves" (*ND,* 78); Katharine Hilbery is "bound to earth by a million fibres" (*ND,* 317); Ralph Denham's mind is a circuitry made of "filament" (*ND,* 61). Indeed, when Mary and a friend part after lunch, they "part . . . on the strip of pavement among the different lines of traffic with a pleasant feeling that they were stepping once more into their separate places in the great and eternally moving pattern of human life" (*ND,* 79).

As in *Mrs. Dalloway,* the streets of London and its "traffic" are among the novel's principal organizing devices and among its principal representations for organization itself, with Mary and friend both securely placed within its field of common influence. For William Rodney, as for Katharine, it is largely literature that structures life, although the narrator is interested in literature here not so much as a system in its own right, but as a system capable of representing systematicity itself: "The books on his shelves were as orderly as regiments of soldiers" (*ND,* 70), she writes, suggesting how "books" organize William's "room" (*ND*, 70) or self, and how even the apparently benevolent order of literature is imperial ("regiments") in the exercise of its power.

Literature in fact is a primary systematic presence throughout the novel, with Katharine's grandfather, the poet Alardyce, presiding over the central scene of the action, the Hilbery household, even in death (the house, of course, is a veritable mausoleum, almost a caricature, however affectionate, of the "House Beautiful"), and providing the book with its pervasive metaphor of texuality as well as with the resonant activity of writing practiced by virtually all the novel's characters: mother's and daughter's biography of Alardyce himself; Rodney's plays and essays; Ralph's law articles and projected history of Disham; Mary's unfinished manuscript on government; Henry Otway's opera; Mr. Hilbery's law review. Indeed, life itself is often described in terms of writing and editing a text (Katharine "ran a bar through half her impressions, as one cancels a badly written sentence, having found the right one" [*ND*, 94]), or reading one ("The book of wisdom lay open," much as "the rules which should govern the behaviour of an unmarried woman are written in red ink, graved upon marble, . . . writing scored upon her heart" [*ND*, 329–30]).

In both a real and a figurative way, then, Katharine's "earliest conceptions of the world" are literary ones, and the names of the poets "made a kind of boundary to her vision of life, and played a considerable part in determining her scale of good and bad" (*ND*, 33). Although she turns to mathematics as an antidote and form of rebellion against her childhood confinement in poetry, it is the function of her central epiphany in the novel to show that mathematics and literature alike are systems or patterns

that provide "some arrangement of life" in an abstract
vision whose contours anticipate *The Waves:*

> Her mind, passing from Mary to Denham, from William
> to Cassandra, and from Denham to herself—if, as she
> rather doubted, Denham's state of mind was con-
> nected with herself—seemed to be tracing out the
> lines of some symmetrical pattern, some arrangement
> of life, which invested, if not herself, at least the
> others, not only with interest, but with a kind of
> tragic beauty. She had a fantastic picture of them
> upholding splendid palaces upon their bent backs.
> They were the lantern-bearers, whose lights, scattered
> among the crowd, wove a pattern, dissolving, joining,
> meeting again in combination. [*ND,* 331–32]

With the discovery of "pattern" again paramount and
consoling, the figures of sewing and knitting, too, are once
again to be found as indices of a notion of systems that
bind life together throughout the novel. Like Helen, Mrs.
Hilbery, the unifying matriarch of *Night and Day,* knits as
well as writes (*ND,* 103), while Cassandra, the cousin who
replaces Mary in the quartet of lovers, actually breeds
silkworms and manufactures silk (*ND,* 219). But even
these metaphors tend to be oblique next to the novel's
more overt figures for system as such. Although Mary
Datchet knits and writes, too (*ND,* 43–44, 281), she also
works for a feminist organization that has a "card-index,"
"files" (*ND,* 271), and "a large scale map of England
dotted with little pins tufted with differently coloured
plumes of hair according to their geographical position"
(*ND,* 269), " 'an enormous system of wires' " (*ND,* 269),
as Mr. Clacton, the group's male director, puts it. Indeed,
this rather literal figure of the map is also subject to
more plainly symbolic usage when the narrator describes

Katharine's attempt to sort out her affair with Ralph as an attempt "to consider their exact position upon the turbulent map of the emotions" (*ND*, 351). The map also returns us to London's "streets" and "traffic": "Katharine was once more irresistibly drawn to gaze upon an imaginary map of London, to follow the twists and turns of unnamed streets" (*ND*, 471), although "it concerned not different streets so much as different streams of thoughts" (*ND*, 284). Mary's "different trains of thought" (*ND*, 177) map out a system of rails, too, much as the implicitly metrical and musical figure of "the new scale of life" (*ND*, 274) with which Mary imagines the future suggests life to be composed of different measures or registers, different circuits or pathways of order, sometimes harmonic or coincident in their various calibrations, sometimes discordant.

If these are the novel's figures for artificial systems of order, its images of natural order are summed up by Mrs. Hilbery's image of the great tree, with roots that clutch deeply and with branches like those that represent "books" in the preface to *Mrs. Dalloway:*[16]

> even now, I seem to see myself stretching out my hands for another present from the great Fairy Tree whose boughs are still hung with enchanting toys, though they are rarer now, perhaps, and between the branches one sees no longer the blue sky, but the stars and the tops of the mountains. [*ND*, 147-48]

And if there seems to be some background discord in a natural image signifying a system of life whose chief properties for Mrs. Hilbery are often literary ones, it is largely resolved by the junction term of dictionary "leaves" (*ND*, 507), which the narrator deploys as a pun in the

16. "Introduction" to *Mrs. Dalloway*, p. vi.

novel's climactic scene when Mrs. Hilbery returns with a "mass of green" leaves (*ND*, 507) from Shakespeare's tomb at Stratford to resolve the lovers' muddle and to pair off the partners like Hymen or Oberon at play's end.

The moral of the tale, of course, is that life hereby imitates art, with the lovers' problems solved by nothing less —and nothing more—than the imitation of Shakespearean comedy. Here life chooses an image for itself among the many in its inventory, and constitutes its present order by means of its specular identification with the green world that precedes and inspires it.

What this immersion in systems disallows, however, is what Ralph calls " 'first hand' " experience (*ND*, 12), that modernist—and Paterian—faith which Katharine has earlier claimed to be her only vantage on "truth": "The only truth which she could discover," says the narrator, "was the truth of what she herself felt" (*ND*, 330). What Katharine and Ralph both feel, however, is often little more than a tangle or collision of the various systems of manners and emotion in which the novel's action is situated. With no real or authentic conclusion to their confusion possible, it is left to Mrs. Hilbery to gather the lovers together under the trope of comedy itself, and so grant to life a harmony and design available only in art.

Although a more overtly liberationist effort than *Night and Day* in its manner, *Jacob's Room* (1922) turns out to be more abundant in the customary figures, too. Although the accent falls heavily on images of natural pattern throughout the novel, some of them already possess a trace of culture: "shifting leaves" (*JR*, 30), with the pun that shifts "leaves" from a natural to a textual referent; "the trees bowing" (*JR*, 56) by the river Cam, perhaps in imitation of courtly manners at Cambridge; the "haze" (*JR*, 66) of the university seen from a distance at night; the "white mist" about the "spires" (*JR*, 120) of St. Paul's; the "branches" (*JR*, 145) of Gray's Inn; the "ebb and flow in our veins" (*JR*, 226); the Aeolian effect of the "wind" as it "roams through . . . twigs" and makes the "air . . . tremulous with breathing" (*JR*, 266) in evidence of some common life in the forest at large. What is interesting about this last description is that it is really a metaphor for London at night, "elastic with filaments" (*JR*, 266) in the "gauze of the air" (*JR*, 267). Nature and culture, in other words, are both systematic: "Only here—in Lombard Street and Fetter Lane and Bedford Square—each insect carries a globe of the world in his head, and the webs of the forest are schemes evolved for the smooth conduct of business" (*JR*, 266).

Thus the world of the novel—and the world into which Jacob Flanders emerges—is a "criss-cross of lines" (*JR*, 24), a "force rushing round geometrical patterns" (*JR*, 249); "flat like a puzzle" (*JR*, 24), but also "mist-wreathed; resonant" (*JR*, 24). Indeed, like the Paterian figure of the "lodging-house" in Cornwall at the start of the book, the world itself is laced with "resonant" or murmuring "pipes" (*JR*, 16) whose secret structure, in Woolf's profoundly deidealizing version of the metaphor, helps to sustain the life of the house in a rather direct and mundane way. Thus, too, the figure of "the corridors of his brain" (*JR*, 62) doubles the way the heart "travelled dark labyrinths" (*JR*, 110), and serves as a clue to the paradigmatic system of order and exchange the narrator finds in the London underground system (*JR*, 107), much as she finds it once again in the system of London streets (*JR*, 155). It is the opera, however, that provides her with a particularly resonant description of the systems she apprehends in life at large, and of the place there of the individual, who, by choosing or occupying any particular position within the network, must sacrifice a thousand other possible sympathies:

> Only to prevent us from being submerged by chaos, nature and society between them have arranged a system of classification which is simplicity itself; stalls, boxes, amphitheatre, gallery. The moulds are filled nightly. There is no need to distinguish details. But the difficulty remains—one has to choose. . . . Never was there a harsher necessity! or one which entails greater pain, more certain disaster; for wherever I seat myself, I die in exile. . . . [*JR*, 110–11]

Although Woolf wants to maintain the half-share that "nature" and "society" each put into "classification," the renunciations in nature and splendor alike that "classification" requires are made abundantly clear in the case of Cowan, Jacob's tutor at Cambridge, who acknowledges the part that system plays in order that knowledge (despite Woolf's just-discernible snicker in the background) be maintained:

> But Cowan sipped his port, his exaltation over, no longer the representative of Virgil. No, the builder, assessor, surveyor, rather; ruling lines between names, hanging lists above doors. Such is the fabric through which the light must shine, if shine it can—the light of all these languages, Chinese and Russian, Persian and Arabic, of symbols and figures, of history, of things that are known and things that are about to be known. [*JR*, 65–66]

Despite Woolf's wish to separate literature ("Virgil") and its hieratic prerogatives from questions of real estate and organization, all that is "known" is nonetheless figured here as a "fabric" of "language," "our stays and props" (*JR*, 150) as the narrator puts it later on: "These lace our days together. . . . And the notes accumulate. And the telephones ring. And everywhere we go wires and tubes surround us to carry the voices that try to penetrate" (*JR*, 150). Here Woolf almost ostentatiously alludes to the "Conclusion" to *The Renaissance* ("that thick wall of personality through which no real voice has ever pierced on its way to us" [*R*, 235]), although her plea for a bridge between self and world is already satisfied, as is Pater's, by the commonalty of the fabric ("lace"), harmonies ("notes"), or circuitry ("telephones," "wires and tubes") by which we represent the world to ourselves, even the "dream of a world" we spin in our "isolation" (*R*, 235). Even more than the house of "classification" represented by the opera, the "enormous mind" possessed by the British Museum is the novel's best emblem for the common life, "hoarded beyond the power of any single mind to possess it" (*JR*, 176), and a consummate figure for the power that allows culture to "continue" (*JR*, 178).

Thus anything individual is of necessity something already inserted within the "wires and tubes" of the "enormous mind" of culture as a whole: "When a child begins to read history one marvels," says the narrator, "sorrowfully, to hear him spell out in his new voice the ancient words" (*JR*, 159). There is, however, little alternative—even Jacob must position himself by means of the image of Virgil: "thankful to be home again in his place, in his line, holding up in his snug little mirror the image of Virgil, all rayed round" (*JR*, 65). And if the narrator's modernist lament for the apparent loss of a natural or original "voice" within these ineluctable systems tends to lose the pungency of its initial accent as the novel proceeds, one reason for it may lie in the book's interrogation

of what the meaning of "one's own impression" really is.
Hardly an informal or organic response to the world or to
a text, the meaning of "one's impression" in a strict sense
is recovered when the narrator uses the example of the
newspaper to suggest how "the impression" is no more
than the sheet or text on which the world leaves its trace:

> These pinkish and greenish newspapers are thin sheets
> of gelatine pressed nightly over the brain and heart of
> the world. They take the impression of the whole.
> [*JR*, 159]

Indeed, even the syntactical uncertainty as to whose property "one's impression" really is—the world's or the self's
—tends to suggest one's impression to be, quite literally
here, the impression or imprint that the world inscribes
upon one. Thus impressionism is really that activity
whereby "mind prints upon mind indelibly" (*JR*, 72),
with the world's trace rendering the individual himself
a text upon which the world has inscribed its own "impression." Even one's "own" experience or "impression,"
then, is a trace that is already there, a text to which one
actually comes belatedly. Instead of a mode of access to
immediate and original vision, impressionism is properly
the work of the texts the world inscribes in each of us
more or less in common.

To the Lighthouse (1927) is also threaded through and
through with the figures for system, pattern, and relation
that we have seen at work in Woolf's four earlier novels.
Mrs. Ramsay's knitting, of course, is the novel's master
metaphor, at least in Part I, with the "criss-cross of steel
needles" at the brown stocking's "mouth" (*TL*, 45)
a paradigm for the "fibre of being" (*TL*, 19) of which the

very "veils of civilisation" (*TL,* 54) are composed. Hence the "phantom net" (*TL,* 108) by which Mrs. Ramsay can plot the relation of harbor and boats at night, and which is doubled by the "map of the Hebrides" (*TL,* 175) that hangs in the house; hence, too, "this admirable fabric of the masculine intelligence, which ran up and down, crossed this way and that, like iron girders spanning the swaying fabric, upholding the world" (*TL,* 164). Indeed, even Mrs. Ramsay's face is closely associated with the structure of the stocking: "she twitched the stocking out, and all the fine gravings came drawn with steel instruments about her lips and forehead" (*TL,* 182). The solace and composure Mrs. Ramsay gains from her work even leads the narrator to liken her peace to the composure of nature itself, with the familiar images of cultural order now exchanged for natural ones: "she grew still like a tree which has been tossing and quivering and now, when the breeze falls, settles, leaf by leaf, into quiet" (*TL,* 182).

Of course, figures for natural order like the "tree" play a considerable role in the novel, too: "the intricacy of the twigs" (*TL,* 59); the "thorn in the tangle of . . . thought" (*TL,* 92); and, in a mixed metaphor in which natural and cultural orders comingle, "the draped branches" (*TL,* 115) of the Ramsays' garden at sunset. This shift or exchange of natural and cultural styles of order can even be seen as the narrator figures Mrs. Ramsay's momentary withdrawal from domestic life in terms of fabric, then flowers, then fabric again: "Mrs. Ramsay seemed to fold herself together, one petal closed in another, and the whole fabric fell in exhaustion upon itself" (*TL,* 64). Indeed, nature and culture alike provide systems in which the self is to be coordinated: Mrs. Ramsay, for example, "used the branches of the elm trees outside to help her to stabilise her position" (*TL,* 174), much as the men after dinner "were taking their bearings," thinks Lily Briscoe, as if "they had gone up on to the bridge of the ship" (*TL,* 174).

Chief among the novel's figures for cultural system are those of languages and codes like the "private code" and "secret language" (*TL,* 12) with which James Ramsay interprets the world even as a child, or like the text that Lily imagines will make the enigmatic Mrs. Ramsay comprehensible to her: "she imagined how in the chambers of the mind and heart of the woman who was, physically, touching her, were stood, like the treasures in the tombs of kings, tablets bearing sacred inscriptions, which if one could spell them out would teach one everything" (*TL,* 82). Significant here, too, is the figure of the alphabet which Mr. Ramsay uses to represent his intellectual failure and which the encyclopedist Bernard will exploit even further as a figure in *The Waves.*

Examples of such codes or languages also include the "code of behaviour" (*TL,* 142) to which Mrs. Ramsay silently appeals during a lull at dinner, as well as the different kinds of "language" (*TL,* 140) within language by which men and women, scientists and poets, try to speak to one another at table. The hope is that such a language will be the "same language" (*TL,* 140), although sometimes, of course, it is not, with the latter alternative creating the impression that "all" is "in scraps and fragments" (*TL,* 141). This Wastelander psychopathology of a world in pieces, however, is really to be interpreted as the collision or discord of fully articulated but different systems of "language" whose orders are largely unconscious. Hence a clash between them, as at the dinner party, may make the world appear to be an assemblage of discrete and unrelated parts when in fact such fragments are each links in chains whose interrelations determine the meaning of any piece or fragment within them.

Along with the stocking and the figures of language, texts, and codes, Lily's painting is the book's primary figure for structure or system, and, even more, it is the novel's primary image of itself. The purpose of Lily's project is in fact the same as the novel's—to make visible the lines of relation that compose the world. Thus "something she remembered in the relations of those lines cutting across, slicing down" (*TL*, 243) provides Lily in Part III with the "running nervous lines" (*TL*, 244) of her painting, which double, as she wishes them to, her perception of the world in Part I: "Looking along his beam," says the narrator of Lily's graphic relation to Mr. Bankes in "The Window," "she added to it her different ray" (*TL*, 79). That such a doubling of art and perception is *aesthesis* in Pater's full sense of the term goes, of course, without saying. The "question" may be put directly in terms of "some relation between those masses" (*TL*, 229), those "unrelated passions" (*TL*, 230) of the Ramsay family which Lily's painting will try to map out by grasping some relation between them.

The narrator's project in Part III, too, is the mapping or triangulation of the novel's hitherto "unrelated" landscape—house, bay, and lighthouse—and it produces the organizing figures of the "veil," "leaf" (*TL*, 285), "fabric," "gauze," and "mesh" (*TL*, 280), of the "sea . . . stretched like silk across the bay" (*TL*, 289). These triumphant figures for order signify the narrator's successful mapping or coordination of the novel's terrain, a success, like Lily's painting, to be related in turn to the expedition to the lighthouse.

Although the thematic possibilities of the Ramsays' voyage are too problematic and complex to pursue here at length, we may at least suggest them to be concerned with the problem of secure identity and self-positioning (the

children's Oedipal struggle with Mr. Ramsay during the
voyage and their apparent resolution of it by journey's end
would suggest as much in its own right). After all, the
aesthetic project of making visible the systems of relation
that organize life is also a project akin to self-making, to
the "bring[ing] . . . together" of "parts" (*TL*, 228), says
the narrator, and to the enclosure of "a space" (*TL*, 244).

Such self-settlement and positioning are necessary following the ruin of the house in "Time Passes," which, like
Septimus's defenestration, is a graphic cipher for the col-
lapse or dissolution of identity, even though here Woolf
addresses the problem in exceedingly abstract terms. In
Part II the narrator tells us of a general breakdown of the
specular machinery by which the self is normally constituted: if "the minds of men" are "mirrors" designed to
"assemble outwardly the scattered parts of the vision
within" (*TL*, 204), the reason "no image . . . comes readily
to hand bringing the night to order" (*TL*, 199) is that "the
mirror was broken" (*TL*, 208). All is eyeless, with "scarcely
anything left . . . by which one could say, 'This is he' or
'This is she' " (*TL*, 196).

Hence Lily's and the narrator's projects in Part III are
both attempts to regain the sense of order and secure self
enigmatically present in Part I, although to regain and re-
draw them with full awareness now of the systematic, if
tangled, relations by which placement and security are
constituted. In short, to make such a map of the world's
relations is to make visible the structures in which the
self emerges.

The cost of such awareness, however, lies in the same
renunciation of " 'first hand' " experience that we have seen
in *Night and Day,* and in the way the "new voice," as
Jacob's Room puts it, can "spell out" only "the ancient
words": "But what she wished to get hold of," says the

narrator of Lily, "was that very jar on the nerves, the thing
itself before it has been made anything" (TL, 297). Woolf,
however, is no Arnoldean—instead of "the thing itself,"
there is, of course, only one's "impression" of it, and in
this difference lies the difference between Mrs. Ramsay
dead (one's belated "impression" of the object) and alive
("the object as in itself it really is"). The death of Mrs.
Ramsay is the death of "the thing itself," which even in
life, as it turns out in retrospect, can only be read belatedly, in terms of the "impression" it makes. Like the
Petrarchan beloved in Shakespeare's ninety-eighth sonnet
(TL, 187), even the beloved Mrs. Ramsay is present
only through the trace or impression that signifies her
absence.

Thus Lily is burdened with that view of experience she
wishes to be free of: "as if she were caught up in one of
those habitual currents which after a certain time forms
experience in the mind, so that one repeats words without
being aware any longer who originally spoke them" (TL,
246). Indeed, Mrs. Ramsay is herself a victim of this same
uneasy experience in which "one repeats words" that are
neither one's own nor anyone else's one can specify:

> It will end. It will end, she said. It will come, it will
> come, when suddenly she added, We are in the hands
> of the Lord.
>
> But instantly she was annoyed with herself for say-
> ing that. Who had said it? not she; she had been
> trapped into saying something she did not mean. She
> looked up over her knitting . . . searching as she alone
> could search into her mind and heart, purifying out
> of existence that lie, any lie. [TL, 101]

Mrs. Ramsay's desire to "purify . . . out of existence that
lie, any lie" is, of course, as impossible an ideal as Pater's

—and Woolf's—to purge away all that is not properly the individual's, since all three are wishes to purify an existence whose very intelligibility is founded upon the residue or impurity of the trace. Hence Mrs. Ramsay is denied the priority and immediate relation to life that everyone in the novel wishes to assign to her as a means of accounting for her power to organize and compose. Like the rest of us, she, too, must be situated within a "cobweb of allusions."

What is gained in this loss, however, is a kind of supra-Paterian art in which systematicity itself is musically and semantically exploited thanks to the very thing that dooms original perception—repetition:

> She was not inventing; she was only trying to smooth out something she had been given years ago folded up; something she had seen. For in the rough and tumble of daily life, with all those children about, all those visitors, one had constantly a sense of repetition—of one thing falling where another had fallen, and so setting up an echo which chimed in the air and made it full of vibrations. [*TL*, 305]

From one point of view the sign of our belatedness as creatures who come to exist within systems erected before our individual births, repetition now becomes the compensatory principle of Woolf's art—"of one thing falling where another had fallen, and so setting up an echo which chimed in the air and made it full of vibrations."[17]

Ironically, *To the Lighthouse* is a far more abstract account of the way the self is situated in the common life than *The Waves* (1931), Woolf's apparently most oblique achievement. Here she is exceedingly concrete: "the streets

17. See also Fleishman (pp. 220 ff.) and McLaurin (pp. 117 ff.).

are laced together with telegraph wires. . . . London is now veiled" (*W*, 66). "My mind hums," says Bernard of the subliminal and structuring murmur of language itself, "with its veil of words for everything" (*W*, 127). Sensation, too, is a network of "membranes, webs of nerve" (*W*, 146). And in school, remembers Rhoda, "we sit herded together under maps of the entire world" (*W*, 35). Indeed, at the reunion late in the novel, Jinny, too, remembers school in terms of "maps" and "geography" (*W*, 135), in terms of the territorial classifications one must learn as a child. And, again as in *Mrs. Dalloway*, these global coordinates also function graphically as the "line" of connection between people: "How strange," says Bernard, "to feel the line that is spun from us lengthening its fine filament across the misty spaces of the intervening world. . . . Between us is this line" (*W*, 95).

Along with maps comes the figure of the text, too: "we decipher the hieroglyphs written on other people's faces," says Jinny, largely because the "common fund of experience" (*W*, 190) provides those grammars by which we may learn to read the languages of everyday life. Indeed, Louis's somewhat guilty reflections about the life of the businessman nonetheless express how the "I" is a function of what is held in common, and how self and system help to strengthen and determine one another:

> Clear-cut and unequivocal am I too. Yet a vast inheritance of experience is packed in me. I have lived thousands of years. . . . I, now a duke, now Plato, companion of Socrates; the tramp of dark men and yellow men migrating east, west, north and south; the eternal procession, women going with attaché cases down the Strand as they went once with pitchers to the Nile; all the furled and close-packed

leaves of my many-folded life are now summed in my
name; incised cleanly and barely on the sheet. . . .
I have helped by my assiduity and decision to score
those lines on the map there by which the different
parts of the world are laced together. [*W*, 181–82]

Using the figures of language and of colonial settlement
coterminously, Bernard even reminds us that "one cannot
despise these phrases laid like Roman roads across the
tumult of our lives, since they compel us to walk in step
like civilised people with the slow and measured tread of
policemen though one may be humming any nonsense
under one's breath at the same time" (*W*, 284). And, in
a dance episode resonant with Symbolist precedent, Jinny
uses the figure of the figure, of the building, and of the
fabric to say how "we are swept now into this large figure;
it holds us together; we cannot step outside its sinuous,
its hesitating, its abrupt, its perfectly encircling walls.
Our bodies, his hard, mine flowing, are pressed together
within its body; it holds us together; and then lengthening
out, in smooth, in sinuous folds, rolls us between it, on
and on" (*W*, 111).

Indeed, the descriptions of infancy at the start of the
novel, like those in "A Sketch of the Past," find the child
emerging into a world of preexistent systems out of which
he will be fashioned. "I am all fibre. All tremors shake me"
(*W*, 10), says the yet-unformed Louis. "I dance. I ripple,"
says Jinny. "I am thrown over you like a net of light"
(*W*, 12). In fact, as children, the six friends "melt into each
other with phrases. We are edged with mist," says Bernard
of the emerging nets on the periphery of childhood vision.
"We make an unsubstantial territory" (*W*, 14–15).

The self, in other words, is not yet mapped and pinioned to a spot in the landscape. Indeed, the landscape

itself has yet to be grasped as such by the child: "There is an order in this world," says Neville; "there are distinctions, there are differences in this world upon whose verge I step" (*W*, 20). Thus the child emerges into a world of "differences" by which order will be constituted, much as the primary level of meaning in the book's section prologues, and the level from which all other meaning is built, is the rather Paterian "difference" between "light" and "shadow" (*W*, 119).

"Thus," says Neville, "we spin round us infinitely fine filaments and construct a system. Plato and Shakespeare are included, also quite obscure people, people of no importance whatsoever" (*W*, 194). Of course, the "system" is largely given rather than created, and often the "lines twist and intersect . . . round us, wrapping us about" (*W*, 194). Stable selfhood means a disentanglement and coordination of these "lines" so that "now," according to Neville, "this room"—this particular self—"seems to me central. . . . Here we are centred" (*W*, 194).

The opposite of selfhood, of course, is shapelessness and fragmentation. "I am broken into separate pieces," says Rhoda in fear; "I am no longer one" (*W*, 114), even though a moment earlier she is "fixed" by the "immense pressure" of "the weight of centuries" (*W*, 114). "Everything," says Neville, "must be done to rebuke the horror of deformity" (*W*, 196).

Selfhood proper, on the other hand, is a specular achievement, as Jinny well knows:

> So I skip up the stairs past them, to the next landing, where the long glass hangs and I see myself entire. I see my body and head in one now; for even in this serge frock they are one, my body and my head. Look, when I move my head I ripple all down my

narrow body; even my thin legs ripple like a stalk in the wind. [*W,* 44]

Rhoda's experience of self is the same as Jinny's: "That is my face . . . in the looking-glass behind Susan's shoulder—that face is my face" (*W,* 45). And to see identity disappear: "I will duck behind her to hide it, for I am not here. I have no face" (*W,* 45). Even late in the novel the same rhythm is repeated: if Jinny sits "before a looking-glass" (*W,* 242), Rhoda counters with the claim, "I have no face" (*W,* 243), and attributes Jinny's "authority" and "fame" to the fact that she is "embedded in a substance made of repeated moments run together" (*W,* 243).

Indeed, the rootedness of achieved selfhood represented by Jinny's "stalk" suggests how, at times, the security of identity is so intoxicating that it can engender the illusion of a natural self as well as the conviction of autogenesis: "My roots," says Louis, "go down to the depths of the world" (*W,* 10); "I, Louis, I, who shall walk the earth these seventy years, am born entire" (*W,* 41). Hence "identity," as Bernard puts it in a figure reminiscent of Leslie Stephen, "becomes robust" (*W,* 282, 286); in a Paterian figure, "robust" identity is instead "the crystal, the globe of life as one calls it" (*W,* 280). "I am," says Bernard, "wedged into my place in the puzzle" (*W,* 236).

Without a self that is natural or autonomous—without a self beyond culture—we are left with Bernard's testimony that "one cannot live outside the machine for more perhaps," in a whimsical attempt at humor, "than half an hour" (*W,* 167). The "machine," of course, is "the rhythm, the throb" (*W,* 165) of life itself, precisely what the dead Percival, at least according to Bernard, "sees . . . no longer" (*W,* 165). Indeed, one section prologue suggests this "machine" to be the very "engine" (*W,* 117) that manufactures the order of nature itself, at least as the human eye construes it. Bernard even sums up the machine's many parts—"intestines" and "tongue," nature and culture compact—and includes among its primary components the body itself: "Muscles, nerves, intestines, blood-vessels, all that makes the coil and spring of our being, the unconscious hum of the engine, as well as the dart and flicker of the tongue" (W, 285). Indeed, when Louis describes the "engine" of the common life in terms of weaving and the image of "corn," Woolf even grazes the deindividuating moments of the "Conclusion" to The Renaissance: "I feel myself woven in and out of the long summers and winters that have made the corn flow and have frozen the streams" (W, 220).

Despite the apparent return to a more customary style of narrative in The Years (1937), the subjugation of the "I" to the systems out of which it emerges persists. With no central or organizing character, the novel is largely tied together by its recurrent use of those figures with which we are now familiar. As usual, these figures suggest how "each person," as Peggy puts it late in the novel, "had a certain line laid down in their minds" and how "one's mind must be criss-crossed," in a figure that recalls Mrs. Ramsay's stocking, "like the palm of one's hand" (Y, 386). There is, in short, something "generalised and solemn" (Y, 50) binding all life together. Even strangers appear as though "caught in a net of light" (Y, 260), a "net" whose structure is as regular and common as those of the doors and windows of London houses, all of which "repeated the same pattern" (Y, 333). Even the "repeated columns" (Y, 357) of Abercorn Terrace, the Pargiter mansion, represent through the figure of the house of which they are a part the way the generations are linked together as the novel moves forward in time, at least until "1913," when the house is sold. Other narrative gestures besides the customary figures accent the common life, too, chief among them the recurrent use of plurals, particularly in the prologues to each section of the narrative;[18] the omnipresence of anonymous street singers, organ grinders, and musicians, all of them recalling the female street-singer in *Mrs. Dalloway;* and the shifting status of personal pronouns that emerges in a close reading of virtually any passage in the novel.

Among the novel's images for natural order are to be included the "mist" (*Y,* 94, 113) and "smoke" (*Y,* 94, 95, 102) in the air in "1891" (sometimes it is "a fine grey veil" [*Y,* 102]); "veins" that "seemed to thread the cold mass" and a "tree" that "put forth branches" with "leaves" (*Y,* 142) in "1907"; "leaves" in "1908" (*Y,* 157) and "branches" (*Y,* 188) in "1910"; "leaves," "trees," "mist," "haze" (*Y,* 206) and "smoke" (*Y,* 207) in "1911"; a "stir of branches" in "1914" that suggests the way the "air" is "laden with murmurs" from a series of networks, cultural as well as natural, overtly signified here by "the rush of wheels" and the "song of a thrush" (*Y,* 258), much as "the murmur" is also signified by "mist" (*Y,* 297) later on in the same year. In "1918," "mist" is "a many-folded veil" that is "fine-meshed" (*Y,* 325). And in "Present Day," the narrator combines all these figures for largely natural systems with the artificial systems of the "traffic" and its "hum" to suggest a common life whose structure extends even to the galaxies as they shine behind "the leaves" (*Y,* 391–92).

With the motif of sewing and embroidering, the novel's images for system include overtly artificial ones, too. In

18. Here Woolf continues her use of a device Naremore points out as early as *The Voyage Out* (pp. 12 ff.).

"1880," Rose Pargiter in London and Kitty's mother in Oxford both work at embroidery (*Y, 26, 85*), while, even thirty years later, Maggie, too, is "stitching" and "sewing" (*Y, 200*), sometimes at a sewing "machine" (*Y, 183*) that provides a link, however inadvertent, with technological images for system like "the engine of the brain" (*Y, 249*), the "apparatus of the mind" (*Y, 350*), and the "engine" of the "mind" (*Y, 434*), all of which resemble in turn the circuitry of the telephone system that plays an increasingly organizing role in the lives of the characters as time proceeds and as the actual presence of technology increases along with it. Of course, even the "jagged roofs" of London as early as "1891" are "laced across and across with wires" (*Y, 119*) in a suggestion of the "customary, rhythmical" nature of life (*Y, 100*), much as in "1914" Martin feels as though "he had trod on a spring" (*Y, 268*) when the footman instantly opens the door at Kitty's.

Stitching and embroidering, meanwhile, are also linked to the narrator's use of cloth and fabric to suggest the systematic quality of life in the novel. Thus "the eternally burning city" is a "fiery gauze" (*Y, 138*) and the sky "a heavy canopy" (*Y, 205*) composed of "folds of silk" (*Y, 204*) like those that Maggie fashions into a dress. Eleanor, thinking of England, feels "as if she were slowly sinking into some fine mesh made of branches . . . and leaves hanging," as one figural system turns into another, "in a fretted pattern . . . like black lace with stars among them" (*Y, 223*). Thus, too, "Present Day" is linked with the past by means of a description of evening "as if a thin veil of gauze hung over it" (*Y, 329*), while "a floating banner of transparent silk" (*Y, 332*) adorns Oxford Street and signifies North's reentry into English society following his imperial sojourn in Africa. Peggy and Eleanor's cab, too, "threaded its way through the traffic" (*Y, 362*) of this same neighborhood, with "the traffic" a sign in its

turn for the ineluctable presence of systematic organization throughout the novel, and one that joins those images
of pathways to be found intersecting the fabric motif in
a figure like the following: "the smooth slope . . . rose and
fell like a breadth of green cloth striped with straight
brown paths" (*Y,* 259). Indeed, the "hot lanes" through
which Eleanor "jolted" (*Y,* 209) on her way to visit Morris
and his family in the country also signify the mnemic
pathways her mind follows into the past simultaneously
with her physical journey. For Kitty, meanwhile, "every
path through the woods" of her estate "had its name"
(*Y,* 299), while, in the case of North, the "background of
traffic noises, of wheels turning and brakes squeaking"
(*Y,* 341), represents the very system of English life from
which he feels alienated on his return home.

Linking with the figure of "traffic" is that of the wheel,
an image for a contained and centered system whose
appearance in the novel usually signifies order and coherence in the swirl of time and life. Hence Eleanor doodles
circular figures with spokes "raying out" (*Y,* 96, 189),
while the "statue of Queen Anne" is able "to preside over
the chaos" of London traffic because it manages "to
supply it with a centre, like the hub of a wheel" (*Y,* 243).
The identification of this hublike "centre" with the order
of British rule, of course, leads us to the figure of territory,
too, North's abandoned ranch in Africa, like Abel Pargiter's
service in India, serving as the grounding instances for
imperial metaphors in the novel. North even thinks of
going to the party that celebrates community at the
novel's close "as if he were riding to the relief of a be-
sieged garrison across a desert" (*Y,* 376).

The need for a center or for territory, of course, is the
need for a secure self, and, as usual, selfhood is by no
means a given in the novel. The sisters Maggie and Sara, for

example, wonder, "Am I that, or am I this? Are we one, or are we separate"? They wonder, in fact, "What's 'I'?" to begin with (*Y*, 150). Eleanor even wonders, like Lily, about the authorship of common texts like the prayers she says before bed ("who said them—when?" [*Y*, 166]), while Rose feels that she is "two different people at the same time" (*Y*, 180). Indeed, as Martin watches the crowd in the park, he feels himself "dispersed," wondering "what would the world be . . . without 'I' in it" (*Y*, 261). Even a momentary remark causes North to "seem different to himself" (*Y*, 397), while Eleanor late in the novel " 'can't describe,' " as she puts it, " 'my own life' " (*Y*, 398). Often, too, the same character is designated by more than a single name—Nicholas the Pole, for example, is known to everyone as Brown, while Sara is also Sally and Sal. Edward Pargiter's face as an old man is an emblem for how the "I" is fashioned by a collective history external to it: "He looked as if his face had been carved and graved," says the narrator in a reminiscence of Mrs. Ramsay, "by a multitude of fine instruments" (*Y*, 437).

It is, of course, the mirror alone that provides characters with a sense of self. Eleanor, for example, confirms her identity by a "glance" in the "looking-glass" (*Y*, 212-13), while Kitty changes her clothes in front of the mirror only to find that the change in her image causes her mind to become "a perfect blank for a moment," as though the circuits are jammed or overloaded during the interim between selves. "Where am I? she wondered. What am I doing? Where am I going?" (*Y*, 288). Thus, too, North, who feels profoundly insecure on his return home, confirms his identity by looking at himself "in the glass" (*Y*, 341) and at last generates some feeling about himself by looking at the image of a couple in love: "As he looked at them, some emotion about himself, about his own life, came over him" (*Y*, 401). Indeed, even the way he notes in the conversation of others "the tricks of speech that were caught at school and college" (*Y*, 435) suggests how one imitates images as a means of gaining a sense of self and location.

As usual, too, the wholeness of a self is an answer to the fear of fragmentation and deformity, the latter signified above all in the novel by the fingers missing from Abel Pargiter's hand. There are, of course, other such examples, whether the literal deformity of the violet-seller with "no nose" (*Y*, 253) or the metaphorical deformity of humanity as a whole during the war, which Eleanor notes, with a Platonic flourish, by thinking of people as "cripples in a cave" (*Y*, 320) during a bombardment of London in "1917."[19]

Such uneasiness about fragmentation also appears in North's feeling that "his mind was a jumble of odds and ends" (*Y*, 332), or in Peggy's awareness of the "odd little gusts of inconsecutive conversations" (*Y*, 415) at the party, although in both cases what is really signified is the collision of various systems whose knotted or tangled intersections obscure the chains that constitute them. Thus North experiences a "blank" or a "block" like Kitty's before the glass when "two thoughts had collided and had stopped the passage of the rest" (*Y*, 446). And in a contrasting moment of pleasure in the crossing of systems, Eleanor feels a sweep of light across the London sky to express "what she was feeling . . . as if another voice were speaking in another language" (*Y*, 323). The mixed metaphor, of course, is the most common example of such crossing or collision—a "picture," says the narrator in an exemplary mixture, "had swum to the surface" (*Y*, 361)— and, from a figural point of view, the paradigmatic example.

19. For a psychological account of the role of shape and shapelessness in Woolf, see Poole, *The Unknown Virginia Woolf*, pp. 56 ff.

The game North, Eleanor, and Renny play with the children at the party at the novel's close presents a graphic account of the way the self is collectively "drawn" together from a series of "odds and ends":

> Each of them had drawn a different part of a picture. On top there was a woman's head like Queen Alexandra, with a fuzz of little curls; then a bird's neck; the body of a tiger; and stout elephant's legs dressed in child's drawers completed the picture. [Y, 420]

The exercise gives Eleanor a curious kind of pleasure, and a glimpse into "a state of being" in which "this fractured world was whole" (Y, 420). Like the Paterian crystal, however, such wholeness signifies a centered perfection that is, strictly speaking, impossible in a world laced together by the inevitably mixed metaphors of life's various languages. Systematic though these languages may be, they tend nevertheless to collide, since each one differs from the next in the style of its knowledge and in the assumptions that characterize it.

Despite its lack of a manifest center, *Between the Acts* (1941), too, is laced together by those figures we have catalogued in all of Woolf's earlier fiction, and in fact gains its own organization by means of its meditation on the nature and possibility of organization itself. It is, of course, the systems of the past that are the most overt instances of system in the novel, and while they may be most apparent in Miss LaTrobe's kaleidoscopic trip through British history and literature in the pageant that functions, like Lily's painting or the books in *Night and Day,* as the most visible doubling text within the text proper, they are also a graphic part of the novel's very landscape. At the start of the book we are told that, from the air, the "scars" of Britons, Romans, and Elizabethans can be seen on the ground surrounding Pointz Hall (*BA*, 8), mapping the region as a surface much as (Wells's?) "Outline of History" (*BA*, 13), read by Mrs. Swithin, maps London vertically or archaeologically (as Julius Slater might have done), and causes her to think of "rhododendron forests in Piccadilly" (*BA*, 13).

Of course, there are also overtly textual, even literary, equivalents to these systems that make up what Isa calls " 'the burden that the past laid on me . . . in the cradle' " (*BA*, 182): the library at Pointz Hall; the snippets of poetry that Isa, like Mr. Ramsay, murmurs to herself throughout the narrative; even the way the servants "have taken indelibly the print of some three hundred years of customary behaviour" (*BA*, 35–36).

Woolf's habitual images for natural order are, of course, abundant, too: "smoke curled up to the nests of the rooks" (*BA*, 11); "flesh and blood . . . a mist" (*BA*, 33); "nets" of fish (*BA*, 37); "brambles" (*BA*, 112); "the many-veined transparent vine leaf" (*BA*, 136); above all, the triumphant figure of the humming tree at the close of the novel, in which it seems "as if each bird plucked," in a musical metaphor that is also a figure for circuitry, "a wire": "The tree became a rhapsody, a quivering cacophony, a whizz and vibrant rapture, branches, leaves, birds syllabling discordantly life, life, life" (*BA*, 245).

As is usual, too, these images of natural order are often associated with depth, particularly with the strata of history in Mrs. Swithin's book and with the "lily pond" (*BA*, 54) on the grounds of Pointz Hall, the latter including the elegiac resonance—and reference to *To the Lighthouse*—compact in "lily." A lady, in fact, "had drowned herself" in that "deep centre, in that black heart" (*BA*, 55). Marginal though it may seem, the lady's suicide—if that is what it is—carries with it a cautionary moral about the very status of natural figures in Woolf's fiction, particularly the figure of a natural self and the depth, or rootedness, associated with it. Naremore reminds us that the pervasive image of watery depths in Woolf's writing is usually associated with death and the loss of self, much as Mrs. Ramsay feels herself "losing personality" as she descends into her "wedge of darkness" (*TL,* 100) in *To the Lighthouse.* So with "looking-glass shame" deriving its guiltiness from its proximity to both narcissism and the prohibition against graven images, the "deep" pool in which the lady drowns recalls the pool of Narcissus for a particular reason. In an extension of the fate of Narcissus himself, the lady's death may well be a warning to all those who believe in the fatal illusion that something real is to be found behind the flat image. To take a trope for reality is frankly suicidal, an inadvertent confrontation with the death that lies beyond illusion. If the self is only an image, to test the waters of reflection is to risk keen disappointment and even extinction.

Woolf, of course, likes to imagine the world in the languages of depth and surface alike, although even in *Between the Acts* her images for deep or natural order tend to merge with images of order that are properly cultural or textual. In both cases, however, what is represented is what is held in common. The human counterpart to the "wire" "plucked" by the birds in the tree, for example, is the "wire" of attraction Isa feels between herself and the farmer Haines, "tingling, tangling, vibrating" (*BA,* 20) like the "thread of life" (*BA,* 24) in old Mr. Oliver, or like the "myriad of hair-thin ties into domesticity" (*BA,* 25) that Isa feels grounding and frustrating her at the same time. Indeed, the "thread" that unites Mrs. Manresa and Giles at lunch is both "visible" and "invisible, like those threads, now seen, now not, that unite trembling grass blades"

(*BA*, 69). Even the remembered image of Mr. Oliver's sister Lucy as a child "winding one long grass stalk round and round" (*BA*, 28) serves as a figure for the pathways of memory down which the old man winds himself—those "corridors and alleys" (*BA*, 14) of the past, as his sister imagines them—full of "strange echoes" and "reverberation" (*BA*, 42) like those that travel through the corridors of Pointz Hall, itself a witness to the systems of the past each of which has added something to its design.

With the figure of the thread, then, nature and culture comingle, too, with nature sometimes fabric-ated so as to make its qualities more readily visible. Hence "the strip of gauze laid upon the distant fields" (*BA*, 66); the "air . . . threaded with sensation" (*BA*, 70); the "invisible threads connecting the bodiless voices" (*BA*, 177) in the pageant; the "thread" of the Reverend Streatfield's "discourse" (even his name joins "street" and "field") by which he tries "to extend the protection of his cloth" (*BA*, 226); or "the random ribbons of birds' voices" (*BA*, 240).

These networks of relation are "the conglomeration of things" that "pressed you flat," although, in a mixed metaphor by which the narrator shifts from a logic of textual surface to one of biological depth, it also "held you fast, like a fish in water" (*BA*, 59). The narrator even uses a pun to link a military or imperial figure for order with a textual one, when Mr. Oliver, a former Indian officer, commands his dog to heel "as if he were commanding a regiment" (*BA*, 18) and then returns to his newspaper "to find his line in the column" (*BA*, 18).

Indeed, when life behaves the way Woolf's text does, the crossing of figural systems can produce the conviction that the world itself is in "scraps and fragments" (*BA*, 50, 251). Of course, such an impression is only the result once again of how mixed or tangled our languages are, like "the

old families who had all intermarried, and lay in their
deaths intertwisted, like the ivy roots, beneath the churchyard wall" (*BA*, 11). Even the scraps of singing in the
pageant or the scraps of conversation in the audience are
simply links in chains whose coils obscure one another
rather than evidence of a world in Eliotic ruins.

That all these systems within which personal identity
must be constellated are themselves no more than sets of
tropes or images is, of course, made abundantly clear when
Miss LaTrobe directs the players to confront the audience
with its own reflection in a series of giant mirrors. Like the
ancestral protraits in Pointz Hall, Mrs. Manresa's pocket
mirror reminds us that "the lady"—any lady, anybody at
all—"was a picture" (*BA*, 46), as Mrs. Manresa herself
takes the pageant's mirrors in stride by simply using them
to powder her nose afresh. Even Mrs. Swithin's notion of
herself as a Christian lies in the question, as her cross
swings about her neck, "How could she weight herself
down by that sleek symbol? How stamp herself, so volatile, so vagrant, with that image?" (*BA*, 90). Without such
a "stamp" or "print" or "symbol" with which to weight
oneself down, one is left volatile and vagrant, in the non-
position of the anonymous voice that says, "what I call
myself was still floating unattached, and didn't settle"
(*BA*, 175).

Like the montage of anonymous conversational fragments toward the pageant's close (*BA*, 230 ff.), the voice
without personality here accents the degree to which personality is embedded in a common life out of which it can
emerge only imperfectly with an identity uniquely its own.
Voice is neither personal nor unique, nor is it natural or,
strictly speaking, expressive, since its utterances are always
fashioned from materials which precede it and which it
only recombines, like so many bones from the tomb of

Marius's ancestors. No one, says another anonymous voice in the tangle of talk in the audience, " 'speaks with a single voice. None with a voice free from the old vibrations. Always I hear corrupt murmurs' " (*BA,* 183). It is, in short, "impossible . . . , even in the heart of the country, to be alone" (*BA,* 47). " 'We live in others,' " says Mrs. Swithin to William Dodge (*BA,* 86), although it is probably more accurate to say that others live in us. Like the "blurred carbon sheet" (*BA,* 184) that serves as a program for the play, all texts, "voice" included, are copies of texts, and all copies are "blurred," corrupt, tangled. As Miss LaTrobe's own history reminds us, "another play always lay behind the play she had just written" (*BA,* 78).

It is nonetheless the audience's increasing anxiety about Miss LaTrobe's unwillingness to come forward at pageant's end to take credit for the play that brings the question of personal identity into focus here as a question of authors and authorship. "Whom could they make responsible?" says the narrator. "Was there no one?" (*BA,* 227). What the audience wants is the reassuring answer of voice, of a personality responsible for, and in control of, the images that have passed before them. It is this reassuring answer that Miss LaTrobe, however, refuses to give; her absence is to be explained in terms of an aesthetic that outlaws the very categories of author and voice. Such an aesthetic also accounts for her use of the megaphone, like the gramophone, as a replacement or, really, as a clarification, for her own natural speaking voice, which is not to be confused with the intelligence that speaks within the play any more than it is to be confused with itself. Even the voices of the players are described as "the voice that was no one's voice" (*BA,* 211), the voice, in short, of the common life of art rather than of the individual actor or author whom the common life fashions. If, in the words of *A Room of*

One's Own, "the experience of the mass is behind the single voice," then, as "A Sketch of the Past" attests, "there is," properly speaking, "no Shakespeare, there is no Beethoven" (*MB,* 72).

As a literary critic, the system that interests Woolf most is language itself, particularly literary language, the neglected "medium," as she puts it in a 1927 essay on Forster's *Aspects of the Novel,* in which the writer works (*CE* II, 54). What is language like? Its behavior is best adduced in "Craftsmanship":

> When we travel on the Tube, for example, when we wait on the platform for a train, there, hung up in front of us, on an illuminated signboard, are the words 'Passing Russell Square.' We look at those words; we repeat them; we try to impress that useful fact upon our minds; the next train will pass Russell Square. We say over and over again as we pace. 'Passing Russell Square, passing Russell Square.' And then as we say them, the words shuffle and change, and we find ourselves saying, 'Passing away saith the world, passing away. . . . The leaves decay and fall, the vapours weep their burthen to the ground. Man comes. . . .' And then we wake up and find ourselves at King's Cross.
> Take another example. Written up opposite us in the railway carriage are the words: 'Do not lean out of the window.' At the first reading the useful meaning, the surface meaning, is conveyed; but soon, as we sit looking at the words, they shuffle, they change; and we begin saying, 'Windows, yes windows—casements opening on the foam of perilous seas in faery lands forlorn.' And before we know what we are

doing, we have leant out of the window; we are looking for Ruth in tears amid the alien corn. The penalty
for that is twenty pounds or a broken neck. (*CE* II,
245-46]

The reason words "shuffle," like a deck of cards, is that "it
is their nature not to express one simple statement but
a thousand possibilities" (*CE* II, 246). And if "it is the
nature of words to mean many things" (*CE* II, 247), it is
"because besides the surface meaning [they] contain . . .
so many sunken meanings":

> The word 'passing' suggested the transiency of things,
> the passing of time and the changes of human life.
> Then the word 'Russell' suggested the rustling of
> leaves and the skirt on a polished floor; also the ducal
> house of Bedford and half the history of England.
> Finally the word 'Square' brings in the sight, the
> shape of an actual square combined with some visual
> suggestion of the stark angularity of stucco. Thus one
> sentence of the simplest kind rouses the imagination,
> the memory, the eye and the ear—all combine in
> reading it.
>   But they combine—they combine unconsciously
> together. . . . In reading we have to allow the sunken
> meanings to remain sunken, suggested, not stated. . . .
> [*CE* II, 247-48]

And even though Woolf claims that "nobody knows" how
or why "words do this" (*CE* II, 248), she provides a clear
explanation for it in the following paragraph:

> Words, English words, are full of echoes, of memo-
> ries, of associations—naturally. They have been out
> and about, on people's lips, in their houses, in the
> streets, in the fields, for so many centuries. And that is

one of the chief difficulties in writing them to-day—
that they are so stored with meanings, with memories, that they have contracted so many famous
marriages. The splendid word 'incarnadine,' for
example—who can use it without remembering also
'multitudinous seas'? In the old days, of course, when
English was a new language, writers could invent new
words and use them. Nowadays it is easy enough to
invent new words—they spring to the lips whenever
we see a new sight or feel a new sensation—but we
cannot use them because the language is old. You
cannot use a brand new word in an old language because of the very obvious yet mysterious fact that
a word is not a single and separate entity, but part
of other words. It is not a word indeed until it is
part of a sentence. Words belong to each other,
although, of course, only a great writer knows that
the word 'incarnadine' belongs to 'multitudinous
seas.' To combine new words with old words is fatal
to the constitution of the sentence. In order to use
new words properly you would have to invent a
new language; and that, though no doubt we shall
come to it, is not at the moment our business. Our
business is to see what we can do with the English
language as it is. How can we combine the old words
in new orders so that they survive, so that they
create beauty, so that they tell the truth? That is the
question [*CE* II, 248-49]

These "stored . . . meanings" are what Woolf calls, in
a chemical figure like Pater's, the "deposit" that "remains
with us" when we read "a great book" (*CE* III, 127).
What this deposit is composed of, then, are those layers
of (unconsciously) retained or remembered meanings

sedimented in the minds of writers and readers alike, with the figure of the "deposit" or sediment joining three figural systems at once—chemistry, geology, and textuality—each of which Woolf can deploy to represent a recovery of the process involved. The figure of the "fossilised" or inscribed trace is probably the most familiar one in Pater and Woolf alike: "There is, to speak metaphorically," says Woolf at the start of "Phases of Fiction," "some design that has been traced upon our minds which reading brings to light" (*CE* II, 56). The same figure emerges in *A Room of One's Own,* too, even though Woolf wishes there to put the burden on "Nature" rather than on language as such: "Nature, in her most irrational mood, has traced in invisible ink on the walls of the mind a premonition which these great artists confirm; a sketch which only needs to be held to the fire of genius to become visible" (*ROO,* 108).

Woolf's most graphic representation of the trace or deposit, however, comes, fittingly enough, in her essay on influence, "The Leaning Tower," written during her work on *Between the Acts.* What is particularly ironic about the essay is that here Woolf berates the writers of her own generation for being copiers, for being "the unconscious inheritors of a great tradition" and therefore "aristocrats" whose influences are too much in books and too little in life: "Put a page of their writing under the magnifying-glass"—for literary criticism is, after all, detective work—"and you will see, far away in the distance, the Greeks, the Romans; coming nearer, the Elizabethans; coming nearer still, Dryden, Swift, Voltaire, Jane Austen, Dickens, Henry James" (*CE* II, 170).

Woolf even has a term in "The Leaning Tower" for this common bed of memory and influence that stamps, inscribes, impresses readers and writers alike with a shared competence in language. It is a surprisingly Germanic term—"the under-mind" (*CE* II, 166)—and, like Pater's "under-texture," it signifies a textual unconscious that serves as that layer of residue, to use Pater's word for Woolf's "deposit," that allows signification itself to emerge.

The way the trace or residue functions, however, is made clearest in a late passage in *Between the Acts:*

> The tune began; the first note meant a second; the second a third. Then down beneath a force was born in opposition; then another. On different levels they diverged. On different levels ourselves went forward; flower gathering some on the surface; others descending to wrestle with the meaning; but all comprehending; all enlisted. The whole population of the mind's immeasurable profundity came flocking; from the unprotected, the unskinned; and dawn rose; and azure; from chaos and cacophony measure; but not the melody of surface sound alone controlled it; but also the warring battle-plumed warriors straining asunder: To part? No. Compelled from the ends of the horizon; recalled from the edge of appalling crevasses; they crashed; solved; united. And some relaxed their fingers; and others uncrossed their legs. [*BA*, 220–21]

In this Paterian conceit of musical relationships, "not the melody of surface sound alone controlled it," of course, since for every "surface sound"—for every "first note"—there is a latent or murmuring sound against which the surface note positions itself as such, either harmonically or discordantly, although to tell which—to hear or read it at all—always requires a note already humming in the memory. This, in other words, is Woolf's version of Lucian's taxonomic exercise—there never can be, never was, a "first note" alone, a "surface sound" alone; there must always be a differential and deferring "under-texture" or "under-mind" functioning as a residue or permanent layer of memory against which every later utterance can be instantly compared so as to judge it syntactically appropriate or discordant, either in harmony or discord with what is already there.

Hence for Woolf, as for Pater, language signifies by means of the very residue that incandescence wishes to burn away. Woolf's "wholeness" and the "globe" that signifies it are as strictly impossible ideals as Pater's luminous crystal, founded as they are on the surplus they mean to refine out of existence. This residue or under-mind of language, moreover, is a paradigm for all those systems into which the individual emerges belatedly in Woolf's fiction, and the particular system into which a writer like Miss LaTrobe emerges in *Between the Acts*.

What makes the corrupt and belated nature of the writer's material doubly hazardous is that semantic discordance is built into the system, too. This is largely because, as Pater puts it, "figure . . . is rarely content to die to thought precisely at the right moment," but will also pick up "quite alien associations," leading to "the metaphor that is mixed in all our speech." Woolf's version of it comes in an essay on Turgenev: "the meaning goes on after the sound has stopped" (*CE* I, 247–48), and, as in the Tube, it will echo down "quite alien" pathways of association. Hence this semantic under-mind is to be located in those "regions," as Woolf puts it in "Phases of Fiction," "deep down in the mind where contradiction prevails" (*CE* II, 86).

What she has in mind here is less an unconscious pool of instinct, of course, than a linguistic or textual unconscious in which a word's semantic inventory, like a psychic memory trace, gets "stored." Here both semantic inventories and the various rhetorical devices that deploy their resources tend to cross and collide in their various ways of

knowing the world thanks to "the strange way," as Woolf
puts it in "The Narrow Bridge of Art," "in which things
that have no apparent connection are associated in [the
writer's] mind" (*CE* II, 222). And with the figure of
physical depth difficult to mix persuasively with the
figure of texts, among Woolf's principal mediatory representations for these unconscious and common pathways
are the labyrinthine, and Paterian, corridors of the "vast
building" (*CE* II, 161) of literature in "How It Strikes
A Contemporary," and the "old house" (*CE* II, 120) of
the English tradition in which the "most impressive" power
of all is, like Chaucer's, the "shaping power, the architect's power" (*CE* III, 14).

With all its contingencies, Woolf's notion of the trace or
under-mind also carries with it a prescriptive or evaluative
standard akin to Pater's notion of the strong writer as
"scholar," although her term for it is "rhythm" (*CE* II,
191), the "rhythm" (or really, harmony) by which the
writer orchestrates the systematic hazards of the language
in which he works in a reflection of the aesthetic virtues
that *To the Lighthouse* discovers in repetition. Thus,
with Chekhov:

> we need a very daring and alert sense of literature to
> make us hear the tune, and in particular those last
> notes which complete the harmony. Probably we
> have to read a great many stories before we feel, and
> the feeling is essential to our satisfaction, that we
> hold the parts together, and that Tchekhov was not
> merely rambling disconnectedly, but struck now this
> note, now that with intention, in order to complete
> his meaning. [*CE* I, 241]

In Shakespeare, the successful juxtaposition of images is
likewise figured as "striking two notes to make one chord"
(*CE* II, 241), although here the context is really painting,

since Woolf is writing on Walter Sickert, thus bringing to bear on writing the two principle Paterian analogues of music and the visual arts: "All great writers," says Woolf, "are great colourists, just as they are musicians into the bargain" (*CE* II, 241). Indeed, it is to the "best critics" that she grants these painterly and musical qualities, although their number here—Dryden, Hazlitt, Lamb—does not, of course, include Pater himself, even though what Woolf praises in her critics in particular is that they "were acutely aware of the mixture of elements"—the Paterian word for it is *Anders-streben* (*R,* 134)—"and wrote of literature with music and painting in their minds" (*CE* II, 242).

It is, moreover, rhythm, or really harmony, that accounts for the power of DeQuincey's "impassioned prose," too: "the train has been laid so deep beneath page after page and chapter after chapter that the single word when it is spoken is enough to start an explosion" (*CE* I, 166). Like the "train" or pathways of language, thought, and emotion in Woolf's novels, the train of DeQuincey's language provides his text with its own kind of (second-order) under-mind or under-texture against which particular words or phrases within it may, in a favorite word, "reverberate" (*CE* I, 170). Coleridge's words, too, "reverberate," and "buzz" in a "labyrinth" of prose like DeQuincey's, which the "reader's net" will hope to catch by becoming coincident with it (*CE* III, 217). And like Sterne, the writer may deploy (or the critic may hear) these reverberations "for some exquisite harmony or for some brilliant discord" (*CE* I, 98). Thus in great writing, says Woolf in "Phases of Fiction," "something is built up which is not the story itself" (*CE* II, 101), a "spectral architecture" (*CE* II, 77), as she puts it in Jane Austen's case, the "dome and column complete" (*CE* II, 101).

If a writer is strong, then, he will orchestrate the residue and discordances of the system in which he works, and, like a strong personality in Woolf's fiction, will strive to fortify and secure his position in the shifting flux of language and its perils. The wordsmith, in other words, needs to be tough-minded, almost a dictator, or at least an imperialist, in keeping his verbal constituency under control. For the Greeks, in fact, it is "only by collecting in companies"—already an implicitly military or imperial metaphor for their power—that "words . . . convey the meaning which each one separately is too weak to express" (*CE* I, 7). And in addition to the sign for literary power compact in "companies," there is also the recognition in it that literary language, like all language, cannot signify by the atom, by the single word, but only by its relations to other words (indeed, the same is true for the morpheme itself, although Woolf does not concern herself with this microscopic level of language). Thus by "the bold and running use of metaphor"—of that necessary relation of one term to another which gives each one its proper meaning and allows the poet to exploit the pathways that connect them—Aeschylus "will amplify," in a strictly stereophonic sense, "and give us, not the thing itself" (for words, like all the languages of life, are "impressions" of things rather than things themselves), "but the reverberation and reflection which, taken into his mind, the thing has made" (*CE* I, 7–8).

Despite the residue and the belatedness that are stipulated in the Greeks' very ability to deploy "reverberation" as a literary technique, Woolf, like Pater, has her myth of presence and beginnings in the Greeks, too. "The stable, the permanent, the original human being is to be found there" (*CE* I, 4), much as "Chaucer's pages" present us with the English equivalent, "the hardness and the freshness of an actual presence" (*CE* III, 9). "There are no schools," says Woolf in "On Not Knowing Greek," "no forerunners; no heirs" (*CE* I, 12). And yet the claim is also put into question by her equally Paterian insistence that behind Greek art there is, after all, an under-mind that forbids the retrospective belief in Greek originality and unmediated vision, "an ancient tradition of manners" (*CE* I, 13), even if there is not, as Pater himself insists in *Plato,* an ancient tradition behind it of literature and philosophy as well.

As we have already seen with Miss LaTrobe, of course, the notion of the artist's natural and original voice is an exceedingly problematic one given the under-mind and its common and already-given materials for self-making. When Woolf deploys the notion of "voice" to describe Meredith, for example, it is profoundly ironic: "to read Meredith is to be conscious of a packed and muscular mind; of a voice booming and reverberating with its own unmistakable accent" (*CE* I, 232). And yet just a few sentences earlier, Woolf has already ascribed the exuberance of Meredith's language—its very ability to reverberate as it does—to the "great ancestry behind it: we cannot," she says, "avoid all memory of Shakespeare" (*CE* I, 232). Thus Meredith's "unmistakable" personal "voice" is to be accounted for by its commerce with voices that are different from it. Unlike (the myth of) DeQuincey's language, which (supposedly) reverberates with the under-text of its own language alone, Meredith's reverberates with the under-text of texts not properly his own at all.

Hence the reoriginating modernist claim in "How It Strikes A Contemporary" that "we are sharply cut off from our predecessors" (*CE* II, 157) is a preposterous one given the hum of a "cobweb of allusions" even denser in post-Renaissance culture than in the Greek. Indeed, when

Woolf tries to account for her supposed rupture between present and past in the passage there which we have already examined under her modernist profile, her figures betray her into acknowledging, however unintentionally, a continuity in culture that is impossible to overlook: "A shift in the scale—the sudden slip of masses held in position for ages—has shaken the fabric from top to bottom, alienated us from the past and made us perhaps too vividly conscious of the present" (*CE* II, 157). Distant we surely are, but past and present are alike positioned in the weave of the same "fabric," in the first of a triply mixed metaphor for the history of culture. In the second metaphor, past and present are sounded, however discordantly, in or on the same "scale," channel, or measure by which utterances have always been sounded. Indeed, the third, geological figure ("slip of masses held in position for ages") even grants the qualities of culture a granite permanence more natural and abiding than those of nature itself.

It should be noted, too, that this "fabric" that represents history can also be folded in different ways by different interpreters, and so constitute the shape of history differently in the hands of each one. With residue a temporal necessity for the use of language, it is also a necessity for constituting the moment, and with a special consequence for the very making and coherence of history, whether the history of the individual or the history of literature. Writing again of Turgenev, Woolf notes that his "scene," as she puts in in a word synonymous with the moment in "A Sketch of the Past," "expands in the mind and lies there giving off fresh ideas, emotions, and pictures much as a moment in real life will sometimes only yield its meaning long after it has passed" (*CE* I, 247). Only "after it has passed," then, does the moment yield its meaning or become intelligible as such at all. Like the need for a second

note to make the first one audible or syntactic in retrospect, the (prior) moment here becomes significant only
later on, when some doubling or repetition of its elements
provides access to the trace it has unknowingly left behind.

The impossibility of direct and immediate experience,
however, is not the only consequence to be drawn from
such deferred action. What is even more important is that
what is early thereby comes into being through the action
of what comes later on. If the moment occurs only "after
it has passed," then one can rewrite or refold—indeed, one
has no choice but to rewrite or rearrange—literary history
to suit one's own belated needs.

If we wish to begin to draw conclusions about the way
Woolf herself is inclined to rewrite literary history for
personal purposes, let us see to what particular use she
puts her theory of the common life or under-mind. With
any writer a latecomer to the lineaments of a personality
he fashions out of materials not his own, we have seen
Woolf eager to insist, as she does in *Between the Acts*, on
the writer's consequent lack of "voice," originality—
indeed, of personality itself. And given the high price
Woolf bestows upon personality elsewhere in her criticism,
we can see how shocking and discordant a theory the
under-mind is when it allows her to situate all individuals
and all artists within so generalized a spectrum of influence
that, as Miss LaTrobe and "A Sketch of the Past" have
both indicated, it is hard to continue speaking of particular selves and particular authors at all in the process. What
advantage such a theory gives Woolf in her struggle with
Pater, however, emerges in "The Leaning Tower": "let us
always remember—influences are infinitely numerous;
writers are infinitely sensitive" (*CE* II, 163). And though
Woolf is willing to claim that there are indeed "families"
(*CE* II, 163) of influence, at the close of the essay she

wishes to elide all such distinctions in favor of a view of literature and culture in its widest and most deindividuating profile:

> Let us trespass at once. Literature is no one's private ground; literature is common ground. It is not cut up into nations; there are no wars there. Let us trespass freely and fearlessly and find our own way for ourselves. [*CE* II, 181]

What is striking here is Woolf's sudden and cavalier endorsement of literary trespassing or poaching, although it seems entirely justified, of course, by the modest remark that influences are "numerous," and that, as Pater himself says through Heine, there can be, strictly speaking, no plagiarism. Indeed, from this point of view the very condition of literature is the condition of influence itself. And yet what Woolf seems to gain by her apparently benign and sincere—and decidedly Paterian—theory of the common life is the right to steal under cover of a collectivist and only secondary critical stance. Whether this is theory alone, or theory motivated by strategy, we will leave to *Three Guineas* to determine.

Three Guineas, of course, is a diatribe against the male vice of "fighting" (*TG,* 14) and the values and ceremonies to which fighting is attached. Indeed, "fighting," as Woolf puts it late in the book, "is a sex characteristic which she," as a woman, "cannot share" (*TG,* 194). As "a woman," says Woolf, "I have no country" nor "the desire to impose 'our' civilization or 'our' dominion upon other people" (*TG,* 197–98). Thus the principal difference in a series that Woolf notes between men and women at the start of the book is that men enjoy the quest for dominion while women do not: "Obviously," she writes, "there is for you some glory, some necessity, some satisfaction in fighting which we have never felt or enjoyed" (*TG,* 14). This is true, of course, largely because women are accustomed to submitting to power rather than wielding it themselves. After all, they are the victims of that "form of slavery" known as the need "to depend upon a father" (*TG,* 31). And this straightforwardly psychological slavery on the level of the family has a literary or intellectual analogue, too, in "the most degrading of all servitudes," as Woolf calls it late in the book, "the intellectual servitude" (*TG,* 203) that is nowhere more evident than at Oxford and Cambridge, the best examples to be found of a patriarchal "society which, while professing to respect liberty, restricts it" (*TG,* 204).

Woolf's very argument, of course, is an attempt to throw off this yoke, to call for liberation from patriarchal influence in the name of "the influence which the educated man's daughter can exert now," that ability to make one's own living which is, in an ironically masculine characterization, "our new weapon" (*TG,* 32). Hence women must fight, too—"fighting together" (*TG,* 187) even against fascism is still fighting—even though women's deployment of the "weapon" of "influence" is presumably designed to issue, not in a new kind of power, but in a world where "competition would be abolished" (*TG,* 63). If men are proprietary, patriotic, dictatorial, women, by contrast, are internationalist, collectivist, and democratic. Thus women's new "influence" should be, strictly speaking, "disinterested" (*TG,* 32), for only in that way will they preserve what distinguishes them from men. In fact, the only way to adjudge truth of any kind, says Woolf, is to strip from the desire for knowledge its "power motive" (*TG,* 175) and so depose that male or imperial intelligence which is "intent upon scoring the floor of the earth with chalk marks, within whose mystic boundaries human beings are penned, rigidly, separately, artificially" (*TG*, 191).

Nonetheless, "they who have our new weapon," says Woolf, have a growing power of their own, "the influence of an independent opinion based upon an independent income, in their possession" (*TG*, 105). Possession, of course, is property, and what is *propre* is what is one's own. So even though the capital dominion of men is, like fighting, something women cannot share with them (*TG*, 194), Woolf still evaluates her position in society as a woman in terms of the dominion, or lack of it, represented by the figure of property itself:

> She will inform herself of the position of her sex and her class in the past. She will inform herself of the amount of land, wealth and property in the possession of her own sex and class in the present—how much of "England" in fact belongs to her. [*TG*, 195]

To be sure, Woolf is fully aware of such contradictions in her argument, and confronts them directly. In particular, she wishes to be careful about "encouraging the very qualities that we wish to prevent" (*TG*, 107). The clear and present danger, of course, is that "we may change our position from being the victims of the patriarchal system . . . to being the champions of the capitalist system." And even though this is "a thought not without its glamour" (*TG*, 123), it would mean accepting "the same conditions," untenable as they are, that men accept (*TG*, 127). "It is," in short, "a choice of evils." (*TG*, 135).

Which "evil"—servitude or property—does Woolf choose? Clearly it is the latter, although it is pursued under the familiar guise of collectivism. In her very zeal to do away with struggle, competition, war, and fascism, Woolf covertly deploys their very methods. Recalling, for exam-

ple, that it was "the lady who could not earn money"
according to the psychopathology of the Victorian household, "the lady," says Woolf, "must be killed" (*TG*, 242).
And in order to rid the air of the odor of struggle which
the word "feminist" happens to carry with it ("Since the
only right, the right to earn a living, has been won," says
a proprietary and bourgeois Woolf, "the word no longer
has a meaning"), Woolf recommends a "new ceremony,"
although it is a far more fearful one than many of the
masculine ceremonies it is designed to replace or supersede. It is the ceremony of word-burning, of burning the
word "feminist" itself: "Let us write that word in large
black letters on a sheet of foolscap," says Woolf, "then
solemnly apply a match to the paper. Look, how it burns!"
(*TG*, 184).

Like the murder of the lady, word-burning is a decidedly
Stalinist means of dealing with opponents, a genuine
attempt at censorship by which memory or record is to be
obliterated. Besides, no one can burn a word anyway, since
words are not things, as Woolf assures us, but brainwaves
set "tolling in memory" (*TG*, 190). Of course, earlier
Woolf has already recommended burning the colleges
down as recompense for their sexist policies, although she
has also assured us there that the idea originates, not with
her, but with "the late head master of Eton, the present
Dean of Durham" (*TG*, 66). She assures us, in other
words, that such violent and fascistic recommendations
can only emanate from the male desire to dominate, a desire alien to women, says Woolf, who forwards her own
imperial designs under cover.

Despite the disguises, then, women are finally no different from men at all since fighting is a "sex characteri-
istic" applicable, as it turns out, to men and women alike.
What, then, distinguishes men from women? Apparently
nothing at all:

> Such is the inconceivable licence of the profession of
> letters that any daughter of an educated man may use
> a man's name—say George Eliot or George Sand—with
> the result that an editor or a publisher, unlike the
> authorities in Whitehall, can detect no difference in
> the scent or savour of a manuscript, or even know
> for certain whether the writer is married or not.
> [*TG*, 163–64]

Where, then, is the difference between men and women
that Woolf insists upon? What in fact is signified by sex?
The answer lies in Woolf's strongest, in fact her only
authentic, liberationist assertion in all of *Three Guineas*,
and yet it is the one that she refuses to exploit:

> What reason or what emotion can make us hesitate to
> become members of a society whose aims we approve,
> to whose funds we have contributed? It may be
> neither reason nor emotion, but something more pro-
> found and fundamental than either. It may be differ-
> ence. Different we are, as facts have proved, both in
> sex and in education. [*TG*, 188]

The only difference between men and women, then, is
difference itself. Even the cultural "difference" between
men and women in terms of "education" is, of course,
itself a product of the more originary difference between
men and women as such. Difference, after all, is "more
profound and fundamental" than either "reason" or "emotion." It precedes them both, just as Pater's originary
aesthetic difference, like Woolf's in "A Sketch of the
Past," precedes all its manifestations as the very condition
of their unfolding. The pure difference, if we can mix
a metaphor, of sexuality itself has that function for Woolf.
And fond as she is of watery depths and the image of
nature, such an originary difference emerges, fittingly

enough, as a biological one, in the pure but constitutive difference between the sexes.

Nonetheless, of course, sex as such is only a differential or figurative quality: even when Orlando's sex changes, it is the mirror that confirms and inscribes the new identity as an image in her mind (*O*, 127). With "difference" the reigning principle in Woolf as well as Pater, there can be no natural or inherent characteristics of any kind, even between the sexes, because all character, all language, even the language of sexuality, emerges by means of a difference from itself. Indeed, in Woolf's other long prose work of this period, the biography of Roger Fry, such a differential notion of culture is central to Fry's aesthetic, and Woolf cites a paragraph from his unpublished papers in which he makes this anti-Arnoldean position abundantly clear by distinguishing it, in his recollection of an Apostolic discussion, from Oliver Strachey's and Leonard Woolf's inability to shake off their common belief in inherence or essence:

> They could not accept the complete relativity of everything to human nature and the impossibility of talking at all about things in themselves. It's curious how difficult it is to root out that mediaeval habit of thinking of 'substances' of things existing apart from all relations, and yet really they have no possible meanings. [*RF*, 270]

Of course, one of the principal consequences of difference, as *Between the Acts* has made abundantly clear, is to release the artist into a common life of literature, with the notion of literary property and selfhood subject to revision at the hands of Woolf's deindividuating argument. Indeed, it is just such a notion of literature that inspires the peroration at the close of *Three Guineas*, and that provides the book with its most generous and commanding vision. We should "listen not to the bark of the guns," writes Woolf,

> but to the voices of the poets, answering each other, assuring us of a unity that rubs out divisions as if they were chalk marks only; to discuss with you the capacity of the human spirit to overflow boundaries and make unity out of multiplicity. But that would be to dream—to dream the recurring dream that has haunted the human mind since the beginning of time; the dream of peace, the dream of freedom. [*TG,* 259]

Here the exemplary individuality of the poet is exchanged for an exemplary commonalty in which the poet's assurance, like that of women, that culture "rubs out" divisions and overflows boundaries succeeds in rubbing out his own individuality, too. As the representative of the common life, the poet thereby succeeds in erasing those "chalk marks" or boundaries inscribed by the patriarchy as the very signature of its power, and in joining women in their collectivist and internationalist crusade. Literature, in other words, is beyond the petty politics of property and boundary-making inhabited by the patriarch, a "common ground" free altogether from the rules of capital and the combat associated with it.

And yet by insisting on power and weaponry for the educated man's daughter in the same moment in which she insists on collectivism and common property, Woolf's own struggle against the patriarchy means nothing less than the erection of new commandments and new moral requirements the search and struggle for which are best expressed by Antigone's desire "not to break the laws," as Woolf puts it, "but to find the law" (*TG,* 250). Despite the Greek context, this latter alternative carries with it a new Mosaic imperative—an answering set of "shall nots" to the patriarchy's (*TG,* 190)—every bit as militant and proprietary as the imperialism it wishes to overthrow. Indeed, Woolf here becomes the lawmaker in her own right, the father of her self, although what this new law is and how she succeeds in subduing it to her own purposes remains to be seen.

If *Three Guineas* is a polemic of property and power for Woolf as woman writer instead of a plain defense of the common life and its common ground, what it needs is a theory of political action that will keep her from "fighting" out in the open like men, but that will nonetheless secure for her the power and position she wishes to achieve. "Therefore let us define culture for our purposes," says Woolf, "as the disinterested pursuit of reading and writing the English language" (*TG*, 164–65). This is "mental chastity" (*TG*, 150), and if the notion carries with it an ironic suggestion of the "monastic" aspects of dread Oxbridge, it also has the more straightforwardly Paterian requirement that, "if you are an artist," your work must be done "for the sake of the art" alone (*TG*, 146). Indeed, the very rhythm and accents of Woolf's argument here are unmistakably Paterian. To rid culture of that falsification " 'by admixture' " known as "adultery of the brain" (*TG*, 170) is an "intellectual liberty" that "may be defined for our purposes," says Woolf, "as the right to say or write what you think in your own words, and in your own way" (*TG*, 165). Thus the "disinterested" stance will issue in the possibility of stasis or incandescence, in that luminous expressiveness achieved by burning away the "admixture" of what is alien to "reading and writing" alike, and which will thereby secure that Paterian ideal denied to the woman writer in *A Room of One's Own*, who is impeded there by the kinetic emotions of fear and anger.

In *Three Guineas,* by contrast, Woolf has apparently burned away such fear and anger—violence, after all, is a "sex characteristic" peculiar to men alone. The reason, of course, lies in the fact that she has at last discovered a political stance consistent with the nonactive and contemplative requirements of Paterian disinterestedness. To this new disinterestedness, Woolf gives the name "indifference" (*TG*, 194 ff.), a strict refusal by women to participate at all in the patriarchal systems of the "private house" and of capitalism alike.

And what is indifference? It is the ideal state to which Gaston aspires (*GL*, 35), and which he sees embodied in Ronsard (*GL*, 67), in Montaigne (*GL*, 99), and, most perfectly, in Bruno (*GL*, 143). As Marius's ideal, too (*M*, 229), it is the ethical counterpart to incandescence, a benign and indifferent stasis on the level of conduct itself, plainly aristocratic on the one hand and, on the other, the stance really of the scientist or objective critic who weighs and balances without getting involved.

Hence Woolf steals Pater's own ideal out from under him, claiming the very virtues that Pater here celebrates to be impossible for the male, whose quest for dominion would supposedly inauthenticate even the monastic ecstasies of Bruno, Marius, or Pater himself, reserving them all instead for Virginia Woolf to claim as her own—as "women's"—belatedly. And, of course, to carry out this literary theft, emblematic as it is of her entire relation to Pater, Woolf must do violence to the anti-imperialist argument that justifies it, since women deserve or earn their "disinterestedness" because they are opposed, by their very nature, to that patriarchal imperialism and property-seeking by which Woolf wins it for them here.[20]

20. There is even a literal trace or clue to the contradictions or impurities of argument at work here in the fact that "mental chastity" is as impossible an ideal for the individual as it is for the languages of the common life themselves. Culture itself functions, after all, by means of the impurity of the trace, by means of the "baser element" or residue which difference requires. Woolf and Pater alike want to elide difference by means of the impossible chastity of "indifference" in order to preserve their naturalizing and quasi-religious notions of the artist in the paradox of his isolation.

So Woolf needs another recourse, another line of defense, a means of erasing or eradicating—of censoring or blotting out—this entire imperial drama, this outlawry by which, as in political imperialism, outlawry itself becomes the law. We haven't far to look, of course, since by now it should be clear that Woolf deploys her theory of the common life for a particular political purpose. What Woolf gains by the common life is a vision of literature without authors and without the need for servitude to a father, an author-rity, among them. What she gains by it, in short, is the claim that there is no literary authority, no single author from whom her own vision might descend, for in the common life there are no authors at all. To look to the past for lines of connection or tracks of influence is therefore impossible, since Woolf has completely rewritten the map of authors and influence as we know it by jettisoning the usual categories by which the map is constituted.

What is most surprising, however, is that even the strategy by which Woolf steals indifference away from Pater is Pater's own. Indeed, it is Woolf's habit to interpret Pater more fully than he interprets himself, absorbing him simply by following out his own instructions, by choosing a latent and deindividuating Pater to counteract the manifest one who celebrates personality and property. In rejecting the "I," Woolf takes Pater at his word, taking one tenet of his work as a means of dissolving the more visible influence of the other, and thereby retaining the precursor and discarding him in one and the same gesture. What is gained under the common life, of course, is the literal erasure—the rubbing out or censorship—of these very operations, since the category of personality by which they are to be tracked or understood is suddenly refined out of existence.

Indeed, with her theory of the common life far more pronounced than its counterpart in Pater, and with the status of the "I" correspondingly subject to more overt deindividuation, too, Woolf helps Pater to see what he wishes not to, the dissolution of his own personality. In fact, Woolf quite literally deepens Pater in order to sink him by extending his figures of archaeology and geology into the figure of full depth, particularly those watery depths that signify selflessness and that provide a destructive element of absorption and effacement into which Woolf can submit and submerge the whole world. As her most prominent deviation from Pater, the figure of biological depth is therefore Woolf's consummate out-Patering—outfathering—of the deindividuating Pater of the "Conclusion," who extends his own vision to a scientific as well as a Heraclitean flux beyond language upon which language inscribes its design so as to colonize and control it. Despite the epistemological dangers of valorizing the images of nature to be found in Woolfian depth, as a trope depth allows Woolf to make this dimension of Pater literally more profound in order to swallow him up in his own consequences.

Thus Woolf overcomes Pater much as she imagines the ego to overcome the world and so establish its authority over it: by absorbing influence through a process of difference and deferral, and thereby rendering those early and determining experiences of influence legible only through the traces they leave. Like Marius at his family mausoleum, Woolf, too, is a proprietary Paterian who rearranges her dead, who reinterprets or reconstellates the trace later on by dislodging it from the telltale sphere of personality in which it resides in order to replace it in the deindividuating air of the common life, thereby relieving it of its determining power by both de-identifying it and dissolving the very logic of its strength.

So behind the wonderfully democratic sentiment, and sentimentality, of a phrase like "literature is common

ground" lies an equally imperial economy of gain and loss
that may well produce the strategy of democratic vision to
begin with. To obliterate the category of the author as
Woolf does is fair and reasonable criticism from one point
of view. But when it is a theory of literature uttered in the
belated retrospect of modernism, it looms ever more strategic as a concept, touting collectivist goals while silently
pursuing proprietary ones.

For Woolf, then, the very means by which she acknowledges influence is the means by which she dissolves any
real or particular claims it may have on her. If Montaigne's
phrases form as literal an under-text for Pascal as Pater's do
for Woolf, that is not, as the theory of the common life
would have it, because the later writer is indebted to the
earlier one, but because, in an expansive reinterpretation
of the Paterian position, the very condition of literature
is a condition of influence which disallows the very categories of author, originality, and indebtedness. Indeed,
Woolf's strategy for a power of her own is not Pater's
alone, or even Pater's at all, since it is the strategy, as she
puts it in *Three Guineas,* of "the boldest of Victorian
sons and daughters" whose mission it is "to cheat the
father, to deceive the father, and then to fly from the
father" (*TG*, 244).

By her own implicit testimony, then, Woolf secures her
own authority by liberation from two fathers in sequence,
and from the literary father only after he has secured her
liberation from the legal or biological father. Indeed,
Woolf's specular origins are really to be figured as one
paternal image superimposed upon another, and both in
turn dissolved, erased, or broken (depending on which of
Woolf's figurative languages we use to describe the process)
by their immersion, insertion, or shattering in the ironically
destructive element of the common life itself.

To imitate Pater well means to outwit him, to overcome his influence by extending his various visions to their logical conclusions in the three different registers or waves of Woolfian assault that we have charted over the course of our discussion. We might call these three waves or registers of denial personality, sexuality, and textuality, and assign to each in turn the corresponding functions of displacement, distortion, and absorption or sublimation. With the theft of personality and the moment comes the covering injunction to rely on the truth of one's own impression and so deny all influence and priority in the name of the originating power of the self and the "right" of the "new" that accompanies and justifies it. Here Pater really displaces himself as an influence by being the very token or action of the influence he means to have, testimony at once to the glory of his manifest project and to the sorrows of its necessary and subsequent effacement at the hands of strong disciples like Woolf, Joyce, or Yeats.

With sexuality comes Woolf's wholesale revision of the initial Paterian project of expressiveness and self-realization into a model for the formulation and formalization of female letters as an adversary aesthetic enterprise. If the truth of personality neutralizes Pater's influence in the very exercise of his recommendations, sexuality neutralizes it by stealing from the literary patriarchy one of the principal—albeit disreputable—weapons in its arsenal, and so turning or distorting what Woolf takes to be a masculine cult of personality and the "I" into the basis of a female vision to rival and overturn it, guerilla or saboteurlike, by blowing up the enemy camp from within, using its own weapons.

And following the partial and uneasy victories of displacement by personality and distortion by sexuality comes the claim that all literature is influence and that

literature itself is common ground. This is still to interpret
Pater, of course, but it is to interpret him where he is least
himself. By unraveling what is already latent and potentially
self-destructive in the precursor, Woolf refines him out of
existence by using his own logic against him. If Pater subverts the individual by difference, Woolf subverts difference by using it to do what it properly cannot—to reinsti-
tutionalize and revitalize personality itself, particularly the
personality of Virginia Woolf, which wields its new strength
and power under the misleading trope of sex.

For Woolf, then, literature is common ground because it
allows her to trespass and to expropriate without paying
the price in unacknowledged influence. It allows her to
seize and colonize a territory not properly her own and so
build up on it a "new house" (*TG,* 152), as she puts it in
Three Guineas, even as she proceeds with—and even as the
result of—her argument for a free and equal distribution of
goods in a world where private property and imperial
power have supposedly been abolished. The gain to be had
in Woolf's defensive system of self-accounting (what we
might call keeping two sets of books at once) is to rout
Pater by routing the notion of literary property itself,
thereby absolving her theft of the Paterian fire by dis-
assembling the very world it fashions. In Woolf's hands,
the tools of its power are also the tools of its disassemblage,
even though they are thereby, paradoxically, the tools of
her new and greater power.

By her compensatory economy, then, Woolf has also
succeeded in bracketing entirely the question and problem
of authority as a whole, overcoming all authority whatsoever by dissolving the very categories by which it, too, is
constituted and distributed in literature. Much as Woolf's
Paterian vision of incandescence and the stance and vocabulary that accompany it protect and secure her from the
threat of strong contemporaries, so in an even more power-

ful extension of Pater in his deindividuating profile can she secure herself from the threat of the past as well.

The risk Virginia Woolf runs, however, is the one to which Pater shrewdly tries to blind himself: the risk of dissolving one's own personality. Although the vision of a world without a self is, for all its ironies, a characteristically Woolfian one, it should nonetheless caution the assurance with which we speak of her, or, indeed, of Pater, as real and coherent voices. In fact, not only are we left with a question about the relative degree of consciousness and unconsciousness with which Woolf approaches or adjudges her various relations to Pater. We are left with the more fundamental question of the stability and coherence, as Woolf and Pater alike remind us, of the notions of author and personality as such. It would be reassuring to say that what we have uncovered here is a drama of conscious, or even unconscious, repression and distortion by Woolf of a decisive influence resolved over the course of her career. But although *Three Guineas* and *Between the Acts*, for example, are both late works, one asserts power despite difference, the other difference despite power, with so little agreement between them that they already forbid us to believe any moment in Woolf's career to be more conclusive than another.

It would be especially reassuring to say that Woolf recognizes her capture in the "chains" of a Paterian under-mind and overcomes it by disengaging her subjectivity from its specular bondage. To speak in such a way, however, is to insist on the coherence of self and author in the face of a discourse that dislocates or decenters them both, that skews the very categories to which our remarks properly refer. Because our argument finally takes us beyond self and author alike, the notion of consciousness, and even of unconsciousness (whose?), is already an asyntactic one. Literature, by Woolf's own testimony, is "the voice that has no voice," the text or inscription that is not the sign of a full and present—a "sincere" and expressive—speaker whose natural voice stands behind it as cause to effect.

Once we emerge on the far side of our writers' deindividuating pathways of argument, then, we reach a terrain that neither Woolf nor Pater is properly in control or possession of. By their own admission, literature itself is a weave or fabric of influence without proper possessors and without a single, authorized shape. Indeed, to describe the very relation we have discovered in these pages has been to double the figures by which Pater and Woolf themselves describe literature and criticism—as fibers or threads, as matrices or maps of figures, with personality itself no more than a locus of tropes to which we assign a name. To speak any longer of particular influence is already to presume that our authors still cohere as such, as proper subjects with proper origins and proper destinies.

The question of Pater's influence on Woolf can never be fully resolved because it can never be fully stated. If the common life covers the tracks of personal influence, then the trope of personality covers the absence of self and author. Woolf and Pater alike turn on this difference or discord, and it is the paradoxical and compensatory rhythm or balance that sustains them both, each notion of art and culture cautioning and correcting the other, and each one bringing the other into being by means of its differences from it. Thus the question of influence leaves us suspended, finally, between two notions of literature itself, one that is profoundly personal, one that puts into question the very coherence of personality. Different from herself, Woolf is different from Pater, too, and so allows us to release her again into the common life of literature as a whole.

Index